KU-746-682

The UCAS Guide to getting into
PSYCHOLOGY

For entry to university and college in 2013

Central Library
Y Llyfrgell Ganolog
☎ 02920 382116

ACC. No: 02856207

378·41

Published by: UCAS Rosehill New Barn Lane Cheltenham GL52 3LZ

Produced in conjunction with GTI Media Ltd

© UCAS 2012

All rights reserved.

UCAS is a registered trade mark.

UCAS, a company limited by guarantee, is registered in England and Wales number: 2839815
Registered charity number: 1024741 (England and Wales) and SC038598 (Scotland)

UCAS reference number: PU039013
Publication reference: 12_049
ISBN: 978-1-908077-20-2
Price £15.99

We have made all reasonable efforts to ensure that the information in this publication was correct at time of publication. We will not, however, accept any liability for errors, omissions or changes to information since publication. Wherever possible any changes will be updated on the UCAS website (www.ucas.com).

UCAS and its trading subsidiary, UCAS Media Limited, accept advertising for publications that promote products and services relating to higher education and career progression. Revenue generated by advertising is invested by UCAS in order to enhance our applications services and to keep the cost to applicants as low as possible. Neither UCAS nor UCAS Media Limited endorse the products and services of other organisations that appear in this publication.

Further copies available from UCAS (p&p charges apply):

contact Publication Services PO Box 130 Cheltenham GL52 3ZF

email: publicationservices@ucas.ac.uk or fax: 01242 544806.

For further information about the UCAS application process go to www.ucas.com.

If you need to contact us, details can be found at www.ucas.com/about_us/contact_us.

UCAS QUALITY AWARDS

Foreword

THINKING ABOUT PSYCHOLOGY?

Finding the course that's right for you at the right university or college can take time and it's important that you use all the resources available to you in making this key decision. We at UCAS have teamed up with TARGETjobs.co.uk to provide you with *The UCAS Guide to getting into Psychology* to show you how you can progress from being a student to careers in psychology. You will find information on what the subject includes, entry routes and real-life case studies on how it worked out for others.

Once you know which subject area you might be interested in, you can use the listings of all the full-time higher education courses in psychology to see where you can study your subject. The course entry requirements are listed so you can check if getting in would be achievable for you. There's also advice on

applying through UCAS, telling you what you need to know at each stage of the application process in just six easy steps to starting university or college.

We hope you find this publication helps you to choose a course and university or college that is right for you.

On behalf of UCAS and TARGETjobs.co.uk, I wish you every success in your research.

Mary Curnock Cook, Chief Executive, UCAS

At TARGETjobs we champion paid work experience for UK university students. Find internships and placements across all sectors, plus take part in the TARGETjobs Undergraduate of the Year awards.

TARGETjobs.co.uk

the best possible start to your career

Why
psychology?

It could be you...

... helping someone overcome anxiety or depression — clinical psychology

... giving an expert opinion and evidence in court about an offender — forensic psychology

... being there for someone going through a difficult life event — counselling psychology

... identifying health risk behaviours in individuals and the general public — health psychology

... working with an athlete to prepare them for competition — sports psychology

... looking at the problems faced by young people in education — educational psychology

... and lots more besides. Psychologists work with a wide variety of people, from young children to the elderly, dealing with a range of problems. They could help people overcome emotional or education issues at school, support them during marital difficulties or bereavement, or counsel them on how to make important lifestyle changes that could affect their physical as well as their mental well-being. Could a career as a psychologist be for you? The aim of this guide is to help you decide.

PSYCHOLOGY IN CONTEXT

The reason why psychology is so fascinating is because it looks at the ways in which people think, act, react and interact. It is the study of human (and animal!) behaviour, and the thoughts and emotions that influence behaviour. At some point we have all been interested in why a friend or relative has behaved in a certain way and psychology can often provide an answer to that question.

Psychologists use the knowledge and understanding that they have gained from their studies and observations to help people deal with a wide variety of problems. For example, in any one day, psychologists in the UK could be looking at any of the following situations (and plenty more besides):

- the most effective way to convey a public health message about the negative side-effects of alcohol
- helping children through the stress of their parents' divorce
- determining whether an eyewitness's account in court is reliable
- enabling a client to overcome a phobia or fear
- working with a track and field athlete to help them achieve their best performance in competitions.

As you can see, psychologists play an important role in many aspects of people's lives.

YOUR PART IN PSYCHOLOGY

Are you good with people? Are you a good listener, who can reflect on what you've heard rather than react in haste? Are your evaluation and observation skills top-notch? Great! Because you will need a wide and varied skills set to work as a psychologist. Many people forget that psychology is a *scientific* study of how people behave and that, to work as a psychologist, you need to learn scientific methods, such as observing, measuring, testing and using statistical evidence to show that your assessment is proven and reliable and not based on a hunch. This is what makes psychology such an interesting career area: it combines personal skills such as empathy and intuition with very scientific approaches to gathering information.

If you're interested in a possible career in psychology, then this guide can help point you further in the right direction. Read on to discover:

- the main areas of work and roles on offer
- what it takes to be a psychologist
- how to get in and the paths to qualification
- advice from trainee and practising psychologists.

A CAREER IN PSYCHOLOGY?

- A psychology trainee working in the NHS could start on £25,528, while a consultant psychologist can earn over £80,000 – see **A career in psychology** on page 13.
- As well as your academic ability, admissions tutors look for people skills, empathy, calmness under pressure and attention to detail – see **The career for you?** on page 37.
- Qualifications are important in psychology. To see what you need to practise as a psychologist, read **Routes to qualification** on page 58.

Why psychology?

Choose a career that is…

VARIED

There are few careers that offer as much variety as psychology, both in the potential areas of work and your day-to-day experiences. Once you've chosen your specialism – such as clinical or forensic – the fact that you will be dealing with both old and new clients means that while you may be facing similar mental conditions, you will need to adapt the way in which you deal with them. No two people are the same so you will have to use your creativity, intuition, empathy, and practical knowledge and experience to decide on how best to help your client, depending on their personality and the seriousness of their condition. As they say, what works for one may not work for another.

VITAL TO SOCIETY

Human behaviour – our own and that of our friends, colleagues and family – affects us all. Sometimes when simple problems escalate beyond the control of individuals, a psychologist can step in and give their expert opinion and advice, working closely with their client to find the best possible solution for everyone. And psychology can help with many – if not all – aspects of life, from educational attainment to performance on stage or sports field; from dealing with depression following the birth of a baby to coping with bereavement.

TECHNICAL *AND* PEOPLE-FOCUSED

Many careers appeal because of the chance to use two different types of skills – the opportunity to use your technical or scientific expertise alongside the chance to work with people. In psychology, you will definitely be required to do this and therefore you will need a balance and interest in both. You'll use the latest research and technology, but you'll also see how these affect real people – **your** clients.

WELL PAID

Many psychologists – for example, clinical, counselling, educational, health, occupational, forensic and neuropsychologists – work, although not exclusively, within the National Health Service under the Agenda for Change pay rates. The following salary guidelines are for clinical and non-clinical psychologists working for the NHS:

Trainee psychologist	£25,528 (lower end)
Qualified psychologist	£30,460
Principal psychologist principal	£38,851
Consultant psychologist	£54,454
Lead/head of psychology services	£97,478 (higher end)

Psychologists who work in education (eg in further education colleges or universities) include teaching and research psychologists, and sports and exercise psychologists. For those working in further education, salary guidelines are as follows (figures apply to 2011):

Qualified lecturer	£23,382–£35,304
Advanced teaching and training	£35,304–£39,729
Leadership and management	£35,304–£88,137

For psychologists working in higher education, the following salary guidelines apply:

Qualified lecturer	£30,122–£44,166
Principal/senior lecturer	£45,486–£52,706
Professorial	£54,283+

ALWAYS IN DEMAND

People of all ages and from all walks of life will always need psychological help, so your skills, knowledge and expertise will never be redundant. The psychology profession has clearly structured career paths and continuous professional development (CPD) opportunities, so you can and should always keep your knowledge up-to-date. Opportunities exist throughout the country, not just in London, and in a variety of settings so you will not be tied to one location.

WHAT DO PSYCHOLOGISTS SAY?

There is never a right answer in psychology; you need to keep a constantly open mind, be inquisitive and ask lots of questions.
Julie Hulme, discipline lead for psychology. page 54

Occupational psychology gives you a broad range of knowledge and skills that are applicable and useful in most organisations, meaning you have the flexibility to choose many career paths.
Adrian Stephen, psychologist, page 48

I really enjoy working with the juvenile population and I strongly believe that targeting this age group can be effective in reducing offending behaviour.
Nicole Kirby, trainee forensic psychologist, page 46

Focus your career with the TARGETjobs Careers Report.

Using biographical data, information about your interests and insightful psychometric testing, the Careers Report gives you a clear picture of jobs that match your skills and personality.

TARGETjobs.co.uk
the best possible start to your career

A career in psychology

A career in psychology

This section aims to give you an overview of the main career choices, specialisms, working conditions and pay for psychologists in the UK today.

If you have an interest in both the arts and the sciences, and a desire to help people, then a career in psychology could be for you. At this stage, you don't need to decide on a particular specialty; most psychology students choose once they've finished their first degree, during which they will have gained some knowledge and had some exposure to the different fields.

PSYCHIATRY, PSYCHOTHERAPY OR PSYCHOLOGY?

Before looking at the main specialisms of psychology itself, it is important to make clear the distinction between **psychology**, **psychiatry** and **psychotherapy**, which can often be confused.

Psychiatrists are medically trained doctors who can prescribe drugs for use in the treatment of serious mental illness. However, they do not have much postgraduate training in psychology, although some will be trained in psychotherapy.

Psychotherapists or **counsellors** are trained to help people through what is often called a 'talking therapy' but they might not have had any formal, recognised training at either undergraduate or postgraduate level in psychology – of the sort that you will read about in this publication. They will usually have extensive knowledge of their chosen, preferred form of therapy but probably not of any or many others.

Psychologists are trained specifically in psychology and, through their three years' postgraduate training, can call themselves doctors of psychology (not of medicine, as psychiatrists can). They have a good overview of different forms of psychological specialisms and can advise patients or clients on the best one for them, often providing the help needed themselves.

FURTHER INFORMATION

This publication deals mainly with careers in psychology. For further information on the other career areas mentioned above, please visit the following websites.

- The Royal College of Psychiatrists **www.rcpsych.ac.uk**
- The UK Council for Psychotherapy **www.psychotherapy.org.uk**
- British Association for Counselling & Psychotherapy **www.bacp.co.uk**

Clinical psychologists

WHAT DO THEY DO?

Clinical psychologists work with health and social care professionals to run clinical tests that gauge the needs of those having problems with mental health, well-being or learning. Their tools of the trade include observation, interviews and performance assessments. Other professionals such as counsellors follow up on the results of the tests.

WHERE DO THEY WORK?

In the main, clinical psychologists are hired by the NHS and located in multidisciplinary practices alongside doctors, nurses and social workers. They're likely to work in health centres or hospitals although some are placed within social services teams or in community health teams.

Because most clinical psychologists are government employees, their terms and conditions are pretty structured and office hours are the norm. Even so, working overtime can happen. Career progression tends to be clear cut, although the routes may be less conventional for the smaller number of clinical psychologists in self-employment or for those employed in the private sector. Some in this profession hold teaching or research posts at academic institutions.

HOW DO I QUALIFY?

A first or 2.1 undergraduate degree in psychology (or a postgraduate conversion course) is a must, followed by a three-year doctorate in clinical psychology. Paid or voluntary relevant work experience is also expected. This might involve time spent as an assistant psychologist, working as a research assistant, summer jobs in care homes or unpaid work with mental health charities.

PROSPECTS

There is a shortage of clinical psychologists, so prospects are good! The number of jobs available varies according to where you are in the country and the area of specialism you'd like to work in. Many clinical psychologists work within the NHS, where they can progress to leading a department. It is also possible to work in higher education, doing teaching or research, or to work within the private sector. To work abroad would usually require further training.

FURTHER INFORMATION

- British Psychological Society (BPS)
  www.bps.org.uk/careers-education-training/how-become-psychologist/types-psychologists/types-psychologists

Counselling psychologists

WHAT DO THEY DO?

This is still a fairly new area in counselling, which looks at the integration of psychological theory and research with therapeutic practice. Practitioners apply the theories of psychology to working with people affected by a range of problems such as bereavement, relationship issues, mental health disorders and illnesses.

Counselling psychologists look at their patients' personal experiences and the underlying issues in order to help empower them to make changes; this makes their approach very much a holistic one. Individuals, couples, families and groups of all ages and from all walks of life seek out the help of counselling psychologists.

WHERE DO THEY WORK?

Anywhere where there are people, basically! Counselling psychotherapists are employed in industry, commerce, the Prison Service and education from primary school all the way to university. About 50% of counselling psychologists are involved with clinical work in health and social care settings, while other career opportunities exist in teaching and research for various academic organisations. They can also work on a self-employed basis as organisational consultants.

Working hours are regular and tend to be from 9am to 5pm, though occasionally longer hours may be necessary. This area is very much one that requires a multidisciplinary approach rather than an individual focus.

HOW DO I QUALIFY?

After completing your undergraduate degree in psychology (or a postgraduate conversion course), you will need to undertake a further three years of postgraduate training in more than two models of psychological therapy. This second stage can either be done at one of the institutions that offer BPS-accredited counselling psychology programmes or by gaining the BPS qualification in counselling psychology through the 'independent route'.

PROSPECTS

Career prospects in both the NHS and Prison Service are good and clearly defined as there is great demand for counselling psychologists who can offer psychological therapies. Employment opportunities exist in the following areas:

- primary care settings
- community mental health teams
- pain management and rehabilitation centres
- audit and research
- eating disorder clinics
- child and family services
- older adults services
- services for people with learning disabilities
- social services
- voluntary organisations
- student counselling services
- Employee Assistance Programmes (EAPs).

FURTHER INFORMATION

- British Psychological Society **www.bps.org.uk/careers-education-training/how-become-psychologist/types-psychologists/types-psychologists**
- British Association for Counselling & Psychotherapy **www.bacp.co.uk**

Educational psychologists

WHAT DO THEY DO?

Educational psychologists concentrate on how children and young people – aged 0–19 years – develop and learn, using their psychological knowledge. They do this by working with other individuals such as teachers, parents and adults in both early years and school settings. Educational psychologists work with children on either an individual or group basis and liaise with parents, carers and other family members, as well as with education officers, social workers and professionals from other child-related organisations. Typical responsibilities include:

- looking at educational issues from a psychological viewpoint
- promoting inclusion
- solving problems
- observing and assessing children
- providing advice to organisations
- research and development.

WHERE DO THEY WORK?

Educational psychologists are normally employed by local authorities. A few work for social or health services, in independent schools or in private practice. They typically work with:

- individual children
- groups of children
- schools and colleges
- providers of early years care
- parents and guardians.

HOW DO I QUALIFY?

As with all careers in psychology, a relevant, accredited degree is required, which will give you graduate basis for registration (GBR). All aspiring educational psychologists must complete a three-year doctorate course. Additionally, relevant work experience with children and young people is essential.

PROSPECTS

As an educational psychologist working within a local authority you could progress to senior and principal education psychologist roles. If you are willing to live in a large city, specialist posts may be available once you have sufficient experience. Beyond working for a local authority other options include working on a freelance basis (including in specialist private schools), working as an adviser in education policy, or taking your skills and expertise into other related areas such as occupational psychology.

FURTHER INFORMATION

- Association of Educational Psychologists **www.aep.org.uk**

Forensic psychologists

WHAT DO THEY DO?

Forensic psychologists are experts on the psychological aspects of legal processes in courts. They also deal with investigative and criminological psychology – basically this means applying psychological theory to criminal investigation, understanding psychological problems associated with criminal behaviour and looking at how criminals are treated. Forensic psychologists deal with a wide variety of people including offenders, their victims, witnesses, judges, juries and prison staff.

Their main duties include the following:

- coming up with and implementing treatment programmes
- changing the behaviour of offenders
- responding to the needs of both prison staff and prisoners, including reducing stress levels
- using research to support practice
- giving an expert opinion in court and advising parole boards
- analysing crime.

In their dealings with offenders, forensic psychologists try to develop rehabilitation programmes, which may include anger management, recommending treatments for drug or alcohol addiction, and using training in social and cognitive skills. When assisting prison staff, forensic psychologists can help advise on stress management and how to deal with bullying.

Recently there have been two development areas: risk assessment procedures with offenders and interventions with sex offenders. The focus with both of these is to try to reduce the risk of re-offending. Child protection work and liaising with social services is also an important area in this field of psychology.

WHERE DO THEY WORK?

Not surprisingly, most forensic psychologists work for HM Prison Service – which also includes the Home Office Research and Development Unit. However, some work for the health service in such settings as rehabilitation units and secure hospitals; in social services (including the police service, young offenders' units, and the probation service); and in academia and private consultancy. Forensic psychologists typically work from 9am to 5pm although weekend and evening work is common due to the nature of this field.

HOW DO I QUALIFY?

As well as having a recognised, accredited psychology degree, potential forensic psychologists must also take the British Psychological Society's diploma in forensic psychology in order to be eligible for registration as a chartered forensic psychologist.

The diploma involves two stages. The first comprises exams and research to assess each trainee's academic ability; students who have already gained an accredited master's in forensic psychology do not have to complete Stage 1. The second stage involves supervised practice, in which trainees must provide examples of applying psychology within a forensic practice. Each of these will show how competently the trainee can produce work that meets the expected standards of a chartered forensic psychologist. A practice diary and supervision log must be completed and will form the portfolio of evidence.

PROSPECTS

Within the prison and probation services it is possible to follow a structured career path, progressing to senior posts for chartered forensic psychologists, where management responsibilities will be a significant part of the role. Forensic psychology is undergoing a boom, and it is becoming increasingly possible to build a freelance career as a consultant.

FURTHER INFORMATION

- The Division of Forensic Psychology (in association with the British Psychological Society) **http://dfp.bps.org.uk**
- HM Prison Service **www.justice.gov.uk/jobs/prisons/on-offer/forensic-psychologist/index.htm**

Health psychologists

WHAT DO THEY DO?

Health psychologists work in a relatively new area of applied psychology, in which they use psychological theories to try to change people's attitudes, behaviour and thinking about health and illness. As such, this is a very broad field in which to practise, involving some of the following responsibilities:

- preventing damaging habits such as smoking, drug addiction and poor diet
- trying to change health-related behaviour in communities and in workplaces
- promoting healthy practices such as exercise, teeth-brushing and healthy eating
- researching things that can explain, predict and change attitudes towards health and illness
- looking at how healthcare practitioners communicate with and relate to their patients
- considering the psychological impact that illnesses have on individuals and their families
- helping patients control their pain.

WHERE DO THEY WORK?

Health psychologists work in a wide variety of settings including hospitals, academic health research units, health authorities and university departments. They often receive referrals from healthcare agencies, NHS Trusts, health authorities, GPs, nurses and rehabilitation therapists.

HOW DO I QUALIFY?

After completing an accredited psychology degree, potential health psychologists must either take an accredited MSc or complete Stage 1 of the British Psychological Society's qualification in health psychology. All trainees will then follow stage 2 of the Society's qualification - two years of supervised practice.

PROSPECTS

Job advertisements might not specifically ask for a health psychologist but instead ask for psychologists with the necessary experience and skills to work within a health arena; this may include clinical or counselling psychologists. The last decade has seen a large increase in the number of health psychology lectureships in universities and in medical and nurse training centres. Additionally there has been an increase in research into the social and behavioural issues in health. Health psychologists could work in a university and then move to a health authority or vice versa or there may be joint jobs between the two.

FURTHER INFORMATION

- Division of Health Psychology (in association with the British Psychological Society)
  www.health-psychology.org.uk

Neuropsychologists

WHAT DO THEY DO?

Neuropsychology is the study of how changes to brain structures relate to thought and behaviour. It's a largely academic discipline that draws upon computing, cognitive psychology, philosophy of the mind and neuroscience. For example, studying electrical brain energy may improve diagnosis and care for those suffering from injuries to the brain and neurological diseases. Other applications are in forensics – informing a legal assessment of someone's behaviour – or in the pharmaceuticals industry, analysing the impact of new drugs upon brain activity.

WHERE DO THEY WORK?

Most neuropsychologists work as academics but can be appointed to clinical posts if their qualifications and experience combine clinical expertise with neuroscience and a good grasp of mental health conditions including diagnosis and treatment from neurological, behavioural and cognitive points of view. The following are the most common workplaces for neuropsychologists:

- **acute/trauma work in a regional centre:** working with surgeons and neurologists
- **rehabilitation centres for people with brain injuries:** helping patients to recuperate within a residential setting
- **community services:** providing aftercare for patients discharged from residential care.

HOW DO I QUALIFY?

You will need a degree in psychology (or a postgraduate conversion qualification) followed by a further three-year doctorate, normally in either clinical or educational psychology, before you can undertake accredited post-qualification training in clinical neuropsychology. Potential nueropsychologists normally need to complete at least two years of formal supervised practice (on the job, while training) and submit case studies, research reports and case reports, research and supervision logs for formal assessment. It is also necessary to sit professional exams, though some candidates will be exempt from these if they have completed an approved part-time postgraduate course.

PROSPECTS

Both the NHS and the private sector employ neuropsychologists in a variety of settings such as private and not-for-profit charitable organisations. Since there is currently a huge shortage of neuropsychologists – particularly in paediatric neuropsychology – opportunities for jobs are very good.

Salaries are generally on the same level as clinical psychologists (see page 11) but those in senior positions can command higher salaries by undertaking private medico-legal work as expert witnesses in such matters as personal injury cases.

FURTHER INFORMATION

- British Psychological Society
  www.bps.org.uk/careers-education-training/how-become-psychologist/types-psychologists/types-psychologists

Occupational psychologists

WHAT DO THEY DO?

Occupational psychologists apply their knowledge of psychology in the workplace. They look at how work duties and the conditions in which people work affect employees – whether they help or hinder them. They can also advise on how different personalities can influence the way in which people do their job. By using their knowledge and expertise, occupational psychologists can identify and resolve issues in the workplace. Typical duties include advising on:

- management of occupational psychology issues
- organisational structure and development
- team development
- career advice
- stress management
- well-being and work/life balance
- learning new technologies and working practices
- ergonomics – ie how people's working environment affects their work
- recruitment and personnel management.

WHERE DO THEY WORK?

Typical workplaces include organisations within both the private and public sector, where occupational psychologists will work in-house. Some work for specialist occupational or business psychology companies and consultancies, while others are self-employed and work as consultants. Finally, some occupational psychologists work in academia, teaching and researching.

HOW DO I QUALIFY?

An accredited undergraduate degree is required, followed by a BPS-accredited master's degree in occupational psychology as the preferred route. The master's qualification can be gained in one year on a full-time study basis or in two years, part-time. Alternatively, you can take the British Psychological Society's qualification in occupational psychology. For you to become a practitioner member and apply for status as a chartered occupational psychologist, you will need to study for Stage 2 of the BPS's qualification.

PROSPECTS

Occupational psychologists tend to work in small units, so there is not a great deal of room for progression to senior posts. However, other options include working in self-employed roles and for other organisations beyond the NHS where their skills could be used in fields such as human resources, training and careers consultancy. Occupational psychologists could also consider business psychology as a potential career option or, with a masters and doctorate, researching and teaching in a higher education institution.

FURTHER INFORMATION

- The Division of Occupational Psychology (in association with the British Psychological Society) **http://dop.bps.org.uk**

Sport and exercise psychologists

WHAT DO THEY DO?

Sport and exercise psychologists work in a fairly new field of the profession – one that is quickly expanding. It deals with the behaviour and mental processes of individuals who are involved in sport and exercise, with professionals dealing predominantly in either sport or exercise psychology, not both.

Sport psychologists help athletes prepare psychologically for competition and cope with the emotional demands of competing and training. This could be either through working with individuals or with entire teams, from amateurs to professionals. They also use psychological principles to help coaches and managers understand how their sportsmen and women are affected by performance issues. Typical duties include:

- helping athletes prepare mentally for the Olympic Games
- counselling referees on how to deal with the stressful nature of their jobs
- advising coaches on how to create a team atmosphere amongst their players
- helping sportsmen and women manage the worries that might strike after being affected by injury.

Exercise psychologists focus on applying psychology to motivate people – for example, the general public – into exercising and to ensure that they benefit from the physiological and psychological rewards that exercise can bring. Typical duties include:

- advising exercise instructors on how to motivate their class participants
- liaising with health promotion workers on ways in which to motivate people to take up exercise
- helping people with specific health problems (for example, heart conditions) to benefit from a tailored exercise regime
- working with individuals on setting exercise goals.

WHERE DO THEY WORK?

Because of the nature of their work, most sport and exercise psychologists work in sport and exercise settings relevant to their specialism. Some sport psychologists are employed by professional teams or national governing bodies for sports, but most will do a mixture of consultancy work and teaching or research in perhaps another field of psychology such as clinical psychology. Some full-time sport psychologist posts are available – and the number is growing – but these sorts of vacancies are still relatively rare at the moment.

Exercise psychologists usually combine consultancy with teaching and/or research. They often deal with referrals from GPs or rehabilitation schemes and will also be responsible for setting up and monitoring exercise programmes in various contexts such as the workplace, in prisons and in psychiatric settings.

As with most psychology fields, this area is very people-centred and varied. Consultancy work can be based in an office but psychologists will often need to go out to visit their clients in such places as training centres, sports venues and rehabilitation settings.

HOW DO I QUALIFY?

The usual route to becoming a sport or exercise psychologist is to complete an accredited psychology degree (or postgraduate conversion course) followed by three further years of training, normally by achieving a postgraduate qualification in sport and exercise psychology.

PROSPECTS

Opportunities for full-time consultancy work are increasing but it is still quite difficult to maintain a practice based entirely on this. Therefore, you need to be prepared to work in a wide range of settings, from a warm office to a cold football pitch! The salary you command will depend on who your clients are and whether you combine consultancy with other duties such as teaching or research.

FURTHER INFORMATION

- British Association of Sport and Exercise Sciences **www.bases.org.uk**
- British Psychological Society **www.bps.org.uk/careers-education-training/how-become-psychologist/types-psychologists/types-psychologists**

Teaching and research psychologists

WHAT DO THEY DO?

Some psychologists want to stay in academia forever while others teach for a while and do some research before returning to careers elsewhere. As with other disciplines, the onus is upon lecturers to publish their findings. However, a job as a lecturer isn't all about seminars and writing for learned journals. It can involve a lot of administration too, such as handling budgets, selecting students, and filling in forms for the government and university bodies.

Psychologists can also teach in secondary schools and sixth form or further education colleges, where the subject is offered as both a GCSE and A level subject. Their job here involves taking their students through a syllabus, so the subject matter is a little narrower in scope, although practical and laboratory work may also be available.

WHERE DO THEY WORK?

Teachers, lecturers and researchers are based mainly in academic institutions. Research scientists are employed by research units, but it is unusual to have a career based only on research.

Working hours are fairly normal. Those working in schools will follow the school's regular timetable, with good holidays. University lecturers will divide their time between teaching (lectures, seminars, practicals and tutorials) and research but tend not to have long working hours and do have a generous holiday allowance.

HOW DO I QUALIFY?

Lecturers and researchers in psychology must first obtain their undergraduate degree from an accredited university, thus gaining the graduate basis for registration (GBR). After this, they must study for a postgraduate qualification in their preferred specialism – normally a PhD. University lecturing and research normally doesn't require any particular teaching qualifications but for those interested in working in state schools, a teaching qualification such as a PGCE (postgraduate certificate in education) is compulsory. Private schools may ask for this but can accept teachers without a teaching qualification.

PROSPECTS

New lecturers will spend much of their time teaching students (an increasing number of universities now offer lecturers proper teaching training), but doing research and producing publications is also a vital way of progressing in academia, as is going to conferences and seminars and giving papers. With a number of years' experience lecturers may find themselves supervising masters and doctoral students, organizing conferences, and helping to run the department and even be involved in fundraising. To reach senior posts, such as senior or principal lecturer, or professor, it's necessary to take on more roles and responsibilities including helping to shape and develop the department's academic direction; at this point time spent doing research and teaching may decrease.

FURTHER INFORMATION

- British Psychological Society **www.bps.org.uk/careers-education-training/how-become-psychologist/types-psychologists/types-psychologists**

Psychotherapists

WHAT DO THEY DO?

Psychotherapists are involved in treating a wide range of mental and physical problems, using many different theoretically developed methods. Patients can include individuals or groups of people suffering from the same condition, and can range in age from children to adults. Psychotherapy can involve different methods of treatment, depending on each individual and their particular problem, but include one-to-one discussions over an extended period of time, intensive interviews over the course of a day or more, or ongoing group sessions in which participants 'act out' problems or express emotions that they might have suppressed. Psychotherapists also help to train other health professionals such as social workers.

Through these methods, psychotherapists help their clients to explore often complex and intense emotional problems, to analyse their past experiences and how they may be influencing current behaviour or thought patterns, and to come up with appropriate coping strategies. Common methods include the following:

- **psychodynamic:** participants look at childhood experiences, dreams and their unconscious mind
- **behavioural:** psychotherapists help their clients 'unlearn' or 'recondition' damaging behaviours
- **cognitive:** a client is challenged to change their negative thought patterns and responses
- **humanistic and integrative:** self-development and personal growth are encouraged, often through spirituality and consciousness
- **person-centred:** the client is encouraged to develop their own inner resources by releasing and expressing any negative emotions with their therapist
- **interpersonal/systemic:** the psychotherapist helps their client to change their behaviour and roles within relationships.

The method used will depend on the model that the particular psychotherapist has trained in.

WHERE DO THEY WORK?

Psychotherapists work in a number of different settings. Some are employed by the NHS, while others work for the private sector or with voluntary organisations. Many work on a self-employed basis, in a practice or in an office in their own homes, and follow normal office hours, ie 9am–5pm, Monday to Friday. However, because they need to fit in around the commitments of their clients, some will work outside these hours, often taking sessions before the normal work day starts or finishes. Consultations usually last from 30 to 60 minutes and part-time work is possible.

HOW DO I QUALIFY?

The British Psychological Society recommends that anyone interested in a career in psychotherapy firstly completes a relevant and accredited degree – and possibly postgraduate degree – in psychology before going on to study psychotherapy as a post-qualification specialisation. The United Kingdom Council for Psychotherapy (UKCP) can give details and advice about possible training routes on their website **www.psychotherapy.org.uk.**

Most psychotherapists will have experience and training in areas related to social work, psychology or one of the other health professions, and tend to move into psychotherapy later as a second or additional career.

PROSPECTS

People will always have problems so psychotherapy offers good opportunities for potential practitioners. However, there are some individuals who practise as a psychotherapist without the relevant qualifications, since there is no single regulatory body responsible for overseeing the work of private-practice psychotherapists. This means that clients seeking help may wish to be reassured by evidence of your training and experience before committing to therapy – a factor that is common and welcomed in this and all areas of psychology practice.

Salaries can be quite high for practitioners in this area, particularly those engaged in private practice.

FURTHER INFORMATION

- British Psychoanalytic Council (BPC) **www.psychoanalytic-council.org**
- Association of Child Psychotherapists **www.childpsychotherapy.org.uk**
- British Association of Psychotherapists (BAP) **www.bap-psychotherapy.org**
- United Kingdom Council for Psychotherapy (UKCP) **www.psychotherapy.org.uk**
- British Association for Counselling & Psychotherapy (BACP) **www.bacp.co.uk**

THINK PSYCHOLOGY
THINK BANGOR

PRIFYSGOL
BANGOR
UNIVERSITY

There are lots of reasons why we think that you should consider studying Psychology with us. Here are just a few:

- In the latest National Student Satisfaction Bangor Psychology was ranked in the **top 5** in the UK with a 95% rating for student satisfaction.

- Bangor Psychology is **ranked 7th** (of 76) in terms or research power based on the most recent Research Assessment Exercise.

- An '**Excellent**' Teaching Quality rating reflected in the fact that over 70% of our students graduate with a 1st or 2:1.

- Bangor Psychology provides students with an excellent mix of embedded transferable skill and **employability** courses giving access to a varied range of professions.

- One of the largest Psychology Schools in the UK, offering students a unique combination of **quality and quantity.**

- Bangor is located on the North Wales coast, between the mountains and the sea and is a compact **friendly city** dominated by over 9000 students.

- **Easy to reach:** Less than 90 minutes from Liverpool or Manchester, 2.5 hours drive from Birmingham and just over 3 hours on the train from London.

Contact: School of Psychology,
Bangor University, Gwynedd, LL57 2AS
E. psychology@bangor.ac.uk
T. 01248 382629

www.bangor.ac.uk/psychology

The career
for you?

Is psychology for you?

Being a successful psychologist – in whatever specialism – calls for more than an in-depth understanding of the relevant discipline. It also requires certain skills and personal qualities or attributes.

To help you decide if a career in psychology is for you, we suggest you consider the following questions:

- What do you want from your future work?
- What does the course typically involve?
- Which skills do psychologists typically need?

Find out what psychology courses usually involve in the **Entry routes** section on pages 57–62. Read on for advice concerning the other two questions.

WHAT DO YOU WANT FROM YOUR CAREER?

You may not have an instant answer for this, but your current studies, work experience to date and even your hobbies can help give you clues about the kind of work you enjoy, and the skills you have already started to develop. Start with a blank sheet of paper and note down the answers to the questions we've provided on the next page to help get you thinking. Be as brutally honest with yourself as you can. Don't write what you think will impress your teachers or parents; write what really matters to you and you'll start to see a pattern emerge.

ANSWER THESE QUESTIONS TO HELP YOU CHOOSE YOUR CAREER

- When you think of your future, in what kind of environment do you see yourself working: office, outdoor, nine-to-five, high-pressure, regular routine?
- What are your favourite hobbies outside school?
- What is it about them you enjoy? Working with people, figuring out how things work?
- What are your favourite subjects in school?
- What is it about them that you enjoy most? Being able to create something, debating, problem-solving, practical hands-on work?
- What do you dislike about the other subjects you're studying? ('The teacher' doesn't count!)
- Which aspects of your work experience have you most enjoyed?

WHICH SKILLS DO PSYCHOLOGISTS TYPICALLY NEED?

Without doubt, admissions tutors for psychology look for **strong academic ability** to prove your ability to cope with a science-based subject, plus clear **evidence of a commitment to psychology** as a career (which can usually be demonstrated through work experience placements).

Psychology, and related fields, are very people centred and therefore require excellent interpersonal and empathic skills. If you love working with people, are a good listener, and can look at problems both from an analytical and personal perspective, you stand a good chance of a successful career in psychology.

However, this alone will not be enough. Psychologists also need the following skills to be accepted onto training courses and then to be a successful practitioner once all the exams have been taken and theory has been learnt:

- the confidence and emotional stamina to explore the painful aspects of a client's life, which can be draining on one's own mental reserves

- empathy, sincerity and sensitivity
- excellent communication skills
- the ability to both listen to and question people
- a genuine interest in people's emotional issues
- a respect for human experience and culture
- a non-judgmental and tolerant approach
- the ability to build rapport with a wide range of people
- an energetic and positive outlook
- an ongoing commitment to self-development
- the ability to maintain a professional distance from your clients.

These are the so-called soft skills. However, psychology is a science-based subject and, therefore, the following hard skills are also essential:

- excellent problem-solving skills
- a logical approach to problems
- an analytical outlook to cope with statistical information
- a methodical approach to your work
- computer literacy.

ALTERNATIVE CAREERS

Many psychology graduates decide to continue with their psychology studies after university, specialising in a particular field such as clinical or forensic psychology.

However, a degree in psychology certainly does not commit you to a career in that field if you decide that you do not wish to pursue further academic research. Some graduates prefer to use the knowledge and skills they have gained from their degree in other related fields such as social work, education, or allied health. It's also common to go into other sectors such as retail, personnel, business and management, in which their skills are in great demand by potential employers.

Professional bodies

Professional bodies are responsible for overseeing a particular profession or career area, ensuring that people who work in the area are fully trained and meet ethical guidelines. Professional bodies may be known as institutions, societies and associations. They generally have regulatory roles: they make sure that members of the profession are able to work successfully in their jobs without endangering lives or abusing their position.

Professional bodies are often involved in training and career development, so courses and workplace training may have to follow the body's guidelines. In order to be fully qualified and licensed to work in your profession of choice, you will have to follow the professional training route. In many areas of work, completion of the professional training results in gaining chartered status – and the addition of some extra letters after your name. Other institutions may award other types of

certification once certain criteria have been met. Chartered or certified members will usually need to take further courses and training to ensure their skills are kept up-to-date.

WHAT PROFESSIONAL BODIES ARE THERE?

Not all career areas have professional bodies. Those jobs that require extensive learning and training are likely to have bodies with a regulatory focus. This includes careers such as engineering, law, construction, health and finance. If you want to work in one of these areas, it's important to make sure your degree course is accredited by the professional body – otherwise you may have to undertake further study or training later on.

Other bodies may play more of a supportive role, looking after the interests of people who work in the sector. This includes journalism, management and arts-based careers. Professional bodies may also be learned bodies, providing opportunities for further learning and promoting the development of knowledge in the field.

CAN I JOIN AS A STUDENT?

Many professional bodies offer student membership – sometimes free or for reduced fees. Membership can be extremely valuable as a source of advice, information and resources. You'll have the opportunity to meet other students in the field, as well as experienced professionals. It will also look good on your CV, when you come to apply for jobs.

See below for a list of professional bodies in the field of psychology.

The British Psychological Society
www.bps.org.uk

Association of Educational Psychologists
www.aep.org.uk

British Association for Counselling & Psychotherapy
www.bacp.co.uk

UK Council for Psychotherapy
www.psychotherapy.org.uk

The Royal College of Psychiatrists
www.rcpsych.ac.uk

British Psychoanalytic Council
www.psychoanalytic-council.org

The Association of Child Psychotherapists
www.childpsychotherapy.org.uk

British Association of Psychotherapists
www.bap-psychotherapy.org

Graduate destinations

Psychology
HESA Destination of Leavers of Higher Education Survey

Each year, comprehensive statistics are collected on what graduates are doing six months after they complete their course. The survey is co-ordinated by the Higher Education Statistics Agency (HESA) and provides information about how many graduates move into employment (and what type of career) or further study and how many are believed to be unemployed.

The full results across all subject areas are published by the Higher Education Careers Service Unit (HECSU) and the Association of Graduate Careers Advisory Services (AGCAS) in *What Do Graduates Do?*, which is available from **www.ucasbooks.com**.

	Psychology
In UK employment	57.8%
In overseas employment	1.2%
Working and studying	9.6%
Studying in the UK for a higher degree	9.2%
Studying in the UK for a teaching qualification	2.4%
Undertaking other further study or training in the UK	2.8%
Studying overseas	0.2%
Not available for employment, study or training	4.1%
Assumed to be unemployed	7.9%
Other	4.7%

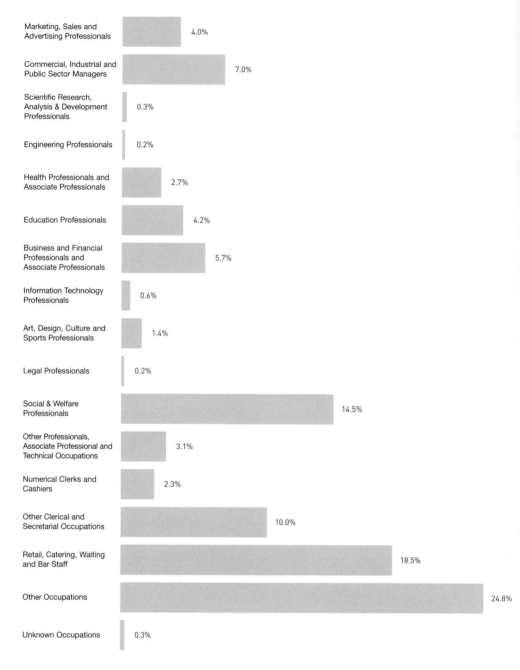

Category	Percentage
Marketing, Sales and Advertising Professionals	4.0%
Commercial, Industrial and Public Sector Managers	7.0%
Scientific Research, Analysis & Development Professionals	0.3%
Engineering Professionals	0.2%
Health Professionals and Associate Professionals	2.7%
Education Professionals	4.2%
Business and Financial Professionals and Associate Professionals	5.7%
Information Technology Professionals	0.6%
Art, Design, Culture and Sports Professionals	1.4%
Legal Professionals	0.2%
Social & Welfare Professionals	14.5%
Other Professionals, Associate Professional and Technical Occupations	3.1%
Numerical Clerks and Cashiers	2.3%
Other Clerical and Secretarial Occupations	10.0%
Retail, Catering, Waiting and Bar Staff	18.5%
Other Occupations	24.8%
Unknown Occupations	0.3%

Reproduced with the kind permission of HECSU/AGCAS, *What Do Graduates Do? 2011*.
All data comes from the HESA Destinations of Leavers of Higher Education Survey 2009/10.

Case studies

JUST WHAT DOES A CAREER IN
PSYCHOLOGY OFFER YOU?

The following profiles show the wealth of exciting
opportunities that are yours for the taking.

Trainee forensic psychologist

HM Prison Service

NICOLE KIRBY

Route into psychology:
A levels – biology, psychology, sociology (2003); BSc psychology, York St John University (2006), MSc applied forensic psychology, University of York (current)

WHY PSYCHOLOGY?

My interest in pursuing a career in psychology came from completing an A level in this area and also from volunteer work that I undertook with a bail support scheme for juvenile offenders in the community. This sparked my interest in the criminal and the forensic arena of psychology, which was further developed by the criminal psychology module that I took as part of my undergraduate degree.

HOW DID YOU GET WHERE YOU ARE TODAY?

After graduating I began looking for psychology-related jobs; in particular, I wanted to focus upon forensic psychology. Due to the competitiveness within this field I decided to gain experience within the forensic setting of the prison service. I applied for the role of a prison officer as it is extremely difficult to gain employment in a psychology-based role within the prison service without prior experience. After successfully completing the prison officer training, I was able to get experience working in a forensic setting. Throughout my time working as a prison officer I continued to look for psychology assistant jobs and I eventually got a position at a Young Offenders' Institute. This role was primarily concerned with delivering offender behaviour programmes to juvenile offenders in custody. I then progressed to my current role of a trainee psychologist.

WHAT DOES YOUR JOB INVOLVE?

My role is more specialised and involves working on an individual basis with people to determine the level of risk for reoffending that they currently pose. I am also responsible for supervising other members of the psychology team, primarily psychology assistants who facilitate the group work programmes. As part of the trainee job role you are expected to work towards becoming a chartered psychologist, which involves two stages: firstly, the MSc in forensic psychology, and secondly, completing four competencies that demonstrate the skills of a forensic psychologist. These include conducting psychology research, communicating psychological knowledge to other professionals, conducting psychological assessments and interventions, and training other professionals in psychological skills.

I work 37 hours per week alongside four psychology assistants, five trainee psychologists and six chartered psychologists. As part of my role I also liaise with other professionals employed within the prison service and in the community including prison officers, healthcare staff, mental health services, probation staff and substance misuse workers.

WHAT HAS BEEN YOUR BIGGEST CHALLENGE?

The populations that forensic psychologists work with can be challenging. We work directly with offenders who have committed a range of offences, some of whom are serving life sentences and whose offences can affect you as a person. You need to utilise the skills and supervision that is offered as part of your role as a forensic psychologist.

AND THE BEST BITS?

My job provides me with the opportunity to meet a diverse range of people and opportunities to learn and progress within my own professional development. In particular, I really enjoy working with the juvenile population and I strongly believe that targeting this age group can be effective in reducing offending behaviour.

NICOLE'S TOP TIPS

Ensure you complete a psychology degree that is recognised by the British Psychological Society as it allows you to progress your psychology studies and is essential if you wish to practise as a psychologist. Gain as much experience as possible within the area that you wish to work in: it can be a long and arduous process to become a forensic psychologist.

Psychologist

Ministry of Defence

ADRIAN STEPHEN

Route into occupational psychology:
A levels – English literature, psychology, sociology (2001); BSc human psychology, Aston University (2005);
MSc occupational psychology, Birkbeck College, University of London (2010)

WHY PSYCHOLOGY?

I first became interested in psychology as a teenager when I heard a story about someone attacked in front of dozens of witnesses where nobody helped or called the police; I wanted to know why. My interest in occupational psychology (OP) grew from wanting to apply my psychology knowledge in a mainstream work setting, rather than working with those with specific psychological difficulties.

HOW DID YOU GET WHERE YOU ARE TODAY?

The important thing for me during my psychology degree was my one-year work placement. This gave me applied experience of psychology in the workplace, as well as future career contacts and something practical to put on my CV to stand out from others. On graduating, I was offered a job at the same place that I did my placement. They paid for me to study part-time for my MSc in OP, which gave me specialist knowledge and theory that I didn't get in my BSc.

WHAT DOES YOUR JOB INVOLVE?

My job is to carry out research on RAF and MoD personnel and any aspect of working for these organisations. After collecting and analysing the findings, I consult academic psychological theory and research and advise my customers of what the findings mean, how they can expect their personnel to behave, and why they might behave as they do. The key skills involved are employing rigorous research methodology, data analysis and statistics, being able to write a thorough report of the findings and making it understandable to someone who has never encountered psychology or statistics before.

I work in an office at RAF Headquarters. My working hours are very reasonable: I usually work 8.30am to 5pm, but I have flexible working hours that allow me to vary my start and finish times so that I can have a good work-life balance.

WHAT HAS BEEN YOUR BIGGEST CHALLENGE?

Working full-time whilst studying for my MSc was the hardest thing I've had to do. The last thing I wanted to do after spending eight to nine hours at work was to come home and spend three hours studying, as well as doing the usual domestic stuff like cooking and washing! I did this for two years though and actually grew to enjoy it. The subject was interesting, I met new people through the university, I knew I was achieving something that was difficult, and it gave me a real sense of achievement. It also helped me to develop my organisation and prioritisation skills.

AND THE BEST BITS?

The best thing about my job is having the opportunity to make a difference to an organisation by using psychology. I love the challenge of taking complex theory and research data, and translating and presenting it to others so that they can use it to improve someone's working life. I get job satisfaction from knowing I influenced that, particularly for such an important organisation as the RAF.

ADRIAN'S TOP TIPS

Actively seek work experiences in your chosen field, even if all you can find is short-term and/or unpaid. This gives you the chance to see how psychology is applied and shows employers that you are dedicated and go the extra mile.

Don't think that by studying psychology you are setting yourself up for a career as a 'shrink'. Occupational psychology gives you a broad range of knowledge and skills that are applicable and useful in most organisations, meaning you have the flexibility to choose many career paths.

Counselling psychologist

Cheltenham Trauma Clinic LLP

JOANNA NOWILL

Route into counselling psychology:
A levels – English, French, music (1976), biology (1990); BA French & Italian, University of Lancaster (1981); BSc psychology, University of Worcester (2005); Doctorate counselling psychology, University of Wolverhampton (2009)

WHY PSYCHOLOGY?

I reached 40 and felt like a major change. I had been editor of a publishing company, had children, and then moved into sales for a big printing firm. I had been interested in mental health for some time and decided to give it a go.

HOW DID YOU GET WHERE YOU ARE TODAY?

I first studied languages and then did psychology later. Interestingly, the languages course has helped me enormously in finding examples and metaphors in literature to help clients understand their dilemmas. For my doctorate, I had to get some first-hand experience of being in a room with someone in distress so I joined the Samaritans and did a mix of telephone and one-to-one work. I also took a part-time job in the NHS. This helped to give me some gravitas in my advertising and also got my name out among GPs and consultants.

Counselling psychology (CP) is very similar on the surface to clinical psychology. However, CP considers the person holistically rather than simply treating the symptoms. Counselling psychologists can work in any environment where there are groups of people. We can be found, for example, in prisons, hospitals, schools, business, and industry. It's a very flexible occupation with many options.

WHAT DOES YOUR JOB INVOLVE?

I use evidence-based therapies like cognitive behavioural therapy to help people find better ways of coping with their psychological problems, such as depression, anxiety, trauma, bereavement, and phobia. My clients usually come to me through GP referrals or insurance companies. I specialise in trauma cases so I might get someone who has suffered a car accident and is having nightmares and flashbacks. I have to work according to the British Psychology Society code of ethics, be registered with the Health Professions Council and make sure that I have regular supervision.

Because I'm in private practice, I'm pretty flexible. I choose to work three days a week, from 10am to about 5pm. I use a clinic room in both a private hospital and a holistic health centre. I undertake some training sessions with the county's GPs and I get asked to write for publications occasionally.

WHAT HAS BEEN YOUR BIGGEST CHALLENGE?

During training I worked in a prison for two-and-a-half years. This was extremely challenging and taught me a lot about human nature and the fragility of personality. I overcame the challenge by setting boundaries – not bringing issues home and knowing that I can't fix everyone all of the time. Developing good therapeutic skills cannot be learnt in the classroom. It takes time to be a competent therapist and I'll never stop learning.

AND THE BEST BITS?

I love meeting people and I'm always curious about their problems. It feels a bit like being 'Sherlock' when you first hear someone's issue, wondering how this happened and trying to piece together the different parts of the problem. It's wonderful when you help someone resolve their difficulties and move on with their lives. I also love running my own business. Luckily this is the sort of job that I can sustain into old age. Indeed, clients seem to feel more comfortable with the older person.

JOANNA'S TOP TIPS

It's a big investment, as counselling psychologists pay for their training. So be sure you want this and that you're robust enough to sit with other people's distress. Get some first-hand experience of working with people who have problems if you can, joining Samaritans or Victim Support, for example.

Child and adolescent psychotherapist

NHS

GABRIELLE LEES

Route into psychotherapy:
A levels – art, biology, English literature (1984), psychology (1985); BA fine art, University of Brighton (1990); PG Dip art therapy, Sheffield Hallam University (1992); MA psychoanalytic infant observational studies, Tavistock Clinic, London (1997); MPhil psychoanalytic psychotherapy, Birmingham Trust for Psychoanalytical Psychotherapy (2005)

WHY PSYCHOTHERAPY?

I was always interested in people, why they did things the way they did, and the communication of feelings. I took a psychology A level in a year out after school, and was particularly interested in child development and psychiatry.

HOW DID YOU GET WHERE YOU ARE TODAY?

I started with a fine art degree and this helped me to think about what was being communicated through art, how it was perceived by the viewer and what it may reveal about the mind of the artist. I took my interest further with a qualification in art therapy. I then went on to work with children and families and became increasingly interested in relationships and childhood development. I did a two-year training course in family therapy, then the three-year master's in infant studies, which is a prerequisite to the full four-year NHS funded training in child and adolescent psychotherapy. I chose child and adolescent psychotherapy as I was always interested in families and early relationships and how this influences the development of the personality, right through life.

WHAT DOES YOUR JOB INVOLVE?

I assess and treat children and adolescents with psychological issues. I try to help children and teenagers overcome their problems, and to improve relationships within families. I also help other people who work with children to understand what is going on and why the children are behaving the way they are. In addition, I work with pregnant women and new parents who have worries about how things are going with their babies.

On a day-to-day basis, I see people in individual sessions, in groups, and meet up with other agencies involved with children, such as social workers, schools and foster parents. Sometimes I see the children on their own, but mostly with their parents or family. Quite a lot of work is done with the parents only. It is essential to have good 'engagement skills' so that people feel comfortable in your presence and don't mind coming back to see you again. I have lots of supervision where I can talk to other therapists who work in the same field.

I work part-time and usually from 9am to 5pm. I am based in health centres and in therapy, play or art rooms, but I also spend a lot of time in an office on a computer.

WHAT HAS BEEN YOUR BIGGEST CHALLENGE?

The biggest challenge is working in an organisation that does not properly fund this kind of work. Things have to get really bad and people are often desperate by the time they get to a service like mine. Lots don't get this service at all in the NHS. This is getting worse as we are expected to see more people, for less time, and with fewer resources.

AND THE BEST BITS?

The privilege of having people share the most difficult and complicated parts of their lives with me, and when things feel better for them because we have understood something and then their lives change for the better.

GABRIELLE'S TOP TIPS

You don't have to do psychology to get into this line of work; you can start with nursing, occupational therapy, speech therapy, social work, medicine, teaching and even music or art (although less so these days). You can then go on to do additional training. In fact, most in this field think it is better to have some life experience before starting in psychotherapy.

Discipline lead for psychology

Higher Education Academy

JULIE HULME

Route into psychology:
A levels – biology, chemistry, physics (1989); BSc psychology and biology, Keele University (1996);
PhD neuroscience, Keele University (2003)

WHY PSYCHOLOGY?

I initially specialised in the biological side of neuroscience. However, although I enjoyed the scientific focus of my work, I wanted to take a more applied approach with an emphasis on people. I was intrigued by the relationship between brain and behaviour and this led to academic psychology, where I became fascinated by the psychology of learning and teaching.

HOW DID YOU GET WHERE YOU ARE TODAY?

I attended university as a mature student with a small baby. My family responsibilities meant I went to a local university, but I liked the idea of the joint honours system at Keele. In my final year, I carried out a research project and was then offered the chance to do a PhD in auditory neuroscience. I studied my PhD part-time, while teaching part-time to support my daughter and myself. My teaching experience in both psychology and bioscience grew into a fascination with teaching and learning. This led to a teaching fellowship in psychology at Keele University, followed by a lectureship at Staffordshire University. I developed my interests further through research into learning and teaching, and was awarded a teaching excellence fellowship in 2008 for my innovative teaching. When an opportunity to work for the Higher Education Academy (HEA) came up, it was just too good to miss!

WHAT DOES YOUR JOB INVOLVE?

Being the discipline lead for psychology at the HEA is massively varied. The HEA are responsible for enhancing learning and teaching practice across the higher education sector in the UK, and my job is to support this within psychology. I visit university psychology departments to advise people on research into psychology learning and teaching, organise and attend events, write papers and reports, and help people to develop best teaching practice. I also still do some research and teaching at Staffordshire University to keep my academic skills sharp. My work involves lots of travel so I can be in a university department, at HEA offices in York, or in my own office at home. I work full-time and often need to put in extra hours, but my job is so rewarding and enjoyable that I don't mind.

The people I work with are diverse, including psychology students, postgraduates, academics, heads of departments, people from the British Psychological Society, and all of my colleagues at the HEA, who have a wide range of subject interests and areas of expertise.

WHAT HAS BEEN YOUR BIGGEST CHALLENGE?

I think probably my biggest challenge was starting university. I wasn't very confident about my abilities and thought everyone else would be brighter than me. I was also very aware of my family responsibilities, and didn't know whether I'd be able to cope with full-time study alongside those.

AND THE BEST BITS?

I love the variety that comes from my job and I love being able to meet new people nearly every day. Most of the people I meet are as passionate about learning and teaching as I am, and I'm constantly exposed to new practices and new ideas, which I find stimulating and exciting.

JULIE'S TOP TIPS

There is never a right answer in psychology; you need to keep a constantly open mind, be inquisitive and ask lots of questions. Challenge everything, and learn from everything you see and experience. Psychology is not just an academic subject – it is happening to you and around you all the time!

The
UCAS Guide
to getting into
University
and College

UCAS

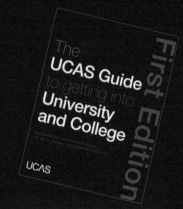

The UCAS Guide to getting into University and College — First Edition

What would 650,000 potential students like to know about UCAS? Everything!

- With rising costs and high competition for places, thorough research and preparation have never been more crucial for future students.

- Relevant throughout the whole year.

- Published by UCAS, a well-known and respected brand with direct access to the most up-to-date information.

- Written in a friendly, step-by-step format, with myth busters, checklists and helpful tips from students and experts at universities and colleges.

'…the most comprehensive guide… completely impartial… offers fabulous tips and advice…'
David Fullerton, Head of Careers

'Absolutely brilliant!'
Debbie Verdino,
Post-16 Manager

Order your copy now…

t +44 (0)1242 544 610

f +44(0)1242 544 806

e publicationservices@ucas.ac.uk

Price: £11.99

Entry routes

Routes to qualification

Qualifying as a psychologist normally involves two main stages:

1 accredited psychology degree or postgraduate conversion course, which confers on you the graduate basis for registration (GBR)
2 further postgraduate training in your preferred specialism.

The postgraduate qualification you take will depend on the field in which you hope to practise once training is complete. As discussed in the 'areas of work' section, the requirements vary according to your chosen field. To research and apply for postgraduate courses, check out **www.ukpass.ac.uk**.

CLINICAL PSYCHOLOGY

1 Psychology degree or conversion course
2 postgraduate accredited training course (three years full-time or equivalent part-time), leading to a **Doctorate in Clinical Psychology**
3 chartered status achieved.

COUNSELLING PSYCHOLOGY

1 Psychology degree or conversion course
2 EITHER three years' full-time (or part-time equivalent) personal development, study, research and practice, leading to a **Doctorate Counselling Psychology** from an accredited university
OR the British Psychological Society's independent training programme, which leads to a **Qualification in Counselling Psychology**
3 chartered status achieved.

EDUCATIONAL PSYCHOLOGY

1 Psychology degree or conversion course
2 EITHER a postgraduate accredited training course (three years full-time or equivalent part-time), leading to a **Doctorate in Educational Psychology** OR, in Scotland, an accredited two-year, full-time **MSc** in Educational Psychology followed by the British Psychology Society's Award in Educational Psychology
3 chartered status achieved.

FORENSIC PSYCHOLOGY

1 Psychology degree or conversion course
2 EITHER a one-year, full-time (or equivalent part-time) **MSc in Forensic Psychology** OR completion of Stage 1 of the British Psychological Society's **Qualification in Forensic Psychology**
3 completion of Stage 2 of the British Psychological Society's **Qualification in Forensic Psychology** (two years of supervised practice)
4 chartered status achieved.
(Note: it is possible to undertake a Doctorate in Forensic Psychology, which covers steps 2 and 3.)

HEALTH PSYCHOLOGY

1 Psychology degree or conversion course
2 EITHER a one-year, full-time (or equivalent part-time) **MSc in Health Psychology** OR completion of Stage 1 of the British Psychological Society's **Qualification in Health Psychology**
3 completion of Stage 2 of the British Psychological Society's **Qualification in Health Psychology** (two years of supervised practice)
4 chartered status achieved.
(Note: it is possible to undertake a Doctorate in Health Psychology, which covers steps 2 and 3.)

NEUROPSYCHOLOGY

1 Psychology degree or conversion course
2 postgraduate accredited training course in clinical neuropsychology or educational neuropsychology
3 completion of the British Psychological Society's **Practitioner Full Membership Qualification in Neuropsychology**
4 chartered status achieved.

OCCUPATIONAL PSYCHOLOGY

1 Psychology degree or conversion course
2 EITHER a one-year, full-time (or equivalent part-time) **MSc in Occupational Psychology** OR completion of Stage 1 of the British Psychological Society's **Qualification in Occupational Psychology**
3 Stage 2 of the British Psychological Society's **Qualification in Occupational Psychology** (two years of supervised practice)
4 chartered status achieved.

SPORT AND EXERCISE PSYCHOLOGY

1 Psychology degree or conversion course
2 EITHER a one-year, full-time (or equivalent part-time) **MSc in Sport and Exercise Psychology** OR Stage 1 of the British Psychological Society's **Qualification in Sport and Exercise Psychology**
3 Stage 2 of the British Psychological Society's **Qualification in Sport and Exercise Psychology** (two years of supervised practice)
4 chartered status achieved.

TEACHING AND RESEARCH PSYCHOLOGISTS

1 Psychology degree or conversion course
2 EITHER a **Doctorate in Psychology** OR, for teachers, a period of full-time experience as a teacher of psychology
3 chartered status achieved.

What does a degree in psychology normally involve?

COURSE INTENSITY

It's important for psychology students to know that while the first stage of their studies lasts the same length of time as other degrees – three years – a further period of study at postgraduate level plus some years of supervised practice is normally required to practise as a fully qualified psychologist. Of course you can decide at the end of your degree that psychology isn't the career for you: you will still be a valuable acquisition for future employers.

COURSE STRUCTURE

All accredited psychology degrees will introduce you to the theories and methods of psychology in order for you to attain the graduate basis for chartered membership (GBC) required by the British Psychological Society for you to progress further with your training in this field. All good courses should also equip you with the relevant IT and communication skills needed for a career in psychology or any other field, as well as a sound understanding of behavioural research.

Courses usually last for three years, full-time, though some four-year courses – including a year's work placement – are available.

In the first year or two, students normally gain a good understanding of psychology by considering the social, developmental, cognitive and biological issues of behaviour and learning how psychology can help with mental and physical health conditions. Modules or learning areas can include the following:

- cognitive neuroscience
- skills for psychology
- research methods
- social psychology
- cognitive psychology
- animal cognition
- statistics in psychology
- developmental psychology
- memory and perception
- quantitative and qualitative methods
- contemporary issues
- social cognition
- brain and behaviour
- language and language development
- thinking and reasoning
- personality theory and intelligence
- abnormal psychology
- parapsychology.

After this general introduction, you will be able to specialise in your final year from a range of topics including health psychology, clinical psychology, and psychology for addictive behaviour. Normally, to consolidate your learning, you will produce a piece of research into your chosen specialisation. Such specialisms could be from the following list:

- the psychology of addiction
- the psychology of racism
- the psychology of language disorders in children
- health psychology
- the psychology of pain
- autism, Asperger's and attentiton deficit hyperactivity disorder (ADHD)
- ergonomics.

Modules and specialisms can vary between universities, so please check with your preferred institutions as to what they offer.

METHODS OF LEARNING AND ASSESSMENT

Teaching in universities normally takes place through a combination of lectures, smaller group seminars, tutorials (often on a one-to-one basis), and practical workshops. Again, this is something to consider when applying for courses as teaching methods can vary.

Equally, assessment methods are different between universities. Some of the more traditional institutions rely on final examinations to award degree classifications, while others will operate an assessment procedure based on either continuous assessment – through projects, for example – or a mixture of final exams and coursework.

ENTRY REQUIREMENTS

Which subjects?

While you don't need to have all three sciences at A level for a psychology degree, most universities prefer at least one out of chemistry, physics, biology or maths. Psychology A level is not a prerequisite although it can be a useful introduction to the subject area. Normally a combination of good, academic A level subjects are accepted, but be aware that general studies is mainly not considered when making offers. Literature A levels can be helpful because of the report writing that you will inevitably be doing, and statistics will help with the analytical component of the degree.

Competition for places on UK psychology courses is intense as the subject is very popular amongst undergraduates. Therefore, it is not uncommon for admissions tutors to request high grades or UCAS Tariff points. Check with each institution for their entry requirements. Tutors may also take GCSE grades into account as another way to filter the growing number of straight-A students.

What others say…

What others say…

These are extracts from case studies in previous editions of this book. They give some insights into the experiences and thoughts of people who were once in the same position as you.

NATHAN SHEARMAN – MASTER'S STUDENT IN FORENSIC PSYCHOLOGY

Nathan did a degree in forensic psychology then chose to do a master's in forensic psychology as a first step towards becoming a chartered forensic psychologist. He says, 'As an undergraduate I worked with offenders in a prison setting, more specifically acting as a mentor for an adult in an open prison to help widen their current support system. I also worked as a paid research assistant for a lecturer in cognitive psychology.

'As part of my master's, I have spent one day a week within a forensic mental health team in a hospital in Middlesbrough, as part of a six-month placement. I have attended ward rounds, meetings and tribunals, discussed cases with members of the multidisciplinary team, and worked directly with mentally disordered offenders, for example administering psychometric tools.

'The first couple of years of my course focused on the theory of psychology and laying the essential foundations of the discipline, including tackling statistics. Although we got a lot of support, it was tough at times and could seem far removed from real life. However, as the course progressed it became increasingly applied and interesting, so it was well worth persevering.'

LARA ZIBARRAS – LECTURER IN PSYCHOLOGY/RESEARCH STUDENT

'I love the variety of my working week, and the fact that I have so much autonomy. As an academic I have the flexibility to pursue what really interests me, rather than being dictated to by clients. As a lecturer, it's great seeing students flourish and leaving with the knowledge to become occupational psychologists. Occupational psychology is about practice, so I'm glad that I have the consultancy side to my work – being able to give real examples also helps in my teaching role.'

Lara's top tip is 'If you are interested in psychology join the British Psychological Society (BPS). You'll receive The Psychologist magazine, from which you can gain so much insight into what kinds of jobs psychologists do. Try to find some work experience or shadowing in the areas that interest you, and make use of your careers service at university.'

REBECCA MCKNIGHT – ACADEMIC FOUNDATION TRAINEE (PSYCHIATRY)

Rebecca studied medicine at Oxford University and explains what she did next.

'When I graduated I applied for a special academic training scheme, which allows me time each year for research in psychiatry. I chose academic psychiatry because I want to spend the rest of my career helping people with severe mental health problems, and discovering some of the causes behind and mechanisms by which these illnesses occur. I like seeing patients over time, getting to know them and their families, and helping them manage with problems in their everyday lives.

'I particularly enjoy learning about my patients and watching their interactions with other people, especially their families. It is very gratifying to discharge someone ill enough to be treated (perhaps involuntarily) from hospital, and see them go back to living a normal life.

'Psychiatry is a very rewarding speciality for those who are interested in people and their problems in a wider sense, but is not for people who like a lot of fast-paced excitement or action.'

SARAH CUDMORE – PRINCIPAL HUMAN FACTORS CONSULTANT

Sarah chose to study human psychology as a degree and did a placement with an applied psychology unit at the Ministry of Defence (MoD) during her sandwich year. After graduating she returned to the MoD as a full-time employee for two years, before leaving to undertake a management training programme in another Government organisation. Since leaving the MoD she has held a series of consultant psychologist roles in defence, safety and risk, process improvement and construction, working with managers to help them improve their organisation's performance. Much of her work has centred around looking at how to help employees do their jobs most effectively: for example, by checking that they have the necessary knowledge, skills, motivation, environment and equipment.

Sarah says 'I find psychology endlessly fascinating and love the fact that I can see the whole world as my laboratory. I can apply psychological tools and theories to anything, everywhere – and sometimes get paid for it!

'Psychology is a great subject to study. As a discipline it spans the arts and science – you'll need to be able to write well as well as do statistics and scientific experiments. You will probably need to undertake further study to find a specialist role in the field.'

DEBORAH LEE – EDUCATION PSYCHOLOGIST

Local authorities employ educational psychologists to assess and advise on children and young people with additional support needs (from birth to 24 years of age). This is what Deborah says.

'When I finished my undergraduate degree I didn't know what I wanted to do – there are so many avenues open to psychology graduates. My PhD was a great way to explore this. At the end of my research, which focused on developing a personal safety curriculum for children with additional support needs, I applied for a master's in educational psychology: it is possible to train as an educational psychologist through a research or teaching route. To get on the course I needed to have had experience of working with children, which I had acquired during my PhD and in other settings, including through voluntary work.

'My work requires me to liaise with other agencies, from local psychiatric services to social workers, and speech and language therapists. As well as contributing to assessments, I may also get involved in helping schools plan whole school or class interventions, running projects related to local authority priorities, or design and organise interventions such as group work and parent groups. To do my job I need to understand educational systems, have good clinical knowledge and use research skills.
'I am responsible for juggling my workload; it can be stressful when demands mount up. Most of the situations educational psychologists are involved in are 'stuck' in some way, so emotions can be high. Ensuring my advice keeps up with current research and literature is a constant challenge.'

Deborah's top tip is: 'Take time to visit psychologists working in different fields, and to find voluntary experience or paid work in contexts that involve working with young people. Know yourself: the job of any psychologist can place you in the 'grey' area of life, so if you like certainty it's maybe not for you! Interpersonal skills and flexibility are perhaps the most important skills for the job. Brush up on your listening skills and seek feedback to ensure you're as good a listener as you think you are!'

LAURA DENNISON – TEACHING FELLOW/RESEARCH ASSISTANT

Laura gained a BSc psychology and a MSc health psychology before embarking on a PhD in health psychology and practice. She explains what being a teaching fellow/research assistant involves:

'As a teaching fellow I teach psychology to undergraduate medical students, mostly to large groups in a lecture format and some small group workshops. I also teach psychology students and supervise final-year research projects.

'My research job involved coordinating a study about improving the psychological adjustment of people with multiple sclerosis (MS). I worked within a team of researchers, including health psychologists, neurologists, health economists and statisticians, to develop a psychological treatment for reducing distress and impairment in patients with MS. We then taught nurses to deliver the therapy and ran a trial to tests its effectiveness. The research from this project has formed part of my PhD and I have published papers on it.'

LEE FROST – SPECIAL ALCOHOL THERAPIST/COUNSELLING PSYCHOLOGIST

Lee studied for a BA psychology and went on to a gain a Doctorate in counselling psychology.

'I took A level psychology by chance, after being advised it would 'fit well' with my other course options. I found it to be a broad and engaging introduction to a vast field of knowledge. It was a natural progression for me to study psychology at degree level.

'Although I gained lots of information and insight from my psychology degree, I wanted to find a course that would allow me to apply this knowledge in a practical way. After completing a foundation counselling qualification, I discovered counselling psychology: a professional approach that integrated numerous psychological approaches and fitted well with my personal philosophy at the time.'

MICHAEL AUSTIN – MANAGING DIRECTOR, SPORT PSYCHOLOGY CONSULTANT

After completing a BSc psychology, Michael went on to gain a MSc sport and exercise psychology, before setting up an applied sports psychology practice.

'My job as a sport psychologist involves advising athletes, coaches and teams on effective mental preparation and performance-enhancement strategies to maximise their true potential. Specifically, we design mental training programmes and personal development plans in the form of educational seminars and workshops and one-to-one consultation sessions. We work regularly with organisations such as UEFA, the Irish Football Association, Swim Ulster and the Gaelic Athletic Association.

'My daily routine varies quite considerably. I could be preparing for a seminar or lecture, designing a workshop, delivering one of our programmes, working with individual clients, organising and attending meetings, or writing an article for a newspaper – there is always something to do and it's always interesting!'

GREG DAVIES – RESEARCH EXECUTIVE

Greg gained a BSc psychology and a MSc organisational psychology. He explains how he got where he is today:

'The optional courses in the final year of my degree gave me a deeper understanding of each area of psychology, and I realised that I wanted to study organisational psychology. I'd always had an interest in business and wanted to apply psychology to work activities as these occupy such a large part of people's lives.

'If you like research and like investigating things (basically, if you're nosey!) organisational psychology could be for you. However, make sure you are clear about what a degree in psychology can involve. Many people view it as an easy option at university, not realising it can include studying science topics, such as neuroscience, as well as statistics.'

BEA ANDERSON – CLINICAL PSYCHOLOGIST

Bea studied for a MA psychology before completing a Doctorate in clinical psychology. She told us about the challenges of her job and what she most likes about it:

'Clinical psychologists work with people who are experiencing difficult thoughts and feelings and may have had very challenging life experiences. While it can be rewarding to help people overcome difficulties, it can also be exhausting and upsetting, so it's important to have a good work-life balance. I also receive supervision from a more senior clinical psychologist, who supports me and offers advice and guidance on professional or clinical issues.

'The most exciting part is making a positive difference to the lives of the children and young people I work with and hopefully contributing to them having happy and fulfilling futures.'

wondering how much higher education costs?

need information about student finance?

Visit www.ucas.com/students/studentfinance
and find sources for all the information on student
money matters you need.

With access to up-to-date information on
bursaries, scholarships and variable fees, plus
our online budget calculator. Visit us today and
get the full picture.

www.ucas.com/students/studentfinance

Applicant
journey

SIX EASY STEPS TO UNIVERSITY AND COLLEGE

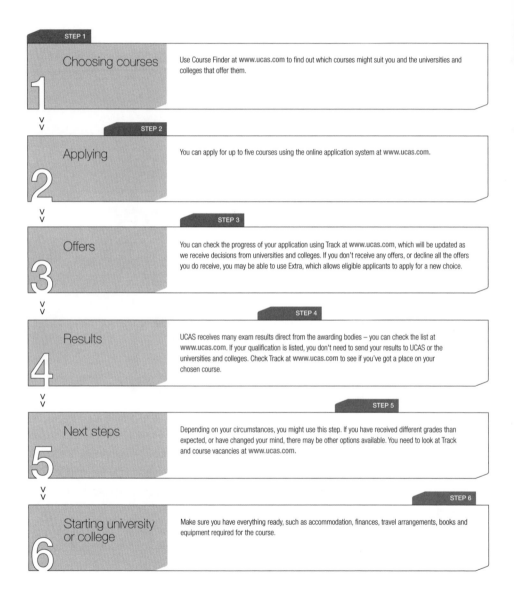

STEP 1

Choosing courses

Use Course Finder at www.ucas.com to find out which courses might suit you and the universities and colleges that offer them.

STEP 2

Applying

You can apply for up to five courses using the online application system at www.ucas.com.

STEP 3

Offers

You can check the progress of your application using Track at www.ucas.com, which will be updated as we receive decisions from universities and colleges. If you don't receive any offers, or decline all the offers you do receive, you may be able to use Extra, which allows eligible applicants to apply for a new choice.

STEP 4

Results

UCAS receives many exam results direct from the awarding bodies – you can check the list at www.ucas.com. If your qualification is listed, you don't need to send your results to UCAS or the universities and colleges. Check Track at www.ucas.com to see if you've got a place on your chosen course.

STEP 5

Next steps

Depending on your circumstances, you might use this step. If you have received different grades than expected, or have changed your mind, there may be other options available. You need to look at Track and course vacancies at www.ucas.com.

STEP 6

Starting university or college

Make sure you have everything ready, such as accommodation, finances, travel arrangements, books and equipment required for the course.

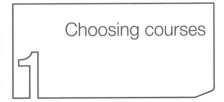

Choosing courses

Step 1 - Choosing courses

USE COURSE FINDER AT WWW.UCAS.COM TO FIND OUT WHICH COURSES MIGHT SUIT YOU, AND THE UNIVERSITIES AND COLLEGES THAT OFFER THEM.

Start thinking about what you want to study and where you want to go. This section will help you, and see what courses are available where in the listings (starting on page 126). Check that the entry requirements required for each course meet your academic expectations.

Use the UCAS website – www.ucas.com has lots of advice on how to find a course. Go to the students' section of the website for the best advice or go straight to Course Finder to see all the courses available through UCAS. Our map of the UK at **www.ucas.com/students/choosingcourses/choosinguni/map/** shows you where all the universities and colleges are located.

Watch UCAStv – at www.ucas.tv there are videos on *How to choose your course*, *Attending events*, and *Open days*, as well as case studies from students talking about their experience of finding a course at university or college.

Attend UCAS conventions – UCAS conventions are held throughout the country. Universities and colleges have exhibition stands where their staff offer information about their courses and institutions. Details of when the conventions are happening, and a convention planner to help you prepare, are shown at **www.ucas.com/conventions**.

Look at university and college websites and prospectuses – universities and colleges have prospectuses and course-specific leaflets on their undergraduate courses. Your school or college library may have copies or go to the university's website to download a copy, or ask them to send one to you.

Go to university and college open days – most institutions offer open days to anyone who wants to attend. See the list of universities and colleges on **www.ucas.com** and the UCAS *Open Days* publication (see the Essential Reading chapter) for information on when they are taking place. Aim to visit all of the universities and colleges you are interested in before you apply. It will help with your expectations of university life and make sure the course is the right one for you.

League tables – these can be helpful but bear in mind that they attempt to rank institutions in an overall order reflecting the views of those that produce them. They may not reflect your views and needs. Examples can be found at **www.thecompleteuniversityguide.co.uk**, **www.guardian.co.uk/education/universityguide**, **www.thetimes.co.uk** (subscription service) and **www.thesundaytimes.co.uk** (subscription service). See page 76 for more information about league tables.

Do your research – speak and refer to as many trusted sources as you can find. Talk to someone already doing the job you have in mind. The section on 'A career in psychology' on pages 13-35 will help you identify the different areas of psychology you might want to enter.

UCAS CARD

At its simplest, the UCAS Card scheme is the start of your UCAS journey. It can save you a packet on the high street with exclusive offers to UCAS Card holders, as well as providing you with hints and tips about finding the best course at the right university or college. If that's not enough you'll also receive these benefits:

- frequent expert help from UCAS, with all the essential information you need on the application process
- free monthly newsletters providing advice, hints, tips and exclusive discounts
- tailored information on the universities and courses you're interested in
- and much more.

If you're in Year 12, S5 or equivalent and thinking about higher education for autumn 2013, sign up for your FREE UCAS Card today to receive all these benefits at **www.ucas.com/ucascard**.

DECIDING ON YOUR COURSE CHOICES

Through UCAS you can initially apply for up to five courses. How do you find out more information to make an informed decision?

Remember you don't have to make five course choices. Only apply for a course if you're completely happy with both the course and the university or college and you would definitely be prepared to accept a place.

How do you narrow down your course choices? First of all, look up course details in this book or on Course Finder at **www.ucas.com**. This will give you an idea of the full range of courses and topics on offer. You may want to study psychology as a single subject, but there

are also many courses which also include additional options, such as a modern language (check out the degree subjects studied by our case studies). You'll quickly be able to eliminate institutions that don't offer the right course, or you can choose a 'hit list' of institutions first, and then see what they have to offer.

Once you've made a short(er) list, look at university or college websites, and generally find out as much as you can about the course, department and institution. Don't be afraid to contact them to ask for more information, request their prospectus or arrange an open day visit.

Choosing courses

1

Choosing your institution

Different people look for different things from their university or college course, but the checklist on the next page sets out the kinds of factors all prospective students should consider when choosing their university. Keep this list in mind on open days, when talking to friends about their experiences at various universities and colleges, or while reading prospectuses and websites.

WHAT TO CONSIDER WHEN CHOOSING YOUR PSYCHOLOGY COURSE

Location	Do you want to stay close to home? Would you prefer to study at a city or campus university or college?
Grades required	Use the Course Finder facility on the UCAS website, www.ucas.com, to view entry requirements for courses you are interested in. Also, check out the university website or call up the admissions office. Some universities specify grades required, eg AAB, while others specify points required, eg 340. If they ask for points, it means they're using the UCAS Tariff system, which awards points to different types and levels of qualification. For example, an A grade at A level = 120 points; a B grade at A level = 100 points. The full Tariff tables are available on pages 101-107 and at www.ucas.com.
Employer links	Ask the course tutor and university or college careers office about links with employers, especially for placements or work experience.
Graduate prospects	Ask the university careers office for their list of graduate 'destinations' to find out what former students are now doing.
Cost	Ask the admissions office about variable tuition fees and financial assistance.
Degree type	Think about whether you want to study psychology on its own (single honours degree) or 50/50 with another subject (joint degree) or as one of a few subjects (combined degree).
Teaching style	How is the course taught? Ask about the number of lectures and tutorials per week, the amount of one-to-one work, and how you will be involved in project work.
Course assessment	What proportion of the assessment is based on project work, written assignments and exams?
Facilities for students	Check out the campus library and computing facilities. Find out if there is a careers adviser dedicated to psychology students.
'Fit'	Even if all the above criteria stack up, this one relies on gut feel – go and visit the psychology department if you can and see if it's 'you'. Also ask about lecturers' own particular interests; many will have personal web pages somewhere on the departmental website.

1 Choosing courses

League tables

The information that follows has been provided by Dr Bernard Kingston of *The Complete University Guide*.

League tables are worth consulting early in your research and perhaps for confirmation later on. But never rely on them in isolation – always use them alongside other information sources available to you. Universities typically report that over a third of prospective students view league tables as important or very important in making their university choices. They give an insight into quality and are mainly based on data from the universities themselves. Somewhat confusingly, tables published in, say, 2012 are referred to as the 2013 tables because they are aimed at applicants going to university in that following year. The well known ones - *The Complete University Guide*, *The Guardian*, *The Times*, and *The Sunday Times* - rank the institutions and the subjects they teach using input measures (eg entry standards), throughput measures (eg student : staff ratios) and output measures (eg graduate prospects). Some tables are free to access whilst others are behind pay walls. All are interactive and enable users to create their own tables based on the measures important to them.

The universities are provided with their raw data for checking and are regularly consulted on methodology. But ultimately it is the compilers who decide what measures to use and what weights to put on them. They are competitors and rarely consult amongst themselves. So, for example, *The Times* tables differ significantly from *The Sunday Times* ones even though both newspapers belong to the same media proprietor.

Whilst the main university rankings tend to get the headlines, we would stress that the individual subject tables are as least as important, if not more so, when deciding where to study. All universities, regardless of their overall ranking, have some academic departments that rank highly in their subjects. Beware also giving much weight to an institution being a few places higher or lower in the tables – this is likely to be of little significance. This is particularly true in the lower half of the main table where overall scores show considerable bunching.

Most of the measures used to define quality come from hard factual data provided by the Higher Education Statistics Agency (HESA) but some, like student satisfaction and peer assessment, are derived from surveys of subjective impressions where you might wish to query sample size. We give a brief overview of the common measures here but please go to the individual websites for full details.

- **Student satisfaction** is derived from the annual National Student Survey (NSS) and is heavily used by *The Guardian* and *The Sunday Times*.
- **Research assessment** comes from a 2008 exercise (RAE) aimed at defining the quality of a university's research (excluded by *The Guardian*).
- **Entry standards** are based on the full UCAS Tariff scores obtained by new students.
- **Student : staff ratio** gives the number of students per member of academic staff.
- **Expenditure figures** show the costs of academic and student services.
- **Good honours** lists the proportion of graduates gaining a first or upper second honours degree.
- **Completion** indicates the proportion of students who successfully complete their studies.
- **Graduate prospects** usually reports the proportion of graduates who obtain a graduate job – not any job – or continue studying within six months of leaving.

- **Peer assessment** is used only by *The Sunday Times* which asks academics to rate other universities in their subjects.
- **Value added** is used only by *The Guardian* and compares entry standards with good honours.

All four main publishers of UK league tables (see Table 1) also publish university subject tables. *The Complete University Guide* and *The Times* are based on four measures: student satisfaction, research quality, entry standards and graduate destinations. *The Sunday Times* uses student satisfaction, entry standards, graduate destinations, graduate unemployment, good degrees and drop-out rate, while *The Guardian* uses student satisfaction (as three separate measures), entry standards, graduate destinations, student-staff ratio, spend per student and value added. This use of different measures is one reason why the different tables can yield different results (sometimes very different, especially in the case of *The Guardian* which has least in common with the other tables).

League tables compiled by *The Complete University Guide* (**www.thecompleteuniversityguide.co.uk**) and *The Guardian* (**www.guardian.co.uk**) are available in spring, those by *The Times* (**www.thetimes.co.uk**) and *The Sunday Times* (**www.thesundaytimes.co.uk**) in the summer.

Table 1 – measures used by the main publishers of UK league tables

	Universities	Measures	Subjects	Measures
The Complete University Guide	116	9	62	4
The Guardian	119	8	46	8
The Sunday Times	122	8	39	6
The Times	116	8	62	4

WHO PUBLISHES PSYCHOLOGY LEAGUE TABLES?

Psychology league tables are published by *The Complete University Guide*, *The Guardian*, *The Times* and *The Sunday Times*. Be aware that the tables make no distinction between universities which offer courses that are accredited by the British Psychological Society and those which do not.

Save with UCAS Card

If you're in Year 12, S5 or equivalent and thinking about higher education, sign up for the **FREE** UCAS Card to receive all these benefits:

- information about courses and unis
- expert advice from UCAS
- exclusive discounts for card holders

UCAS

Register today at
www.ucas.com/ucascard

find us on
Facebook

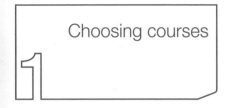

1 Choosing courses

How will they choose you?

Most psychology admissions departments will have different entry criteria, so make sure that you check prospectuses, websites and all other materials thoroughly before you apply. Even better, why not give them a call and discuss their entry requirements with them directly? Not only will it leave you better prepared to submit a targeted application, but it will also demonstrate that you're self-motivated.

It's unlikely that you'll have to sit an entry test. This means that if there is an interview (and in many cases there will be) it is particularly important.

THE INTERVIEW

Talk to someone who has been – or is currently – on the course that you are applying for. What was their interview like? What kinds of questions were they asked? Be prepared and if possible do a mock interview with a friend, teacher or a careers adviser before you go for the real thing.

Each university will have its own format of interview but you can prepare for typical questions. Interviewers will want to find out whether you possess the skills and attributes needed for a career in psychology. These include empathy, communication skills and analytical skills. Take a look at the skills listed in **Is psychology for you?** (page 38) and try to come up with an example for each one. There's also some advice in the personal statement section (page 90). Tutors will also want to know why you are interested in psychology, so be ready to explain why you chose the course. If you have done any work experience, this will also support your case. Good preparation is the best way to success at interview.

1

Choosing courses

The cost of higher education

The information in this section was up-to-date when this book was published. You should visit the websites mentioned in this section for the very latest information.

THE COST OF STUDYING IN THE UK

As a student, you will usually have to pay for two things: tuition fees for your course, which for most students do not need to be paid for up front, and living costs such as rent, food, books, transport and entertainment. Fees charged vary between courses, between universities and colleges and also according to your normal country of residence, so it's important to check these before you apply. Course fee information is supplied to UCAS by the universities and is displayed in Course Finder at **www.ucas.com**.

STUDENT LOANS

The purpose of student loans from the Government is to help cover the costs of your tuition fees and basic living costs (rent, bills, food and so on). Two types are available: a tuition fee loan to cover the tuition charges and a maintenance loan to help with accommodation and other living costs. Both types of student loan are available to all students who meet the basic eligibility requirements. Interest will be charged at inflation plus a fixed percentage while you are studying. In addition, many other commercial loans are available to students studying at university or college but the interest rate can vary considerably. Loans to help with living costs will be available for all eligible students, irrespective of family income.

Find out more information from the relevant sites below:

England: Student Finance England –
www.direct.gov.uk/studentfinance
Northern Ireland: Student Finance Northern Ireland –
www.studentfinanceni.co.uk
Scotland: Student Awards Agency for Scotland –
www.saas.gov.uk
Wales: Student Finance Wales –
www.studentfinancewales.co.uk or
www.cyllidmyfyrwyrcymru.co.uk

BURSARIES AND SCHOLARSHIPS

- The National Scholarships Programme gives financial help to students studying in England. The scheme is designed to help students whose families have lower incomes.
- Students from families with lower incomes will be entitled to a non-repayable maintenance grant to help with living costs.
- Many universities and colleges also offer non-repayable scholarships and bursaries to help students cover tuition and living costs whilst studying.
- All eligible part-time undergraduates who study for at least 25% of their time will be able to apply for a loan to cover the costs of their tuition, which means they no longer have to pay up front.

There will be extra support for disabled students and students with child or adult dependants. For more information, visit the country-specific websites listed above.

Choosing courses

1

International students

APPLYING TO STUDY IN THE UK

Deciding to go to university or college in the UK is very exciting. You need to think about what course to do, where to study, and how much it will cost. The decisions you make can have a huge effect on your future but UCAS is here to help.

HOW TO APPLY

Whatever your age or qualifications, if you want to apply for any of over 35,000 courses listed at 300 universities and colleges on the UCAS website, you must apply through UCAS at **www.ucas.com**. If you are unsure, your school, college, adviser, or local British Council office will be able to help. Further advice and a video guide for international students can be found on the non-UK students' section of the UCAS website at **www.ucas.com/international**.

Students may apply on their own or through their school, college, adviser, or local British Council if this is registered with UCAS to use Apply. If you choose to use an education agent's services, check with the British Council to see if they hold a list of certificated or registered agents in your country. Check also on any charges you may need to pay. UCAS charges only the application fee (see below) but agents may charge for additional services.

HOW MUCH WILL MY APPLICATION COST?

If you choose to apply to more than one course, university or college you need to pay UCAS £23 GBP when you apply. If you only apply to one course at one university or college, you pay UCAS £12 GBP.

WHAT LEVEL OF ENGLISH?

UCAS provides a list of English language qualifications and grades that are acceptable to most UK universities and colleges, however you are advised to contact the institutions directly as each have their own entry requirement in English. For more information go to **www.ucas.com/students/wheretostart/nonukstudents/englangprof.**

INTERNATIONAL STUDENT FEES

If you study in the UK, your fee status (whether you pay full-cost fees or a subsidised fee rate) will be decided by the UK university or college you plan to attend. Before you decide which university or college to attend, you need to be absolutely certain that you can pay the full cost of:

- your tuition fees (the amount is set by universities and colleges, so contact them for more information – visit their websites where many list their fees. Fee details will also be included on Course Finder at www.ucas.com)
- the everyday living expenses for you (and your family) for the whole time that you are in the UK, including accommodation, food, gas and electricity bills, clothes, travel and leisure activities
- books and equipment for your course
- travel to and from your country.

You must include everything when you work out how much it will cost. You can get information to help you do this accurately from the international offices at universities and colleges, UKCISA (UK Council for International Student Affairs) and the British Council. There is a useful website tool to help you manage your money at university – **www.studentcalculator.org.uk**.

Scholarships and bursaries are offered at some universities and colleges and you should contact them for more information. In addition, you should check with your local British Council for additional scholarships available to students from your country who want to study in the UK.

LEGAL DOCUMENTS YOU WILL NEED

As you prepare to study in the UK, it is very important to think about the legal documents you will need to enter the country.

Everyone who comes to study in the UK needs a valid passport, details of which will be collected either in your UCAS application or later through Track. If you do not yet have a passport, you should apply for one as soon as possible. People from certain countries also need visas before they come into the UK. They are known as 'visa nationals'. You can check if you require a visa to travel to the UK by visiting the UK Border Agency website and selecting 'Studying in the UK', so please check the UK Border Agency website at **www.ukba.homeoffice.gov.uk** for the most up-to-date guidance and information about the United Kingdom's visa requirements.

When you apply for your visa you need to make sure you have the following documents:

- A confirmation of acceptance for studies (CAS) number from the university or college where you are going to study. The university or college must be on the UKBA Register of Sponsors in order to accept international students.
- A valid passport.
- Evidence that you have enough money to pay for your course and living costs.
- Certificates for all qualifications you have that are relevant to the course you have been accepted for and for any English language qualifications.

You will also have to give your biometric data.

Do check for further information from your local British Embassy or High Commission. Guidance information for international students is also available from UKCISA and from UKBA.

ADDITIONAL RESOURCES

There are a number of organisations that can provide further guidance and information to you as you prepare to study in the UK:

- British Council
  www.britishcouncil.org
- Education UK (British Council website dealing with educational matters)
  www.educationuk.org
- English UK (British Council accredited website listing English language courses in the UK)
  www.englishuk.com
- UK Border Agency (provides information on visa requirements and applications)
  www.ukba.homeoffice.gov.uk
- UKCISA (UK Council for International Student Affairs)
  www.ukcisa.org.uk
- Directgov (the official UK Government website)
  www.direct.gov.uk
- Prepare for Success
  www.prepareforsuccess.org.uk

Applying

2

Step 2 – Applying

You apply through UCAS using the online application system, called Apply, at **www.ucas.com**. You can apply for a maximum of five choices, but you don't have to use them all if you don't want to. If you apply for fewer than five choices, you can add more at a later date if you want to. But be aware of the course application deadlines. You can find these in Course Finder at **www.ucas.com**.

IMPORTANT DATES FOR 2012 ENTRY	
Early June 2012	UCAS Apply opens for 2013 entry registration.
Mid-September 2012	Applications can be sent to UCAS.
15 October 2012	Application deadline for the receipt at UCAS of applications for all medicine, dentistry, veterinary medicine and veterinary science courses and for all courses at the universities of Oxford and Cambridge.
15 January 2013	Application deadline for the receipt at UCAS of applications for all courses except those listed above with a 15 October deadline, and some art and design courses with a 24 March deadline.
25 February 2013	Extra starts (see page 96 for more information about Extra).
24 March 2013	Application deadline for the receipt at UCAS of applications for art and design courses except those listed on Course Finder at www.ucas.com with a 15 January deadline.
31 March 2013	If you apply by 15 January, the universities and colleges should aim to have sent their decisions by this date (but they can take longer).
9 May 2013	If you apply by 15 January, universities and colleges need to send their decisions by this date. If they don't, UCAS will make any outstanding choices unsuccessful on their behalf.
30 June 2013	If you send your application to us by this date, we will send it to your chosen universities and colleges. Applications received after this date are entered into Clearing (see page 110 for more information about Clearing).
3 July 2013	Last date to apply through Extra.
August 2013 (date to be confirmed)	Scottish Qualifications Authority (SQA) results are published.
15 August 2013	GCE and Advanced Diploma results are published (often known as 'A level results day'). Adjustment opens for registration (see page 111 for more information about Adjustment).

DON'T FORGET...

Universities and colleges guarantee to consider your application only if we receive it by the appropriate deadline. Check application deadlines for your courses on Course Finder at www.ucas.com.

If you send it to UCAS after the deadline but before 30 June 2013, universities and colleges will consider your application only if they still have places available.

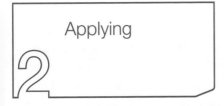

Applying

How to apply

You apply online at **www.ucas.com** through Apply – a secure, web-based application service that is designed for all our applicants, whether they are applying through a UCAS-registered centre or as an individual, anywhere in the world. Apply is:

- easy to access – all you need is an internet connection
- easy to use – you don't have to complete your application all in one go: you can save the sections as you complete them and come back to it later
- easy to monitor – once you've applied, you can use Track to check the progress of your application, including any decisions from universities or colleges. You can also reply to your offers using Track.

Watch the UCAStv guide to applying through UCAS at **www.ucas.tv**.

You can submit only one UCAS application in each year's application cycle.

APPLICATION FEE

The fee for applying through UCAS is £23 for two or more choices and £12 for one choice.

DEFERRED ENTRY

If you want to apply for deferred entry in 2014, perhaps because you want to take a year out between school or college and higher education, you should check that the university or college will accept a deferred entry application. Occasionally, tutors are not happy to accept students who take a gap year, because it interrupts the flow of their learning. If you apply for deferred entry, you must meet the conditions of any offers by 31 August 2013 unless otherwise agreed by the university or college. If you accept a place for 2014 entry and then change your mind, you cannot reapply through us in the 2014 entry cycle unless you withdraw your original application.

APPLYING THROUGH YOUR SCHOOL OR COLLEGE

1 GET SCHOOL OR COLLEGE 'BUZZWORD'

Ask your UCAS application coordinator (may be your sixth form tutor) for your school or college UCAS 'buzzword'. This is a password for the school or college.

2 REGISTER

Go to **www.ucas.com/students/apply** and click on **Register/Log in to use Apply** and then **register**. After you have entered your registration details, the online system will automatically generate a username for you, but you'll have to come up with a password and answers to security questions.

3 COMPLETE SEVEN SECTIONS

Complete all the sections of the application. To access any section, click on the section name at the left of the screen and follow the instructions. The sections are:

Personal details – contact details, residential status, disability status

Additional information – only UK applicants need to complete this section

Student finance – UK students can share some of their application details with their student finance company. Finance information is provided for other EU and international applicants

Choices – which courses you'd like to apply for

Education – your education and qualifications

Employment – eg work experience, holiday jobs

Statement – see page 90 for personal statement advice.

Before you can send your application you need to go to the **View all details** screen and tick the **section completed** box.

4 PASS TO REFEREE

Once you've completed all the sections, send your application electronically to your referee (normally your form tutor). They'll check it, approve it and add their reference to it, and will then send it to UCAS on your behalf.

USEFUL INFORMATION ABOUT APPLY

- Important details like date of birth and course codes will be checked by Apply. It will alert you if they are not valid.
- We strongly recommend that the personal statement and reference are written in a word processing package and pasted in to Apply.
- If you want to, you can enter European characters into certain areas of Apply.
- You can change your application at any time before it is completed and sent to UCAS.
- You can print and preview your application at any time. Before you send it you need to go to the **View all details** screen and tick the **section completed** box.
- Your school, college or centre can choose different payment methods. For example, they may want us to bill them, or you may be able to pay online by debit or credit card.

NOT APPLYING THROUGH A SCHOOL OR COLLEGE

If you're not currently studying, you'll probably be applying as an independent applicant rather than through a school, college or other UCAS-registered centre. In this case you won't be able to provide a 'buzzword', but we'll ask you a few extra questions to check you are eligible to apply.

If you're not applying through a UCAS-registered centre, the procedure you use for obtaining a reference will depend on whether or not you want your reference to be provided through a registered centre. For information on the procedures for providing references, visit www.ucas.com/students/applying/howtoapply/reference.

INVISIBILITY OF CHOICES

Universities and colleges cannot see details of the other choices on your application until you reply to any offers or you are unsuccessful at all of your choices.

APPLICATION CHECKLIST

We want this to run smoothly for you and we also want to process your application as quickly as possible. You can help us to do this by remembering to do the following:

✓ check the closing dates for applications – see page 86

✓ check the student information at www.ucas.com/students/studentfinance/ and course fees information in Course Finder at www.ucas.com

✓ start early and allow plenty of time for completing your application – including enough time for your referee to complete the reference section

✓ read the online instructions carefully before you start

✓ consider what each question is actually asking for - use the 'help'

✓ pay special attention to your personal statement (see page 90) and start drafting it early

✓ ask a teacher, parent, friend or careers adviser to review your draft application – particularly the personal statement

✓ if you get stuck, watch our videos on YouTube where we answer your frequently asked questions on completing a UCAS application at www.youtube.com/ucasonline

✓ if you have extra information that will not fit on your application, send it direct to your chosen universities or colleges after we have sent you your Welcome letter with your Personal ID – don't send it to us

✓ print a copy of the final version of your application, in case you are asked questions on it at an interview.

> Applying

2

The personal statement

Next to choosing your courses, this section of your application will be the most time-consuming. It is of immense importance as many universities and colleges make their selection relying solely on the information in the UCAS application, rather than interviews and admissions tests. The personal statement can be the deciding factor in whether or not they offer you a place. If it is an institution that interviews, your statement could be the deciding factor in whether you get invited for interview.

Keep a copy of your personal statement – if you are called for interview, you will almost certainly be asked questions based on it.

Tutors will look carefully at your exam results, actual and predicted, your reference and your personal statement. Remember, they are looking for reasons to offer you a place – try to give them every opportunity to do so!

A SALES DOCUMENT

The personal statement is your opportunity to sell yourself, so do so. The university or college admissions tutor wants to get a rounded picture of you to decide whether you will make an interesting member of the university or college both academically and socially. They want to know more about you than the subjects you are studying at school.

HOW TO START

At **www.ucas.com** you'll find several tools to help you write a good personal statement.

- Personal statement timeline, to help you do all your research and plan your statement over several drafts and checks.
- Personal statement mind map, which gives you reminders and hints on preparation, content and presentation, with extra hints for mature and international applicants.
- Personal statement worksheet, which gets you to start writing by asking relevant questions so that you include everything you need. You can also check your work against a list dos and don'ts.

Include things such as hobbies and work experience, and try to link the skills you have gained to the type of course you are applying for. Describe your career plans and goals. Have you belonged to sports teams or orchestras or held positions of responsibility in the community?

Try to give evidence of your ability to undertake higher level study successfully by showing your commitment and maturity. If you left full-time education a while ago, talk about the work you have done and the skills you have gathered or how you have juggled bringing up a family with other activities – that is solid evidence of time management skills. Whoever you are, make sure you explain what appeals to you about the course you are applying for.

You may not have studied psychology prior to applying so provide evidence that you are well informed about the subject including how scientific it is.

Visit www.ucas.tv to view the video to help guide you through the process and address the most common fears and concerns about writing a personal statement.

WHAT ADMISSIONS TUTORS LOOK FOR	WHAT TO TELL THEM
<ul><li>Your reasons for wanting to take this subject in general and this particular course.</li><li>Your communication skills – not only what you say but how you say it. Your grammar and spelling must be perfect.</li><li>Relevant experience – practical things you've done that are related to your choice of course.</li><li>Evidence of your teamworking ability, leadership capability, independence.</li><li>Evidence of your skills, for example: IT skills, empathy and people skills, debating and public speaking, research and analysis.</li><li>Other activities that show your dedication and ability to apply yourself and maintain your motivation.</li></ul>	<ul><li>Why you want to do this subject – how you know it is the subject for you.</li><li>What experience you already have in this field – for example work experience, school projects, hobbies, voluntary work.</li><li>The skills and qualities you have as a person that would make you a good student, for example anything that shows your dedication, communication ability, academic achievement, initiative.</li><li>Examples that show you can knuckle down and apply yourself, for example running a marathon or your Extended Project.</li><li>If you're taking a gap year, why you've chosen this and (if possible) what you're going to do during it.</li><li>About your other interests and activities away from studying – to show you're a rounded person. (But remember that it is mainly your suitability for the particular course that they're looking to judge.)</li></ul>

WORK EXPERIENCE

How much does it count for? Ask any psychology admissions tutor about the importance of work experience on a candidate's application and they'll probably say that work experience shows a real, rather than theoretical, interest in your chosen profession. An absence of work experience might make tutors question your commitment to your choice of career.

Work experience is especially useful to help you find out what you want to do. Since psychology is a people-centred profession, work experience in a setting where you are dealing with a variety of individuals could help you find out early on if a career in this area is really for you. Relevant work experience could be in any field where human contact is required, and especially in any kind of 'caring' setting. Here are some pointers to get you started on finding relevant work experience:

- Your local NHS trust – you may be able to secure a work placement, shadow a psychologist or help with administrative work.
- Mental health charities, such as Mind.
- Children's charities – eg Barnados, The Autistic Society.
- Local schools – see if you can volunteer as an assistant in after-school or holiday clubs.
- Regular work with children who have special needs, eg children with autism or Downs Syndrome.
- Nursing homes and daycare centres.
- Check out **www.do-it.org.uk** for more volunteering opportunities, as well as The British Psychological Society – a good source of information on organisations and possible vacancies. Check out their website at **www.bps.org.uk**. You could also try **http://vinspired.com/**, an organisation that specialises in helping 14- to 25-year-olds to volunteer.

Setting up a work placement in this field can take a while, so be proactive, start early and be persistent. Note that work experience sustained over a few months, even if it's just a few hours a week, is more useful to you and looks better than a one-off week in the holidays. The main thing is what you get out of it: keep a diary so that you will be able to think about your experiences and draw on them when writing your personal statement and at interview.

HOW CAN RELEVANT WORK EXPERIENCE HELP YOUR PERSONAL STATEMENT?

In your personal statement you'll need to write about yourself, setting out which subject you'd like to study, why you'd like to study it, and what skills and experience you possess that would make you a good student for the course and a great potential psychologist. This is where your work experience will help you stand out because you will be able to provide examples from real-life experience.

MAKING THE MOST OF OTHER WORK EXPERIENCE

Hopefully if you follow the tips above, finding some relevant work experience won't be a problem! If you don't manage this, however, it will still be useful to include other work experience you have had. The trick is to pull out the professional and personal skills you have developed that are of relevance to the work of a psychologist. These could be in jobs where you have had to deal with people in potentially difficult or stressful situations (think sales assistants or waitressing), for example. Good social, communication, problem-solving and team-working skills are also pertinent to working in psychology and can be developed from all sorts of working environments.

> ③ | Offers

Step 3 – Offers

Once we have sent your application to your chosen universities and colleges, they will each consider it independently and tell us whether or not they can offer you a place. Some universities and colleges will take longer to make decisions than others. You may be asked to attend an interview, sit an additional test or provide a piece of work, such as an essay, or art portfolio before a decision can be made.

INTERVIEWS

Many universities (particularly the more popular ones, running competitive courses) use interviews as part of their selection process. Universities will want to find out why you want to study your chosen course at their institution, and they want to judge whether the course is suitable for you and your future career plans. Interviews also give you an opportunity to visit the university and ask any questions you may have about the course or their institution.

If you are called for interview, the key areas they are likely to cover will be:

- evidence of your academic ability
- your capacity to study hard
- your awareness of current issues in the news that may have an impact on your chosen field of study
- your logic and reasoning ability.

A lot of the interview will be based on information on your application, especially your personal statement. See page 90 for tips about the personal statement.

Whenever a university or college makes a decision about your application, we record it and let you know. You can check the progress of your application using Track at **www.ucas.com**. This is our secure online service which gives you access to your application, using the same username and password you used when you applied. You use it to find out if you have been invited for an interview or need to provide an additional piece of work, and you can check to see if you have received any offers. Whenever there is any change in your application status, we email you to advise you to check Track.

TYPES OF OFFER

Universities can make two types of offer: conditional or unconditional.

Conditional offer

A conditional offer means the university or college will offer you a place if you meet certain conditions – usually based on exam results. The conditions may be based on Tariff points (for example, 300 points from three A levels), or specify certain grades in named subjects (for example, A in economics, B in accounting, C in business studies).

Unconditional offer

If you've met all the academic requirements for the course and the university or college wants to accept you, they will make you an unconditional offer. If you accept this you'll have a definite place. However, there might be other requirements, such as medical or financial conditions, that you need to meet before you can start your course.

REPLYING TO OFFERS

When you have received decisions for all your choices, you must decide which offers you want to accept. You will be given a deadline in Track by which you have to make your replies. Before replying, get advice from family, friends or advisers, but remember that you're the one taking the course so it's your decision.

Firm acceptance

- Your firm acceptance is your first choice - this is your preferred choice out of all the offers you have received. You can only have one firm acceptance.

- If you accept an unconditional offer, you are entering a contract that you will attend the course, so you must decline any other offers.

- If you accept a conditional offer, you are agreeing that you will attend the course at that university or college if you meet the conditions of the offer. You can accept another offer as an insurance choice.

Insurance acceptance

- If your firm acceptance is a conditional offer, you can accept another offer as an insurance choice. Your insurance choice can be conditional or unconditional and acts as a back-up, so if you don't meet the conditions for your firm choice but meet the conditions for your insurance, you will be committed to the insurance choice. You can only have one insurance choice.

- The conditions for your insurance choice would usually be lower than your firm choice.

- You don't have to accept an insurance choice if you don't want one; you need to be certain that it's an offer you would be happy to accept.

For more information watch our video guides *How to use Track*, *Making sense of your offers*, and *How to reply to your offers* at **www.ucas.tv**.

WHAT IF YOU HAVE NO OFFERS?

If you have used all five choices on your application and either received no offers, or decided to turn down any offers you have received, you may be eligible to apply for another choice through Extra. Find out more about Extra on page 96.

If you are not eligible for Extra, in the summer you can contact universities and colleges with vacancies in Clearing. See page 110 for more information.

Offers

3

Extra

Extra allows you to make additional choices, one at a time, without having to wait for Clearing in July. It is completely optional and free, and is designed to encourage you to continue researching and choosing courses if you are holding no offers. You can search for courses available through Extra on Course Finder, at **www.ucas.com**. The Extra service is available to eligible applicants from 25 February to early July 2013 through Track at **www.ucas.com**.

WHO IS ELIGIBLE?

You will be eligible for Extra if you have already made five choices and:

- you have had unsuccessful or withdrawal decisions from all five of your choices, or
- you have cancelled your outstanding choices and hold no offers, or
- you have received decisions from all five choices and have declined all offers made to you.

HOW DOES IT WORK?

We contact you and explain what to do if you are eligible for Extra. If you are eligible a special Extra button will be available on your Track screen. If you want to use Extra you should:

- tick the 'Available in extra' box in the study options section when looking for courses on Course Finder
- choose a course that you would like to apply for and enter the details on your Track screen.

When you have chosen a course the university or college will be able to view your application and consider you for a place.

WHAT HAPPENS NEXT?

We give universities and colleges a maximum of 21 days to consider your Extra application. During this time, you cannot be considered by another university or college. If you have not heard after 21 days you can apply to a different university or college if you wish, but it is a good idea to ring the one currently considering you before doing so. If you are made an offer, you can choose whether or not to accept it.

If you accept any offer, conditional or unconditional, you will not be able to take any further part in Extra.

If you are currently studying for examinations, any offer that you receive is likely to be an offer conditional on exam grades. If you already have your examination results, it is possible that a university or college may make an unconditional offer. If you accept an unconditional offer, you will be placed. If you decide to decline the offer or the university or college decides they cannot make you an offer, you will be given another opportunity to use Extra, time permitting. Your Extra button on Track will be reactivated.

Once you have accepted an offer in Extra, you are committed to it in the same way as you would be with an offer through the main UCAS system. Conditional offers made through Extra will be treated in the same way as other conditional offers, when your examination results become available.

If your results do not meet the conditions and the university or college decides that they cannot confirm your Extra offer, you will automatically become eligible for Clearing if it is too late for you to be considered by another university or college in Extra.

If you are unsuccessful, decline an offer, or do not receive an offer, or 21 days has elapsed since choosing a course through Extra, you can use Extra to apply for another course, time permitting.

ADVICE

Do some careful research and seek guidance on your Extra choice of university or college and course as you did for your initial choices. If you applied to high-demand courses and institutions in your original application and were unsuccessful, you could consider related or alternative subjects or perhaps apply for the subject you want in combination with another. Your teachers or careers advisers, or the universities and colleges themselves can provide useful guidance. Course Finder at **www.ucas.com** is another important source of information. Be flexible, that is the key to success. But you are the only one who knows how flexible you are prepared to be.

Visit **www.ucas.tv** to watch the video guide on how to use Extra.

Offers

3

The Tariff

Finding out what qualifications are needed for different higher education courses can be very confusing.

The UCAS Tariff is the system for allocating points to qualifications used for entry to higher education. Universities and colleges can use the UCAS Tariff to make comparisons between applicants with different qualifications. Tariff points are often used in entry requirements, although other factors are often taken into account. Information on Course Finder at www.ucas.com provides a fuller picture of what admissions tutors are seeking.

The tables on the following pages show the qualifications covered by the UCAS Tariff. There may have been changes to these tables since this book was printed. You should visit www.ucas.com to view the most up-to-date tables.

FURTHER INFORMATION?

Although Tariff points can be accumulated in a variety of ways, not all of these will necessarily be acceptable for entry to a particular higher education course. The achievement of a points score therefore does not give an automatic entitlement to entry, and many other factors are taken into account in the admissions process.

The Course Finder facility at www.ucas.com is the best source of reference to find out what qualifications are acceptable for entry to specific courses. Updates to the Tariff, including details on how new qualifications are added, can be found at www.ucas.com/students/ucas_tariff/.

HOW DOES THE TARIFF WORK?

- Students can collect Tariff points from a range of different qualifications, eg GCE A level with BTEC Nationals.
- There is no ceiling to the number of points that can be accumulated.
- There is no double counting. Certain qualifications within the Tariff build on qualifications in the same subject. In these cases only the qualification with the higher Tariff score will be counted. This principle applies to:
    - GCE Advanced Subsidiary level and GCE Advanced level
    - Scottish Highers and Advanced Highers
    - Speech, drama and music awards at grades 6, 7 and 8.
- Tariff points for the Advanced Diploma come from the Progression Diploma score plus the relevant Additional and Specialist Learning (ASL) Tariff points. Please see the appropriate qualification in the Tariff tables to calculate the ASL score.
- The Extended Project Tariff points are included within the Tariff points for Progression and Advanced Diplomas. Extended Project points represented in the Tariff only count when the qualification is taken outside of these Diplomas.
- Where the Tariff tables refer to specific awarding organisations, only qualifications from these awarding organisations attract Tariff points. Qualifications with a similar title, but from a different qualification awarding organisation do not attract Tariff points.

HOW DO UNIVERSITIES AND COLLEGES USE THE TARIFF?

The Tariff provides a facility to help universities and colleges when expressing entrance requirements and when making conditional offers. Entry requirements and conditional offers expressed as Tariff points will often require a minimum level of achievement in a specified subject (for example, '300 points to include grade A at A level chemistry', or '260 points including SQA Higher grade B in mathematics').

Use of the Tariff may also vary from department to department at any one institution, and may in some cases be dependent on the programme being offered.

In July 2010, UCAS announced plans to review the qualifications information provided to universities and colleges. You can read more about the review at **www.ucas.com/qireview**.

WHAT QUALIFICATIONS ARE INCLUDED IN THE TARIFF?

The following qualifications are included in the UCAS Tariff. See the number on the qualification title to find the relevant section of the Tariff table.

1   AAT NVQ Level 3 in Accounting
2   AAT Level 3 Diploma in Accounting (QCF)
3   Advanced Diploma
4   Advanced Extension Awards
5   Advanced Placement Programme (US and Canada)
6   Arts Award (Gold)
7   ASDAN Community Volunteering qualification
8   Asset Languages Advanced Stage
9   British Horse Society (Stage 3 Horse Knowledge & Care, Stage 3 Riding and Preliminary Teacher's Certificate)
10 BTEC Awards (NQF)
11 BTEC Certificates and Extended Certificates (NQF)
12 BTEC Diplomas (NQF)
13 BTEC National in Early Years (NQF)
14 BTEC Nationals (NQF)
15 BTEC QCF Qualifications (Suite known as Nationals)
16 BTEC Specialist Qualifications (QCF)
17 CACHE Award, Certificate and Diploma in Child Care and Education
18 CACHE Level 3 Extended Diploma for the Children and Young People's Workforce (QCF)
19 Cambridge ESOL Examinations
20 Cambridge Pre-U
21 Certificate of Personal Effectiveness (COPE)
22 CISI Introduction to Securities and Investment
23 City & Guilds Land Based Services Level 3 Qualifications
24 Graded Dance and Vocational Graded Dance
25 Diploma in Fashion Retail
26 Diploma in Foundation Studies (Art & Design; Art, Design & Media)
27 EDI Level 3 Certificate in Accounting, Certificate in Accounting (IAS)
28 Essential Skills (Northern Ireland)
29 Essential Skills Wales
30 Extended Project (stand alone)
31 Free-standing Mathematics
32 Functional skills
33 GCE (AS, AS Double Award, A level, A level Double Award and A level (with additional AS))
34 Hong Kong Diploma of Secondary Education (from 2012 entry onwards)
35 ifs School of Finance (Certificate and Diploma in Financial Studies)
36 iMedia (OCR level Certificate/Diploma for iMedia Professionals)
37 International Baccalaureate (IB) Diploma
38 International Baccalaureate (IB) Certificate
39 Irish Leaving Certificate (Higher and Ordinary levels)
40 IT Professionals (iPRO) (Certificate and Diploma)
41 Key Skills (Levels 2, 3 and 4)
42 Music examinations (grades 6, 7 and 8)
43 OCR Level 3 Certificate in Mathematics for Engineering
44 OCR Level 3 Certificate for Young Enterprise
45 OCR Nationals (National Certificate, National Diploma and National Extended Diploma)
46 Principal Learning Wales
47 Progression Diploma
48 Rockschool Music Practitioners Qualifications
49 Scottish Qualifications
50 Speech and Drama examinations (grades 6, 7 and 8 and Performance Studies)
51 Sports Leaders UK
52 Welsh Baccalaureate Advanced Diploma (Core)

Updates on the Tariff, including details on the incorporation of any new qualifications, are posted on **www.ucas.com**.

UCAS TARIFF TABLES

2

AAT NVQ LEVEL 3 IN ACCOUNTING

GRADE	TARIFF POINTS
PASS	160

AAT LEVEL 3 DIPLOMA IN ACCOUNTING

GRADE	TARIFF POINTS
PASS	160

3

ADVANCED DIPLOMA

Advanced Diploma = Progression Diploma plus Additional & Specialist Learning (ASL). Please see the appropriate qualification to calculate the ASL score. Please see the Progression Diploma (Table 47) for Tariff scores

4

ADVANCED EXTENSION AWARDS

GRADE	TARIFF POINTS
DISTINCTION	40
MERIT	20

Points for Advanced Extension Awards are over and above those gained from the A level grade

6

ADVANCED PLACEMENT PROGRAMME (US & CANADA)

GRADE	TARIFF POINTS
Group A	
5	120
4	90
3	60
Group B	
5	50
4	35
3	20

Details of the subjects covered by each group can be found at www.ucas.com/students/ucas_tariff/tarifftables

ARTS AWARD (GOLD)

GRADE	TARIFF POINTS
PASS	35

7

ASDAN COMMUNITY VOLUNTEERING QUALIFICATION

GRADE	TARIFF POINTS
CERTIFICATE	50
AWARD	30

ASSET LANGUAGES ADVANCED STAGE

GRADE	TARIFF POINTS	GRADE	TARIFF POINTS
Speaking		Listening	
GRADE 12	28	GRADE 12	25
GRADE 11	20	GRADE 11	18
GRADE 10	12	GRADE 10	11
Reading		Writing	
GRADE 12	25	GRADE 12	25
GRADE 11	18	GRADE 11	18
GRADE 10	11	GRADE 10	11

9

BRITISH HORSE SOCIETY

GRADE	TARIFF POINTS
Stage 3 Horse Knowledge & Care	
PASS	35
Stage 3 Riding	
PASS	35
Preliminary Teacher's Certificate	
PASS	35

Awarded by Equestrian Qualifications (GB) Ltd (EQL)

10

BTEC AWARDS (NQF) (EXCLUDING BTEC NATIONAL QUALIFICATIONS)

GRADE	TARIFF POINTS		
	Group A	Group B	Group C
DISTINCTION	20	30	40
MERIT	13	20	26
PASS	7	10	13

Details of the subjects covered by each group can be found at www.ucas.com/students/ucas_tariff/tarifftables

1

BTEC CERTIFICATES AND EXTENDED CERTIFICATES (NQF) (EXCLUDING BTEC NATIONAL QUALIFICATIONS)

GRADE	TARIFF POINTS				
	Group A	Group B	Group C	Group D	Extended Certificates
DISTINCTION	40	60	80	100	60
MERIT	26	40	52	65	40
PASS	13	20	26	35	20

Details of the subjects covered by each group can be found at www.ucas.com/students/ucas_tariff/tarifftables

12

BTEC DIPLOMAS (NQF) (EXCLUDING BTEC NATIONAL QUALIFICATIONS)

GRADE	TARIFF POINTS		
	Group A	Group B	Group C
DISTINCTION	80	100	120
MERIT	52	65	80
PASS	26	35	40

Details of the subjects covered by each group can be found at www.ucas.com/students/ucas_tariff/tarifftables

UCAS TARIFF TABLES

13

BTEC NATIONAL IN EARLY YEARS (NQF)					
GRADE	TARIFF POINTS	GRADE	TARIFF POINTS	GRADE	TARIFF POINTS
Theory				Practical	
Diploma		Certificate		D	120
DDD	320	DD	200	M	80
DDM	280	DM	160	P	40
DMM	240	MM	120		
MMM	220	MP	80		
MMP	160	PP	40		
MPP	120				
PPP	80				

Points apply to the following qualifications only: BTEC National Diploma in Early Years (100/1279/5); BTEC National Certificate in Early Years (100/1280/1)

14

BTEC NATIONALS (NQF)					
GRADE	TARIFF POINTS	GRADE	TARIFF POINTS	GRADE	TARIFF POINTS
Diploma		Certificate		Award	
DDD	360	DD	240	D	120
DDM	320	DM	200	M	80
DMM	280	MM	160	P	40
MMM	240	MP	120		
MMP	200	PP	80		
MPP	160				
PPP	120				

15

BTEC QUALIFICATIONS (QCF) (SUITE OF QUALIFICATIONS KNOWN AS NATIONALS)					
EXTENDED DIPLOMA	DIPLOMA	90 CREDIT DIPLOMA	SUBSIDIARY DIPLOMA	CERTIFICATE	TARIFF POINTS
D*D*D*					420
D*D*D					400
D*DD					380
DDD					360
DDM					320
DMM	D*D*				280
	D*D				260
MMM	DD				240
		D*D*			210
MMP	DM	D*D			200
		DD			180
MPP	MM	DM			160
			D*		140
PPP	MP	MM	D		120
		MP			100
	PP		M		80
			D*		70
		PP	D		60
			P	M	40
				P	20

16

BTEC SPECIALIST (QCF)			
GRADE	TARIFF POINTS		
	Diploma	Certificate	Award
DISTINCTION	120	60	20
MERIT	80	40	13
PASS	40	20	7

UCAS TARIFF TABLES

17

CACHE LEVEL 3 AWARD, CERTIFICATE AND DIPLOMA IN CHILD CARE & EDUCATION

AWARD		CERTIFICATE		DIPLOMA	
GRADE	TARIFF POINTS	GRADE	TARIFF POINTS	GRADE	TARIFF POINTS
A	30	A	110	A	360
B	25	B	90	B	300
C	20	C	70	C	240
D	15	D	55	D	180
E	10	E	35	E	120

18

CACHE LEVEL 3 EXTENDED DIPLOMA FOR THE CHILDREN AND YOUNG PEOPLE'S WORKFORCE (QCF)

GRADE	TARIFF POINTS
A*	420
A	340
B	290
C	240
D	140
E	80

19

CAMBRIDGE ESOL EXAMINATIONS

GRADE	TARIFF POINTS
Certificate of Proficiency in English	
A	140
B	110
C	70
Certificate in Advanced English	
A	70

20

CAMBRIDGE PRE-U

GRADE	TARIFF POINTS	GRADE	TARIFF POINTS	GRADE	TARIFF POINTS
Principal Subject		Global Perspectives and Research		Short Course	
D1	TBC	D1	TBC	D1	TBC
D2	145	D2	140	D2	TBC
D3	130	D3	126	D3	60
M1	115	M1	112	M1	53
M2	101	M2	98	M2	46
M3	87	M3	84	M3	39
P1	73	P1	70	P1	32
P2	59	P2	56	P2	26
P3	46	P3	42	P3	20

21

CERTIFICATE OF PERSONAL EFFECTIVENESS (COPE)

GRADE	TARIFF POINTS
PASS	70

Points are awarded for the Certificate of Personal Effectiveness (CoPE) awarded by ASDAN and CCEA

22

CISI INTRODUCTION TO SECURITIES AND INVESTMENT

GRADE	TARIFF POINTS
PASS WITH DISTINCTION	60
PASS WITH MERIT	40
PASS	20

23

CITY AND GUILDS LAND BASED SERVICES LEVEL 3 QUALIFICATIONS

GRADE	TARIFF POINTS			
	EXTENDED DIPLOMA	DIPLOMA	SUBSIDIARY DIPLOMA	CERTIFICATE
DISTINCTION*	420	280	140	70
DISTINCTION	360	240	120	60
MERIT	240	160	80	40
PASS	120	80	40	20

24

GRADED DANCE AND VOCATIONAL GRADED DANCE

GRADE	TARIFF POINTS	GRADE	TARIFF POINTS	GRADE	TARIFF POINTS
Graded Dance					
Grade 8		Grade 7		Grade 6	
DISTINCTION	65	DISTINCTION	55	DISTINCTION	40
MERIT	55	MERIT	45	MERIT	35
PASS	45	PASS	35	PASS	30
Vocational Graded Dance					
Advanced Foundation		Intermediate			
DISTINCTION	70	DISTINCTION	65		
MERIT	55	MERIT	50		
PASS	45	PASS	40		

25

DIPLOMA IN FASHION RETAIL

GRADE	TARIFF POINTS
DISTINCTION	160
MERIT	120
PASS	80

Applies to the NQF and QCF versions of the qualifications awarded by ABC Awards

UCAS TARIFF TABLES

26

DIPLOMA IN FOUNDATION STUDIES (ART & DESIGN AND ART, DESIGN & MEDIA)	
GRADE	TARIFF POINTS
DISTINCTION	285
MERIT	225
PASS	165

Awarded by ABC, Edexcel, UAL and WJEC

27

EDI LEVEL 3 CERTIFICATE IN ACCOUNTING, CERTIFICATE IN ACCOUNTING (IAS)	
GRADE	TARIFF POINTS
DISTINCTION	120
MERIT	90
PASS	70

28

ESSENTIAL SKILLS (NORTHERN IRELAND)	
GRADE	TARIFF POINTS
LEVEL 2	10

Only allocated at level 2 if studied as part of a wider composite qualification such as 14-19 Diploma or Welsh Baccalaureate

29

ESSENTIAL SKILLS WALES	
GRADE	TARIFF POINTS
LEVEL 4	30
LEVEL 3	20
LEVEL 2	10

Only allocated at level 2 if studied as part of a wider composite qualification such as 14-19 Diploma or Welsh Baccalaureate

30

EXTENDED PROJECT (STAND ALONE)	
GRADE	TARIFF POINTS
A*	70
A	60
B	50
C	40
D	30
E	20

Points for the Extended Project cannot be counted if taken as part of Progression/Advanced Diploma

31

FREE-STANDING MATHEMATICS	
GRADE	TARIFF POINTS
A	20
B	17
C	13
D	10
E	7

Covers free-standing Mathematics - Additional Maths, Using and Applying Statistics, Working with Algebraic and Graphical Techniques, Modelling with Calculus

32

FUNCTIONAL SKILLS	
GRADE	TARIFF POINTS
LEVEL 2	10

Only allocated if studied as part of a wider composite qualification such as 14-19 Diploma or Welsh Baccalaureate

33

GCE AND VCE									
GRADE	TARIFF POINTS	GRADE	TARIFF POINTS	GRADE	TARIFF POINTS	GRADE	TARIFF POINTS	GRADE	TARIFF POINTS
GCE & AVCE Double Award		GCE A level with additional AS (9 units)		GCE A level & AVCE		GCE AS Double Award		GCE AS & AS VCE	
A*A*	280	A*A	200	A*	140	AA	120	A	60
A*A	260	AA	180	A	120	AB	110	B	50
AA	240	AB	170	B	100	BB	100	C	40
AB	220	BB	150	C	80	BC	90	D	30
BB	200	BC	140	D	60	CC	80	E	20
BC	180	CC	120	E	40	CD	70		
CC	160	CD	110			DD	60		
CD	140	DD	90			DE	50		
DD	120	DE	80			EE	40		
DE	100	EE	60						
EE	80								

34

HONG KONG DIPLOMA OF SECONDARY EDUCATION					
GRADE	TARIFF POINTS	GRADE	TARIFF POINTS	GRADE	TARIFF POINTS
All subjects except mathematics		Mathematics compulsory component		Mathematics optional components	
5**	No value	5**	No value	5**	No value
5*	130	5*	60	5*	70
5	120	5	45	5	60
4	80	4	35	4	50
3	40	3	25	3	40

No value for 5** pending receipt of candidate evidence (post 2012)

35

IFS SCHOOL OF FINANCE (NQF & QCF)

GRADE	TARIFF POINTS	GRADE	TARIFF POINTS
Certificate in Financial Studies (CeFS)		Diploma in Financial Studies (DipFS)	
A	60	A	120
B	50	B	100
C	40	C	80
D	30	D	60
E	20	E	40

Applicants with the ifs Diploma cannot also count points allocated to the ifs Certificate. Completion of both qualifications will result in a maximum of 120 UCAS Tariff points

36

LEVEL 3 CERTIFICATE / DIPLOMA FOR iMEDIA USERS (iMEDIA)

GRADE	TARIFF POINTS
DIPLOMA	66
CERTIFICATE	40

Awarded by OCR

37

INTERNATIONAL BACCALAUREATE (IB) DIPLOMA

GRADE	TARIFF POINTS	GRADE	TARIFF POINTS
45	720	34	479
44	698	33	457
43	676	32	435
42	654	31	413
41	632	30	392
40	611	29	370
39	589	28	348
38	567	27	326
37	545	26	304
36	523	25	282
35	501	24	260

38

INTERNATIONAL BACCALAUREATE (IB) CERTIFICATE

GRADE	TARIFF POINTS	GRADE	TARIFF POINTS	GRADE	TARIFF POINTS
Higher Level		Standard Level		Core	
7	130	7	70	3	120
6	110	6	59	2	80
5	80	5	43	1	40
4	50	4	27	0	10
3	20	3	11		

39

IRISH LEAVING CERTIFICATE

GRADE	TARIFF POINTS	GRADE	TARIFF POINTS
Higher		Ordinary	
A1	90	A1	39
A2	77	A2	26
B1	71	B1	20
B2	64	B2	14
B3	58	B3	7
C1	52		
C2	45		
C3	39		
D1	33		
D2	26		
D3	20		

40

IT PROFESSIONALS (iPRO)

GRADE	TARIFF POINTS
DIPLOMA	100
CERTIFICATE	80

Awarded by OCR

41

KEY SKILLS

GRADE	TARIFF POINTS
LEVEL 4	30
LEVEL 3	20
LEVEL 2	10

Only allocated at level 2 if studied as part of a wider composite qualification such as 14-19 Diploma or Welsh Baccalaureate

42

MUSIC EXAMINATIONS					
GRADE	TARIFF POINTS	GRADE	TARIFF POINTS	GRADE	TARIFF POINTS
Practical					
Grade 8		Grade 7		Grade 6	
DISTINCTION	75	DISTINCTION	60	DISTINCTION	45
MERIT	70	MERIT	55	MERIT	40
PASS	55	PASS	40	PASS	25
Theory					
Grade 8		Grade 7		Grade 6	
DISTINCTION	30	DISTINCTION	20	DISTINCTION	15
MERIT	25	MERIT	15	MERIT	10
PASS	20	PASS	10	PASS	5

Points shown are for the ABRSM, LCMM/University of West London, Rockschool and Trinity Guildhall/Trinity College London Advanced Level music examinations

43

OCR LEVEL 3 CERTIFICATE IN MATHEMATICS FOR ENGINEERING	
GRADE	TARIFF POINTS
A*	TBC
A	90
B	75
C	60
D	45
E	30

44

OCR LEVEL 3 CERTIFICATE FOR YOUNG ENTERPRISE	
GRADE	TARIFF POINTS
DISTINCTION	40
MERIT	30
PASS	20

45

OCR NATIONALS					
GRADE	TARIFF POINTS	GRADE	TARIFF POINTS	GRADE	TARIFF POINTS
National Extended Diploma		National Diploma		National Certificate	
D1	360	D	240	D	120
D2/M1	320	M1	200	M	80
M2	280	M2/P1	160	P	40
M3	240	P2	120		
P1	200	P3	80		
P2	160				
P3	120				

46

PRINCIPAL LEARNING WALES	
GRADE	TARIFF POINTS
A*	210
A	180
B	150
C	120
D	90
E	60

47

PROGRESSION DIPLOMA	
GRADE	TARIFF POINTS
A*	350
A	300
B	250
C	200
D	150
E	100

Advanced Diploma = Progression Diploma plus Additional & Specialist Learning (ASL). Please see the appropriate qualification to calculate the ASL score

48

ROCKSCHOOL MUSIC PRACTITIONERS QUALIFICATIONS

GRADE	TARIFF POINTS				
	Extended Diploma	Diploma	Subsidiary Diploma	Extended Certificate	Certificate
DISTINCTION	240	180	120	60	30
MERIT	160	120	80	40	20
PASS	80	60	40	20	10

49

SCOTTISH QUALIFICATIONS

GRADE	TARIFF POINTS	GRADE	TARIFF POINTS	GRADE	TARIFF POINTS	GROUP	TARIFF POINTS
Advanced Higher		Higher		Scottish Interdisciplinary Project		Scottish National Certificates	
A	130	A	80	A	65	C	125
B	110	B	65	B	55	B	100
C	90	C	50	C	45	A	75
D	72	D	36				
Ungraded Higher		NPA PC Passport					
PASS	45	PASS	45				
		Core Skills					
		HIGHER	20				

Details of the subjects covered by each Scottish National Certificate can be found at www.ucas.com/students/ucas_tariff/tarifftables

50

SPEECH AND DRAMA EXAMINATIONS

GRADE	TARIFF POINTS	GRADE	TARIFF POINTS	GRADE	TARIFF POINTS	GRADE	TARIFF POINTS
PCertLAM		Grade 8		Grade 7		Grade 6	
DISTINCTION	90	DISTINCTION	65	DISTINCTION	55	DISTINCTION	40
MERIT	80	MERIT	60	MERIT	50	MERIT	35
PASS	60	PASS	45	PASS	35	PASS	20

Details of the Speech and Drama Qualifications covered by the Tariff can be found at www.ucas.com/students/ucas_tariff/tarifftables

51

SPORTS LEADERS UK

GRADE	TARIFF POINTS
PASS	30

These points are awarded to Higher Sports Leader Award and Level 3 Certificate in Higher Sports Leadership (QCF)

52

WELSH BACCALAUREATE ADVANCED DIPLOMA (CORE)

GRADE	TARIFF POINTS
PASS	120

These points are awarded only when a candidate achieves the Welsh Baccalaureate Advanced Diploma

Results

4

Step 4 – Results

You should arrange your holidays so that you are at home when your exam results are published because, if there are any issues to discuss, admissions tutors will want to speak to you in person.

We receive many exam results direct from the exam boards – check the list at **www.ucas.com**. If your qualification is listed, we send your results to the universities and colleges that you have accepted as your firm and insurance choices. If your qualification is not listed, you must send your exam results to the universities and colleges where you are holding offers.

After you have received your exam results check Track to find out if you have a place on your chosen course.

If you have met all the conditions for your firm choice, the university or college will confirm that you have a place. Occasionally, they may still confirm you have a place even if you have not quite met all the offer conditions; or they may offer you a place on a similar course.

If you have not met the conditions of your firm choice and the university or college has not confirmed your place, but you have met all the conditions of your insurance offer, your insurance university or college will confirm that you have a place.

When a university or college tells us that you have a place, we send you confirmation by letter.

RE-MARKED EXAMS

If you ask for any of your exams to be re-marked, you must tell the universities and colleges where you're holding offers. If a university or college cannot confirm your place based on the initial results, you should ask them if they would be able to reconsider their decision after the re-mark. They are under no obligation to reconsider their position even if your re-mark results in higher grades. Don't forget that re-marks may also result in lower grades.

The exam boards tell us about any re-marks that result in grade changes. We then send the revised grades to the universities and colleges where you're holding offers. As soon as you know about any grade changes, you should also tell these universities and colleges.

'CASHING IN' A LEVEL RESULTS

If you have taken A levels, your school or college must certificate or 'cash in' all your unit scores before the exam board can award final grades. If when you collect your A level results you have to add up your unit scores to find out your final grades, this means your school or college has not 'cashed in' your results.

We only receive cashed in results from the exam boards, so if your school or college has not cashed in your results, you must ask them to send a 'cash in' request to the exam board. You also need to tell the universities and colleges where you're holding offers that there'll be a delay in receiving your results and call our Customer Service Unit to find out when your results have been received.

When we receive your 'cashed in' results from the exam board we send them straight away to the universities and colleges where you're holding offers.

WHAT IF YOU DON'T HAVE A PLACE?

If you have not met the conditions of either your firm or insurance choice, and your chosen universities or colleges have not confirmed your place, you are eligible for Clearing. In Clearing you can apply for any courses that still have vacancies (but remember that admissions tutors will still be reading your original personal statement). Clearing operates from mid-July to late September 2012 (page 110).

BETTER RESULTS THAN EXPECTED?

If you obtain exam results that meet and exceed the conditions of the offer for your firm choice, you can for a short period use a process called adjustment to look for an alternative place, whilst still keeping your original firm choice. See page 111 for information about Adjustment.

> Next steps

5

Step 5 – Next steps

You might find yourself with different exam results than you were expecting, or you may change your mind about what you want to do. If so, there may be other options open to you.

CLEARING

Clearing is a service that helps people without a place find suitable course vacancies. It runs from mid-July until the end of September, but most people use it after the exam results are published in August.

You could consider related or alternative subjects or perhaps combining your original choice of subject with another. Your teachers or careers adviser, or the universities and colleges themselves, can provide useful guidance.

Course vacancies are listed at **www.ucas.com** and in the national media following the publication of exam results in August. **Once you have your exam results**, if you're in Clearing you need to look at the vacancy listings and then contact any university or college you are interested in.

Talk to the institutions; don't be afraid to call them. Make sure you have your Personal ID and Clearing Number ready and prepare notes on what you will say to them about:

- why you want to study the course
- why you want to study at their university or college
- any relevant employment or activities you have done that relate to the course
- your grades.

Accepting an offer - you can contact as many universities and colleges as you like through Clearing, and you may informally be offered more than one place. If this happens, you will need to decide which offer you want to accept. If you're offered a place you want to be formally considered for, you enter the course details in Track, and the university or college will then let you know if they're accepting you.

ADJUSTMENT

If you receive better results than expected, and meet and exceed the conditions of your conditional firm choice, you have the opportunity to reconsider what and where you want to study. This process is called Adjustment.

Adjustment runs from A level results day on 15 August 2013 until the end of August. Your individual Adjustment period starts on A level results day or when your conditional firm choice changes to unconditional firm, whichever is the later. You then have a maximum of five calendar days to register and secure an alternative course, if you decide you want to do this. If you want to try to find an alternative course you must register in Track to use Adjustment, so universities and colleges can view your application.

There are no vacancy listings for Adjustment, so you'll need to talk to the institutions. When you contact a university or college make it clear that you are applying through Adjustment, not Clearing. If they want to consider you they will ask for your Personal ID, so they can view your application.

If you don't find an alternative place then you remain accepted at your original firm choice.

Adjustment is entirely optional; remember that nothing really beats the careful research you carried out to find the right courses before you made your UCAS application. Talk to a careers adviser at your school, college or local careers office, as they can help you decide if registering to use Adjustment is right for you.

More information about Adjustment and Clearing is available at www.ucas.com. You can also view UCAStv video guides on how to use Adjustment and Clearing at www.ucas.tv.

IF YOU ARE STILL WITHOUT A PLACE TO STUDY

If you haven't found a suitable place, or changed your mind about what you want to do, there are lots of other options. Ask for advice from your school, college or careers office. Here are some suggestions you might want to consider:

- studying a part-time course (there's a part-time course search at www.ucas.com from July until September)
- studying a foundation degree
- re-sit your exams
- getting some work experience
- studying in another country
- reapplying next year to university or college through UCAS
- taking a gap year
- doing an apprenticeship (you'll find a vacancy search on the National Apprenticeship Service (NAS) website at www.apprenticeships.org.uk)
- finding a job
- starting a business.

More advice and links to other organisations can be found on the UCAS website at www.ucas.com/students/nextsteps/advice.

6

Starting university
or college

Step 6 – Starting university or college

Congratulations! Now that you have confirmed your place at university or college you will need to finalise your plans on how to get there, where to live and how to finance it. Make lists of things to do with deadlines, and start contacting people whose help you can call on. Will you travel independently or can your parents or relatives help with transport? If you are keeping a car at uni, have you checked out parking facilities and told your insurance company?

Freshers week will help you settle in and make friends, but don't forget you are there to study. You may find the teaching methods rather alien at first, but remember there are plenty of sources of help, including your tutors, other students or student mentors, and the Students' Union.

Make sure you have everything organised, including travel arrangements, essential documents and paperwork, books and equipment required for the course. The university will send you joining information – contact the Admissions Office or the Students' Union if you have questions about anything to do with starting your course.

Where to live - unless you are planning to live at home, your university or college will usually provide you with guidance on how to find somewhere to live. The earlier you contact them the better your chance of finding a suitable range of options, from hall to private landlords. Find out what facilities are available at the different types of accommodation, and check whether it fits within your budget. Check also what you need to bring with you and what is supplied. Don't leave it all to the last minute – especially things like arranging a bank account, checking what proof of identity you might need, gathering together a few essentials like a mug and supplies of coffee, insurance cover, TV licence etc.

Student finance - you will need to budget for living costs, accommodation, travel and books (and tuition fees if you are paying them up front). Learn about budgeting by visiting **www.ucas.com** where you will find further links to useful resources to help you manage your money. Remember that if you do get into financial difficulties the welfare office at the university will help you change tack and manage better in future, but it is always better to live within your means from the outset. If you need help, find it before the situation gets stressful.

Useful contacts

CONNECTING WITH UCAS

You can follow UCAS on Twitter at www.twitter.com/ucas_online, and ask a question or see what others are asking on Facebook at www.facebook.com/ucasonline. You can also watch videos of UCAS advisers answering frequently asked questions on YouTube at www.youtube.com/ucasonline.

There are many UCAStv video guides to help with your journey into higher education, such as *How to choose your courses, Attending events, Open days,* and *How to apply.* These can all be viewed at www.ucas.tv or in the relevant section of www.ucas.com.

If you need to speak to UCAS, please contact the Customer Service Unit on 0871 468 0 468 or 0044 871 468 0 468 from outside the UK. Calls from BT landlines within the UK will cost no more than 9p per minute. The cost of calls from mobiles and other networks may vary.

If you have hearing difficulties, you can call the Text Relay service on 18001 0871 468 0 468 (outside the UK 0044 151 494 1260). Calls are charged at normal rates.

CAREERS ADVICE

The Directgov Careers Helpline for Young People is for you if you live in England, are aged 13 to 19 and want advice on getting to where you want to be in life.

Careers advisers can give you information, advice and practical help with all sorts of things, like choosing subjects at school or mapping out your future career options. They can help you with anything that might be affecting you at school, college, work or in your personal or family life.

Contact a careers adviser at
www.direct.gov.uk/en/youngpeople/index.htm.

Skills Development Scotland provides a starting point for anyone looking for careers information, advice or guidance.
www.myworldofwork.co.uk.

Careers Wales – Wales' national all-age careers guidance service.
www.careerswales.com or **www.gyrfacymru.com**.

Northern Ireland Careers Service website for the new, all-age careers guidance service in Northern Ireland.
www.nidirect.gov.uk/careers.

If you're not sure what job you want or you need help to decide which course to do, give learndirect a call on 0800 101 901 or visit
www.learndirect.co.uk.

GENERAL HIGHER EDUCATION ADVICE

National Union of Students (NUS) is the national voice of students, helping them to campaign, get cheap student discounts and provide advice on living student life to the full - **www.nus.org.uk**.

STUDENTS WITH DISABILITIES

If you have a disability or specific learning difficulty, you are strongly encouraged to make early direct contact with individual institutions before submitting your application. Most universities and colleges have disability coordinators or advisers. You can find their contact details and further advice on the Disability Rights UK website - **www.disabilityalliance.org**.

There is financial help for students with disabilities, known as Disabled Students' Allowances (DSAs). More information is available on the Directgov website at **www.direct.gov.uk/disabledstudents**.

YEAR OUT

For useful information on taking a year out, see **www.gap-year.com**.

The Year Out Group website is packed with information and guidance for young people and their parents and advisers. **www.yearoutgroup.org**.

Essential reading

UCAS has brought together the best books and resources you need to make the important decisions regarding entry to higher education. With guidance on choosing courses, finding the right institution, information about student finance, admissions tests, gap years and lots more, you can find the most trusted guides at **www.ucasbooks.com**.

The publications listed on the following pages and many others are available through **www.ucasbooks.com** or from UCAS Publication Services unless otherwise stated.

UCAS PUBLICATION SERVICES

UCAS Publication Services
PO Box 130, Cheltenham, Gloucestershire GL52 3ZF

f: 01242 544 806
e: publicationservices@ucas.ac.uk
// www.ucasbooks.com

ENTIRE RESEARCH AND APPLICATION PROCESS EXPLAINED

The UCAS Guide to getting into University and College

This guide contains advice and up-to-date information about the entire research and application process, and brings together the expertise of UCAS staff, along with insights and tips from well known universities including Oxford and Cambridge, and students who are involved with or have experienced the process first-hand.

The book clearly sets out the information you need in an easy-to-read format, with myth busters, tips from students, checklists and much more; this book will be a companion for applicants throughout their entire journey into higher education.
Published by UCAS
Price £11.99
Publication date January 2011

NEED HELP COMPLETING YOUR APPLICATION?

How to Complete your UCAS Application 2013
A must for anyone applying through UCAS. Contains advice on the preparation needed, a step-by-step guide to filling out the UCAS application, information on the UCAS process and useful tips for completing the personal statement.
Published by Trotman
Price £12.99
Publication date May 2012

Insider's Guide to Applying to University
Full of honest insights, this is a thorough guide to the application process. It reveals advice from careers advisers and current students, guidance on making sense of university information and choosing courses. Also includes tips for the personal statement, interviews, admissions tests, UCAS Extra and Clearing.
Published by Trotman
Price £12.99
Publication date June 2011

How to Write a Winning UCAS Personal Statement
The personal statement is your chance to stand out from the crowd. Based on information from admissions tutors, this book will help you sell yourself. It includes specific guidance for over 30 popular subjects, common mistakes to avoid, information on what admissions tutors look for, and much more.
Published by Trotman
Price £12.99
Publication date March 2010

CHOOSING COURSES

Progression Series 2013 entry
The 'UCAS Guide to getting into…' titles are designed to help you access good quality, useful information on some of the most competitive subject areas. The books cover advice on applying through UCAS, routes to qualifications, course details, job prospects, case studies and career advice.

New for 2013: information on the pros and cons of league tables and how to read them.

The UCAS Guide to getting into…
Art and Design
Economics, Finance and Accountancy
Engineering and Mathematics
Journalism, Broadcasting, Media Production and
    Performing Arts
Law
Medicine, Dentistry and Optometry
Nursing, Healthcare and Social Work
Psychology
Sports Science and Physiotherapy
Teaching and Education
Published by UCAS
Price £15.99 each
Publication date June 2012

UCAS Parent Guide
Free of charge.
Order online at **www.ucas.com/parents**.
Publication date February 2012

Open Days 2012

Attending open days, taster courses and higher education conventions is an important part of the application process. This publication makes planning attendance at these events quick and easy.
Published annually by UCAS.
Price £3.50
Publication date January 2012

Heap 2013: University Degree Course Offers

An independent, reliable guide to selecting university degree courses in the UK.

The guide lists degree courses available at universities and colleges throughout the UK and the grades, UCAS points or equivalent that you need to achieve to get on to each course listed.
Published by Trotman
Price £32.99
Publication date May 2012

ESSENTIAL READING

Choosing Your Degree Course & University

With so many universities and courses to choose from, it is not an easy decision for students embarking on their journey to higher education. This guide will offer expert guidance on the questions students need to ask when considering the opportunities available.
Published by Trotman
Price £24.99
Publication date April 2012

Degree Course Descriptions

Providing details of the nature of degree courses, the descriptions in this book are written by heads of departments and senior lecturers at major universities. Each description contains an overview of the course area, details of course structures, career opportunities and more.
Published by COA
Price £12.99
Publication date September 2011

CHOOSING WHERE TO STUDY

The Virgin Guide to British Universities

An insider's guide to choosing a university or college. Written by students and using independent statistics, this guide evaluates what you get from a higher education institution.
Published by Virgin
Price £15.99
Publication date May 2011

Times Good University Guide 2013

How do you find the best university for the subject you wish to study? You need a guide that evaluates the quality of what is available, giving facts, figures and comparative assessments of universities. The rankings provide hard data, analysed, interpreted and presented by a team of experts.
Published by Harper Collins
Price £16.99
Publication date June 2012

A Parent's Guide to Graduate Jobs

A must-have guide for any parent who is worried about their child's job prospects when they graduate.

In this guide, the graduate careers guru, Paul Redmond, advises parents how to help their son or daughter:

- increase their employability
- boost their earning potential
- acquire essential work skills
- use their own contacts to get them ahead
- gain the right work experience.

Published by Trotman
Price £12.99
Publication date January 2012

Which Uni?

One person's perfect uni might be hell for someone else. Picking the right one will give you the best chance of future happiness, academic success and brighter job prospects. This guide is packed with tables from a variety of sources, rating universities on everything from the quality of teaching to the make-up of the student population and much more.
Published by Trotman
Price £14.99
Publication date September 2011

Getting into the UK's Best Universities and Courses

This book is for those who set their goals high and dream of studying on a highly regarded course at a good university. It provides information on selecting the best courses for a subject, the application and personal statement, interviews, results day, timescales for applications and much more.
Published by Trotman
Price £12.99
Publication date June 2011

FINANCIAL INFORMATION

Student Finance - e-book

All students need to know about tuition fees, loans, grants, bursaries and much more. Covering all forms of income and expenditure, this comprehensive guide is produced in association with UCAS and offers great value for money.
Published by Constable Robinson
Price £4.99
Publication date May 2012

CAREERS PLANNING

A-Z of Careers and Jobs

It is vital to be well informed about career decisions and this guide will help you make the right choice. It provides full details of the wide range of opportunities on the market, the personal qualities and skills needed for each job, entry qualifications and training, realistic salary expectations and useful contact details.
Published by Kogan Page
Price £16.99
Publication date March 2012

The Careers Directory

An indispensable resource for anyone seeking careers information, covering over 350 careers. It presents up-to-date information in an innovative double-page format. Ideal for students in years 10 to 13 who are considering their futures and for other careers professionals.
Published by COA
Price £14.99
Publication date September 2011

Careers with a Science Degree

Over 100 jobs and areas of work for graduates of biological, chemical and physical sciences are described in this guide.

Whether you have yet to choose your degree subject and want to know where the various choices could lead, or are struggling for ideas about what to do with your science degree, this book will guide and inspire you. The title includes: nature of the work and potential employers, qualifications required for entry, including personal qualities and skills; training routes and opportunities for career development and postgraduate study options.
Published by Lifetime Publishing
Price £12.99
Publication date September 2010

Careers with an Arts and Humanities Degree

Covers careers and graduate opportunities related to these degrees.

The book describes over 100 jobs and areas of work suitable for graduates from a range of disciplines including: English and modern languages, history and geography, music and the fine arts. The guide highlights: graduate opportunities, training routes, postgraduate study options and entry requirements.
Published by Lifetime Publishing
Price £12.99
Publication date September 2010

'Getting into...' guides

Clear and concise guides to help applicants secure places. They include qualifications required, advice on applying, tests, interviews and case studies. The guides give an honest view and discuss current issues and careers.

Getting into Oxford and Cambridge
Publication date April 2011
Getting into Veterinary School
Publication date February 2011
Published by Trotman
Price £12.99 each

DEFERRING ENTRY

Gap Years: The Essential Guide

The essential book for all young people planning a gap year before continuing with their education. This up-to-date guide provides essential information on specialist gap year programmes, as well as the vast range of jobs and voluntary opportunities available to young people around the world.
Published by Crimson Publishing
Price £9.99
Publication date April 2012

Gap Year Guidebook 2012

This thorough and easy-to-use guide contains everything you need to know before taking a gap year. It includes real-life traveller tips, hundreds of contact details, realistic advice on everything from preparing, learning and working abroad, coping with coming home and much more.
Published by John Catt Education
Price £14.99
Publication date November 2011

Summer Jobs Worldwide 2012
This unique and specialist guide contains over
40,000 jobs for all ages. No other book includes
such a variety and wealth of summer work
opportunities in Britain and aboard. Anything from
horse trainer in Iceland, to a guide for nature walks
in Peru, to a yoga centre helper in Greece, to an
animal keeper for London Zoo, can be found.
Published by Crimson Publishing
Price £14.99
Publication date November 2011

Please note all publications incur a postage and packing
charge. All information was correct at the time of
printing.

For a full list of publications, please visit
www.ucasbooks.com.

UCAS HIGHER EDUCATION CONVENTIONS

Meet face-to-face with over 100 UK university representatives, attend seminars on How to Apply through UCAS and Financing yourself through university.

For further details visit
www.ucas.com/conventions

Courses

Courses

Keen to get started on your career in psychology? This section contains details of the various degree courses available at UK institutions.

EXPLAINING THE LIST OF COURSES

The list of courses has been divided into subject categories (see over for the list of subjects). We list the universities and colleges by their UCAS institution codes. Within each institution, courses are listed first by award type (such as BA, BSc, FdA, HND, MA and many others), then alphabetically by course title.

You might find some courses showing an award type '(Mod)', which indicates a combined degree that might be modular in design. A small number of courses have award type '(FYr)'. This indicates a 12-month foundation course, after which students can choose to apply for a degree course. In either case, you should contact the university or college for further details.

Generally speaking, when a course comprises two or more subjects, the word used to connect the subjects indicates the make-up of the award: 'Subject A and Subject B' is a joint award, where both subjects carry equal weight; 'Subject A with Subject B' is a major/minor award, where Subject A accounts for at least 60% of your study. If the title shows 'Subject A/Subject B', it may indicate that students can decide on the weighting of the subjects at the end of the first year. You should check with the university or college for full details.

Each entry shows the UCAS course code and the duration of the course. Where known, the entry contains details of the minimum qualification requirements for the course, as supplied to UCAS by the universities and colleges. Bear in mind that possessing the minimum qualifications does not guarantee acceptance to the course: there may be far more applicants than places. You may be asked to attend an interview, present a portfolio or sit an admissions test.

Courses with entry requirements that require applicants to disclose information about spent and unspent convictions and may require a Criminal Records Bureau (CRB) check, are marked '**CRB Check:** Required'.

Before applying for any course, you are advised to contact the university or college to check any changes in entry requirements and to see if any new courses have come on stream since the lists were approved for publication. To make this easy, each institution's entry starts with their address, email, phone and fax details, as well as their website address.

LIST OF SUBJECT CATEGORIES

The list of courses in this section has been divided into the following subject categories.

PSYCHOLOGY

A20 THE UNIVERSITY OF ABERDEEN
UNIVERSITY OFFICE
KING'S COLLEGE
ABERDEEN AB24 3FX
t: +44 (0) 1224 273504 f: +44 (0) 1224 272034
e: sras@abdn.ac.uk
// www.abdn.ac.uk/sras

C803 BSc Behavioural Studies
Duration: 4FT Hon
Entry Requirements: *GCE:* BBB. *SQAH:* BBBB. *IB:* 30.

C800 BSc Psychology
Duration: 4FT Hon
Entry Requirements: *GCE:* 240. *SQAH:* BBBB. *SQAAH:* BCC. *IB:* 28.

C80A BSc Psychology (International Foundation)
Duration: 4FT Hon
Entry Requirements: Contact the institution for details.

C801 MA Behavioural Studies
Duration: 4FT Hon
Entry Requirements: Contact the institution for details.

C802 MA Psychology
Duration: 4FT Hon
Entry Requirements: *GCE:* BBB. *SQAH:* BBBB. *IB:* 30.

A30 UNIVERSITY OF ABERTAY DUNDEE
BELL STREET
DUNDEE DD1 1HG
t: 01382 308080 f: 01382 308081
e: sro@abertay.ac.uk
// www.abertay.ac.uk

C890 BSc Behavioural Science
Duration: 4FT Hon
Entry Requirements: *GCE:* CC. *SQAH:* BBB. *IB:* 26.

C800 BSc Psychology
Duration: 4FT Hon
Entry Requirements: *GCE:* CC. *SQAH:* ABB. *IB:* 26.

A40 ABERYSTWYTH UNIVERSITY
ABERYSTWYTH UNIVERSITY, WELCOME CENTRE
PENGLAIS CAMPUS
ABERYSTWYTH
CEREDIGION SY23 3FB
t: 01970 622021 f: 01970 627410
e: ug-admissions@aber.ac.uk
// www.aber.ac.uk

C800 BSc Psychology
Duration: 3FT Hon
Entry Requirements: *GCE:* 280. *IB:* 28.

A60 ANGLIA RUSKIN UNIVERSITY
BISHOP HALL LANE
CHELMSFORD
ESSEX CM1 1SQ
t: 0845 271 3333 f: 01245 251789
e: answers@anglia.ac.uk
// www.anglia.ac.uk

C800 BSc Psychology
Duration: 3FT Hon
Entry Requirements: *GCE:* 240. *SQAH:* BBBC. *SQAAH:* BB. *IB:* 30.

A80 ASTON UNIVERSITY, BIRMINGHAM
ASTON TRIANGLE
BIRMINGHAM B4 7ET
t: 0121 204 4444 f: 0121 204 3696
e: admissions@aston.ac.uk (automatic response)
// www.aston.ac.uk/prospective-students/ug

C800 BSc Psychology
Duration: 3FT Hon
Entry Requirements: *GCE:* AAB-ABB. *SQAH:* AABBB. *SQAAH:* AAB. *IB:* 33.

C801 BSc Psychology (4 year sandwich)
Duration: 4SW Hon
Entry Requirements: *GCE:* AAB-ABB. *SQAH:* AABBB. *SQAAH:* AAB. *IB:* 33.

B06 BANGOR UNIVERSITY
BANGOR UNIVERSITY
BANGOR
GWYNEDD LL57 2DG
t: 01248 388484 f: 01248 370451
e: admissions@bangor.ac.uk
// www.bangor.ac.uk

C802 BA Psychology
Duration: 3FT Hon
Entry Requirements: *GCE:* 280-320. *IB:* 28.

C800 BSc Psychology
Duration: 3FT Hon
Entry Requirements: *GCE:* 280-320. *IB:* 28.

B16 UNIVERSITY OF BATH
CLAVERTON DOWN
BATH BA2 7AY
t: 01225 383019 f: 01225 386366
e: admissions@bath.ac.uk
// www.bath.ac.uk

C800 BSc Psychology (Sandwich)
Duration: 4SW Hon
Entry Requirements: *GCE:* A*AA. *SQAAH:* AAA. *IB:* 38.

B20 BATH SPA UNIVERSITY
NEWTON PARK
NEWTON ST LOE
BATH BA2 9BN
t: 01225 875875 f: 01225 875444
e: enquiries@bathspa.ac.uk
// www.bathspa.ac.uk/clearing

C800 BSc Psychology
Duration: 3FT Hon
Entry Requirements: *GCE:* 220-280. *IB:* 24.

C801 DipHE Psychology
Duration: 2FT Dip
Entry Requirements: *GCE:* 220-280. *IB:* 24.

B22 UNIVERSITY OF BEDFORDSHIRE
PARK SQUARE
LUTON
BEDS LU1 3JU
t: 0844 8482234 f: 01582 489323
e: admissions@beds.ac.uk
// www.beds.ac.uk

C800 BSc Psychology
Duration: 3FT Hon
Entry Requirements: *Foundation:* Pass. *GCE:* 240. *SQAH:* BBBB-BBBC. *SQAAH:* BCC. *IB:* 24. *OCR ND:* D *OCR NED:* M3

C801 CertHE Psychology
Duration: 1FT Cer
Entry Requirements: Contact the institution for details.

B24 BIRKBECK, UNIVERSITY OF LONDON
MALET STREET
LONDON WC1E 7HX
t: 020 7631 6316
e: webform: www.bbk.ac.uk/ask
// www.bbk.ac.uk/ask

C800 BSc Psychology
Duration: 3FT Hon
Entry Requirements: *GCE:* ABB. *SQAH:* AAAA-AABB. *IB:* 30. Interview required.

B25 BIRMINGHAM CITY UNIVERSITY
PERRY BARR
BIRMINGHAM B42 2SU
t: 0121 331 5595 f: 0121 331 7994
// www.bcu.ac.uk

C800 BSc Psychology
Duration: 3FT Hon
Entry Requirements: *GCE:* 280. *IB:* 26.

B32 THE UNIVERSITY OF BIRMINGHAM
EDGBASTON
BIRMINGHAM B15 2TT
t: 0121 415 8900 f: 0121 414 7159
e: admissions@bham.ac.uk
// www.birmingham.ac.uk

C800 BSc Psychology
Duration: 3FT Hon
Entry Requirements: *GCE:* AAA-AAB. *SQAH:* AAAAB-AABBB. *SQAAH:* AA. *IB:* 36.

C801 MSci Psychology and Psychological Practice
Duration: 4FT Hon
Entry Requirements: *GCE:* AAA. *SQAH:* AAAAB-AAABB. *SQAAH:* AA. *IB:* 36. Interview required.

B44 UNIVERSITY OF BOLTON
DEANE ROAD
BOLTON BL3 5AB
t: 01204 903903 f: 01204 399074
e: enquiries@bolton.ac.uk
// www.bolton.ac.uk

C801 BSc Psychology
Duration: 3FT Hon
Entry Requirements: *GCE:* 300. Interview required.

C80D BSc Psychology (1+2)
Duration: 3FT Hon
Entry Requirements: *GCE:* 300. Interview required.

B50 BOURNEMOUTH UNIVERSITY
TALBOT CAMPUS
FERN BARROW
POOLE
DORSET BH12 5BB
t: 01202 524111
// www.bournemouth.ac.uk

C800 BSc Psychology
Duration: 3FT Hon
Entry Requirements: *GCE:* 320. *IB:* 32.

B54 BPP UNIVERSITY COLLEGE OF PROFESSIONAL STUDIES LIMITED
142-144 UXBRIDGE ROAD
LONDON W12 8AW
t: 02031 312 298
e: admissions@bpp.com
// undergraduate.bpp.com/

C800 BSc (Hons) Psychology
Duration: 3FT Hon
Entry Requirements: Contact the institution for details.

C801 BSc (Hons) Psychology (Accelerated)
Duration: 2FT Hon
Entry Requirements: Contact the institution for details.

B56 THE UNIVERSITY OF BRADFORD
RICHMOND ROAD
BRADFORD
WEST YORKSHIRE BD7 1DP
t: 0800 073 1225 f: 01274 235585
e: course-enquiries@bradford.ac.uk
// www.bradford.ac.uk

C801 BSc Psychology
Duration: 3FT Hon
Entry Requirements: *GCE:* 260. *IB:* 24.

B78 UNIVERSITY OF BRISTOL
UNDERGRADUATE ADMISSIONS OFFICE
SENATE HOUSE
TYNDALL AVENUE
BRISTOL BS8 1TH
t: 0117 928 9000 f: 0117 331 7391
e: ug-admissions@bristol.ac.uk
// www.bristol.ac.uk

C801 BSc Psychology
Duration: 3FT Hon
Entry Requirements: *GCE:* A*AA-AAB. *SQAH:* AAAAA-AAABB.
SQAAH: AA.

B80 UNIVERSITY OF THE WEST OF ENGLAND, BRISTOL
FRENCHAY CAMPUS
COLDHARBOUR LANE
BRISTOL BS16 1QY
t: +44 (0)117 32 83333 f: +44 (0)117 32 82810
e: admissions@uwe.ac.uk
// www.uwe.ac.uk

C800 BSc Psychology
Duration: 3FT Hon
Entry Requirements: *GCE:* 340.

B84 BRUNEL UNIVERSITY
UXBRIDGE
MIDDLESEX UB8 3PH
t: 01895 265265 f: 01895 269790
e: admissions@brunel.ac.uk
// www.brunel.ac.uk

C801 BSc Psychology
Duration: 3FT Hon
Entry Requirements: *GCE:* AAB. *SQAAH:* AAB. *IB:* 35. *BTEC SubDip:* D. *BTEC Dip:* D*D. *BTEC ExtDip:* D*D*D.

C800 BSc Psychology (4 year Thin SW)
Duration: 4SW Hon
Entry Requirements: *GCE:* AAB. *SQAAH:* AAB. *IB:* 35. *BTEC SubDip:* D. *BTEC Dip:* D*D. *BTEC ExtDip:* D*D*D.

B90 THE UNIVERSITY OF BUCKINGHAM
YEOMANRY HOUSE
HUNTER STREET
BUCKINGHAM MK18 1EG
t: 01280 820313 f: 01280 822245
e: info@buckingham.ac.uk
// www.buckingham.ac.uk

C800 BSc Psychology
Duration: 2FT Hon
Entry Requirements: *GCE:* BBB. *SQAH:* ABBB. *SQAAH:* BBB. *IB:* 34.

B94 BUCKINGHAMSHIRE NEW UNIVERSITY
QUEEN ALEXANDRA ROAD
HIGH WYCOMBE
BUCKINGHAMSHIRE HP11 2JZ
t: 0800 0565 660 f: 01494 605 023
e: admissions@bucks.ac.uk
// bucks.ac.uk

C800 BSc Psychology
Duration: 3FT Hon
Entry Requirements: *GCE:* 240-280. *IB:* 25. *OCR ND:* D *OCR NED:* M2

C05 UNIVERSITY OF CAMBRIDGE
CAMBRIDGE ADMISSIONS OFFICE
FITZWILLIAM HOUSE
32 TRUMPINGTON STREET
CAMBRIDGE CB2 1QY
t: 01223 333 308 f: 01223 746 868
e: admissions@cam.ac.uk
// www.study.cam.ac.uk/undergraduate/

C800 BA Psychological and Behavioural Sciences
Duration: 3FT Hon
Entry Requirements: *GCE:* A*AA. *SQAAH:* AAA-AAB. Interview required.

C10 CANTERBURY CHRIST CHURCH UNIVERSITY
NORTH HOLMES ROAD
CANTERBURY
KENT CT1 1QU
t: 01227 782900 f: 01227 782888
e: admissions@canterbury.ac.uk
// www.canterbury.ac.uk

C800 BSc Psychology
Duration: 3FT Hon   CRB Check: Required
Entry Requirements: *GCE:* 260. *IB:* 24. Interview required.

C802 BSc Psychology 'International Only'
Duration: 4FT Hon
Entry Requirements: *GCE:* 260. *IB:* 24.

C15 CARDIFF UNIVERSITY
PO BOX 927
30-36 NEWPORT ROAD
CARDIFF CF24 0DE
t: 029 2087 9999 f: 029 2087 6138
e: admissions@cardiff.ac.uk
// www.cardiff.ac.uk

C800 BSc Psychology
Duration: 3FT Hon
Entry Requirements: *GCE:* AAA-AAB. *SQAH:* AAAAB. *SQAAH:* AA.
IB: 35. Interview required.

C20 CARDIFF METROPOLITAN UNIVERSITY (UWIC)
ADMISSIONS UNIT
LLANDAFF CAMPUS
WESTERN AVENUE
CARDIFF CF5 2YB
t: 029 2041 6070 f: 029 2041 6286
e: admissions@cardiffmet.ac.uk
// www.cardiffmet.ac.uk

C800 BSc Psychology
Duration: 3FT Hon
Entry Requirements: *GCE:* 280. *IB:* 25. *BTEC ExtDip:* DMM. *OCR NED:* M2

C801 BSc Psychology (4 years including Foundation)
Duration: 4FT Hon
Entry Requirements: *Foundation:* Pass. *GCE:* 80. *IB:* 24. *BTEC Dip:* PP. *BTEC ExtDip:* PPP. *OCR ND:* P3 *OCR NED:* P3

C30 UNIVERSITY OF CENTRAL LANCASHIRE
PRESTON
LANCS PR1 2HE
t: 01772 201201 f: 01772 894954
e: uadmissions@uclan.ac.uk
// www.uclan.ac.uk

C800 BSc Psychology
Duration: 3FT Hon
Entry Requirements: *Foundation:* Distinction. *GCE:* 260-300.
SQAH: BBBBC-BBCCC. *IB:* 30. *OCR NED:* M2

C55 UNIVERSITY OF CHESTER
PARKGATE ROAD
CHESTER CH1 4BJ
t: 01244 511000 f: 01244 511300
e: enquiries@chester.ac.uk
// www.chester.ac.uk

C800 BSc Psychology
Duration: 3FT Hon
Entry Requirements: *Foundation:* Pass. *GCE:* 260-300. *SQAH:* BBBB. *IB:* 28.

C58 UNIVERSITY OF CHICHESTER
BISHOP OTTER CAMPUS
COLLEGE LANE
CHICHESTER
WEST SUSSEX PO19 6PE
t: 01243 816002 f: 01243 816161
e: admissions@chi.ac.uk
// www.chiuni.ac.uk

C800 BSc Psychology
Duration: 3FT Hon
Entry Requirements: *GCE:* BBB. *SQAAH:* BBB. *IB:* 30. *BTEC Dip:* DD. *BTEC ExtDip:* DDM.

C60 CITY UNIVERSITY
NORTHAMPTON SQUARE
LONDON EC1V 0HB
t: 020 7040 5060 f: 020 7040 8995
e: ugadmissions@city.ac.uk
// www.city.ac.uk

C800 BSc Psychology
Duration: 3FT Hon
Entry Requirements: *GCE:* AAA. *SQAH:* BBBBC. *IB:* 35.

C85 COVENTRY UNIVERSITY
THE STUDENT CENTRE
COVENTRY UNIVERSITY
1 GULSON RD
COVENTRY CV1 2JH
t: 024 7615 2222 f: 024 7615 2223
e: studentenquiries@coventry.ac.uk
// www.coventry.ac.uk

C800 BSc Psychology
Duration: 3FT/4SW Hon
Entry Requirements: *GCE:* BBB. *SQAH:* BBBBC. *IB:* 28. *BTEC ExtDip:* DDM. *OCR NED:* M1

D26 DE MONTFORT UNIVERSITY
THE GATEWAY
LEICESTER LE1 9BH
t: 0116 255 1551 f: 0116 250 6204
e: enquiries@dmu.ac.uk
// www.dmu.ac.uk

C800 BSc Psychology
Duration: 3FT Hon
Entry Requirements: *GCE:* 300. *IB:* 30. *BTEC ExtDip:* DDM. *OCR NED:* M1

D39 UNIVERSITY OF DERBY
KEDLESTON ROAD
DERBY DE22 1GB
t: 01332 591167 f: 01332 597724
e: askadmissions@derby.ac.uk
// www.derby.ac.uk

C800 BSc Psychology
Duration: 3FT Hon
Entry Requirements: *GCE:* 300. *IB:* 28. *BTEC Dip:* D*D*. *BTEC ExtDip:* DMM. *OCR NED:* M1 Interview required.

D65 UNIVERSITY OF DUNDEE
NETHERGATE
DUNDEE DD1 4HN
t: 01382 383838 f: 01382 388150
e: contactus@dundee.ac.uk
// www.dundee.ac.uk/admissions/
undergraduate/

C800 BSc Psychology
Duration: 4FT Hon
Entry Requirements: *GCE:* BBB. *SQAH:* ABBB. *IB:* 30.

C801 MA Psychology
Duration: 4FT Hon
Entry Requirements: *GCE:* BCC. *SQAH:* ABBB. *IB:* 30.

D86 DURHAM UNIVERSITY
DURHAM UNIVERSITY
UNIVERSITY OFFICE
DURHAM DH1 3HP
t: 0191 334 2000 f: 0191 334 6055
e: admissions@durham.ac.uk
// www.durham.ac.uk

C800 BSc Psychology
Duration: 3FT Hon
Entry Requirements: *GCE:* AAA. *SQAH:* AAAAB. *SQAAH:* AAA. *IB:* 37.

E14 UNIVERSITY OF EAST ANGLIA
NORWICH NR4 7TJ
t: 01603 591515 f: 01603 591523
e: admissions@uea.ac.uk
// www.uea.ac.uk

C800 BSc Psychology
Duration: 3FT Hon   CRB Check: Required
Entry Requirements: *GCE:* AAB. *SQAAH:* AAB. *IB:* 33. *BTEC ExtDip:* DDD. Interview required.

E28 UNIVERSITY OF EAST LONDON
DOCKLANDS CAMPUS
UNIVERSITY WAY
LONDON E16 2RD
t: 020 8223 3333 f: 020 8223 2978
e: study@uel.ac.uk
// www.uel.ac.uk

C800 BSc Psychology
Duration: 3FT Hon
Entry Requirements: *GCE:* 240. *IB:* 24.

C801 BSc Psychology Extended
Duration: 4FT Hon
Entry Requirements: *GCE:* 80. *IB:* 24. Interview required.

E42 EDGE HILL UNIVERSITY
ORMSKIRK
LANCASHIRE L39 4QP
t: 01695 657000 f: 01695 584355
e: study@edgehill.ac.uk
// www.edgehill.ac.uk

C800 BSc Psychology
Duration: 3FT Hon
Entry Requirements: *GCE:* 280. *IB:* 26. *OCR ND:* D *OCR NED:* M2

E56 THE UNIVERSITY OF EDINBURGH
STUDENT RECRUITMENT & ADMISSIONS
57 GEORGE SQUARE
EDINBURGH EH8 9JU
t: 0131 650 4360 f: 0131 651 1236
e: sra.enquiries@ed.ac.uk
// www.ed.ac.uk/studying/undergraduate/

C800 BSc Psychology
Duration: 4FT Hon
Entry Requirements: *GCE:* AAA-BBB. *SQAH:* AAAA-BBBB. *IB:* 34.

C801 MA Psychology
Duration: 4FT Hon
Entry Requirements: *GCE:* AAA-BBB. *SQAH:* AAAA-BBBB. *IB:* 34.

E59 EDINBURGH NAPIER UNIVERSITY
CRAIGLOCKHART CAMPUS
EDINBURGH EH14 1DJ
t: +44 (0)8452 60 60 40 f: 0131 455 6464
e: info@napier.ac.uk
// www.napier.ac.uk

C800 BA Psychology
Duration: 3FT/4FT Ord/Hon
Entry Requirements: *GCE:* 230.

C801 BSc Psychology
Duration: 3FT/4FT Ord/Hon
Entry Requirements: *GCE:* 230.

E70 THE UNIVERSITY OF ESSEX
WIVENHOE PARK
COLCHESTER
ESSEX CO4 3SQ
t: 01206 873666 f: 01206 874477
e: admit@essex.ac.uk
// www.essex.ac.uk

C802 BA Psychology
Duration: 3FT Hon
Entry Requirements: *GCE:* ABB. *SQAH:* AAAB. *IB:* 34.

C801 BA Psychology (Including Year Abroad)
Duration: 4FT Hon
Entry Requirements: Contact the institution for details.

C804 BA Psychology (including foundation year)
Duration: 4FT Hon
Entry Requirements: Contact the institution for details.

C800 BSc Psychology
Duration: 3FT Hon
Entry Requirements: *GCE:* ABB. *SQAH:* AAAB. *IB:* 34.

C803 BSc Psychology (Including Year Abroad)
Duration: 4FT Hon
Entry Requirements: Contact the institution for details.

C805 BSc Psychology (including foundation year)
Duration: 4FT Hon
Entry Requirements: Contact the institution for details.

E84 UNIVERSITY OF EXETER
LAVER BUILDING
NORTH PARK ROAD
EXETER
DEVON EX4 4QE
t: 01392 723044 f: 01392 722479
e: admissions@exeter.ac.uk
// www.exeter.ac.uk

C802 BSc Psychology
Duration: 3FT Hon
Entry Requirements: *GCE:* AAA-AAB. *SQAH:* AAAAB-AAABB. *SQAAH:* AAB-ABB. *BTEC ExtDip:* DDM.

G14 UNIVERSITY OF GLAMORGAN, CARDIFF AND PONTYPRIDD
ENQUIRIES AND ADMISSIONS UNIT
PONTYPRIDD CF37 1DL
t: 08456 434030 f: 01443 654050
e: enquiries@glam.ac.uk
// www.glam.ac.uk

C800 BSc Psychology
Duration: 3FT Hon
Entry Requirements: *GCE:* BBC. *IB:* 25. *BTEC SubDip:* M. *BTEC Dip:* D*D*. *BTEC ExtDip:* DMM.

G28 UNIVERSITY OF GLASGOW
71 SOUTHPARK AVENUE
UNIVERSITY OF GLASGOW
GLASGOW G12 8QQ
t: 0141 330 6062 f: 0141 330 2961
e: student.recruitment@glasgow.ac.uk
// www.glasgow.ac.uk

C803 BSc Psychological Studies
Duration: 3FT Ord
Entry Requirements: *GCE:* AAA. *SQAH:* AAAA-AABB. *IB:* 36.

C800 BSc Psychology
Duration: 4FT Hon
Entry Requirements: *GCE:* ABB. *SQAH:* AAAA-AABB. *IB:* 36.

C801 MA Psychology
Duration: 4FT Hon
Entry Requirements: *GCE:* ABB. *SQAH:* AAAB-ABBB. *IB:* 36.

C802 MA Psychology
Duration: 4FT Hon
Entry Requirements: *GCE:* ABB. *SQAH:* AAAA-AABB. *IB:* 36.

G42 GLASGOW CALEDONIAN UNIVERSITY
STUDENT RECRUITMENT & ADMISSIONS SERVICE
CITY CAMPUS
COWCADDENS ROAD
GLASGOW G4 0BA
t: 0141 331 3000 f: 0141 331 8676
e: undergraduate@gcu.ac.uk
// www.gcu.ac.uk

C800 BSc Psychology
Duration: 4FT Hon
Entry Requirements: *GCE:* ABB. *SQAH:* ABBBB-ABBB. *IB:* 28. *OCR NED:* M1

C800 BSc Psychology option - Biology
Duration: 4FT Hon
Entry Requirements: *GCE:* CCC. *SQAH:* BBBB. *SQAAH:* BBC. *IB:* 28.

C800 BSc Psychology option - Chemistry
Duration: 4FT Hon
Entry Requirements: *GCE:* CCC. *SQAH:* BBBB. *SQAAH:* BBC. *IB:* 28.

C800 BSc Psychology option - Economics
Duration: 4FT Hon
Entry Requirements: *GCE:* CCC. *SQAH:* BBBB. *SQAAH:* BBC. *IB:* 28.

C800 BSc Psychology option - Environmental Science
Duration: 4FT Hon
Entry Requirements: *GCE:* CCC. *SQAH:* BBBB. *SQAAH:* BBC. *IB:* 28.

C800 BSc Psychology option - Mathematics
Duration: 4FT Hon
Entry Requirements: *GCE:* CCC. *SQAH:* BBBB. *SQAAH:* BBC. *IB:* 28.

C800 BSc Psychology option - Media Studies
Duration: 4FT Hon
Entry Requirements: *GCE:* CCC. *SQAH:* BBBB. *SQAAH:* BBC. *IB:* 28.

C800 BSc Psychology option - Politics
Duration: 4FT Hon
Entry Requirements: *GCE:* CCC. *SQAH:* BBBB. *SQAAH:* BBC. *IB:* 28.

C800 BSc Psychology option - Consumer Studies
Duration: 4FT Hon
Entry Requirements: *GCE:* CCC. *SQAH:* BBBB. *SQAAH:* BBC. *IB:* 28.

C800 BSc Psychology option - History
Duration: 4FT Hon
Entry Requirements: *GCE:* CCC. *SQAH:* BBBB. *SQAAH:* BBC. *IB:* 28.

C800 BSc Psychology option - European Languages
Duration: 4FT Hon
Entry Requirements: *GCE:* CCC. *SQAH:* BBBB. *SQAAH:* BBC. *IB:* 28.

C800 BSc Psychology option - Sociology
Duration: 4FT Hon
Entry Requirements: *GCE:* CCC. *SQAH:* BBBB. *SQAAH:* BBC. *IB:* 28.

G50 THE UNIVERSITY OF GLOUCESTERSHIRE
PARK CAMPUS
THE PARK
CHELTENHAM GL50 2RH
t: 01242 714501 f: 01242 714869
e: admissions@glos.ac.uk
// www.glos.ac.uk

C800 BSc Psychology
Duration: 3FT Hon
Entry Requirements: *GCE:* 280-300.

G53 GLYNDWR UNIVERSITY
PLAS COCH
MOLD ROAD
WREXHAM LL11 2AW
t: 01978 293439 f: 01978 290008
e: sid@glyndwr.ac.uk
// www.glyndwr.ac.uk

C800 BSc Psychology
Duration: 3FT Hon
Entry Requirements: *GCE:* 260.

G56 GOLDSMITHS, UNIVERSITY OF LONDON
GOLDSMITHS, UNIVERSITY OF LONDON
NEW CROSS
LONDON SE14 6NW
t: 020 7048 5300 f: 020 7919 7509
e: admissions@gold.ac.uk
// www.gold.ac.uk

C800 BSc Psychology
Duration: 3FT Hon
Entry Requirements: *GCE:* ABB. *SQAH:* BBBBB. *SQAAH:* BBB. *IB:* 30. Interview required.

C801 BSc Psychology with Foundation Year (Integrated Degree)
Duration: 4FT Hon
Entry Requirements: Interview required.

G70 UNIVERSITY OF GREENWICH
GREENWICH CAMPUS
OLD ROYAL NAVAL COLLEGE
PARK ROW
LONDON SE10 9LS
t: 020 8331 9000 f: 020 8331 8145
e: courseinfo@gre.ac.uk
// www.gre.ac.uk

C800 BSc Psychology
Duration: 3FT Hon
Entry Requirements: *GCE:* 320. *IB:* 24.

G80 GRIMSBY INSTITUTE OF FURTHER AND HIGHER EDUCATION
NUNS CORNER
GRIMSBY
NE LINCOLNSHIRE DN34 5BQ
t: 0800 328 3631
e: headmissions@grimsby.ac.uk
// www.grimsby.ac.uk

C800 BA Psychological Studies
Duration: 3FT Hon
Entry Requirements: *GCE:* 120-240. HND required.

H24 HERIOT-WATT UNIVERSITY, EDINBURGH
EDINBURGH CAMPUS
EDINBURGH EH14 4AS
t: 0131 449 5111 f: 0131 451 3630
e: ugadmissions@hw.ac.uk
// www.hw.ac.uk

C800 BSc Psychology
Duration: 4FT Hon
Entry Requirements: *GCE:* BBB. *SQAH:* BBBBC. *SQAAH:* BB. *IB:* 27.

H36 UNIVERSITY OF HERTFORDSHIRE
UNIVERSITY ADMISSIONS SERVICE
COLLEGE LANE
HATFIELD
HERTS AL10 9AB
t: 01707 284800
// www.herts.ac.uk

C800 BSc Psychology
Duration: 3FT Hon
Entry Requirements: *GCE:* 320.

H49 UNIVERSITY OF THE HIGHLANDS AND ISLANDS
UHI EXECUTIVE OFFICE
NESS WALK
INVERNESS
SCOTLAND IV3 5SQ
t: 01463 279000 f: 01463 279001
e: info@uhi.ac.uk
// www.uhi.ac.uk

C800 BSc Psychology
Duration: 4FT Hon
Entry Requirements: *GCE:* BC. *SQAH:* BBC.

H60 THE UNIVERSITY OF HUDDERSFIELD
QUEENSGATE
HUDDERSFIELD HD1 3DH
t: 01484 473969 f: 01484 472765
e: admissionsandrecords@hud.ac.uk
// www.hud.ac.uk

C800 BSc Psychology
Duration: 3FT Hon
Entry Requirements: *GCE:* 300. *SQAH:* BBBB.

H72 THE UNIVERSITY OF HULL
THE UNIVERSITY OF HULL
COTTINGHAM ROAD
HULL HU6 7RX
t: 01482 466100 f: 01482 442290
e: admissions@hull.ac.uk
// www.hull.ac.uk

C800 BSc Psychology
Duration: 3FT Hon
Entry Requirements: *GCE:* 280. *IB:* 32. *BTEC ExtDip:* DMM.

K12 KEELE UNIVERSITY
KEELE UNIVERSITY
STAFFORDSHIRE ST5 5BG
t: 01782 734005 f: 01782 632343
e: undergraduate@keele.ac.uk
// www.keele.ac.uk

C802 BA Psychology with Social Science Foundation Year
Duration: 4FT Hon
Entry Requirements: Contact the institution for details.

C801 BSc Psychology (Major with 2nd subject)
Duration: 3FT Hon
Entry Requirements: *GCE:* BBC.

C800 BSc Psychology with Science Foundation Year
Duration: 4FT Hon
Entry Requirements: *GCE:* CC.

K24 THE UNIVERSITY OF KENT
RECRUITMENT & ADMISSIONS OFFICE
REGISTRY
UNIVERSITY OF KENT
CANTERBURY, KENT CT2 7NZ
t: 01227 827272 f: 01227 827077
e: information@kent.ac.uk
// www.kent.ac.uk

C800 BSc Psychology
Duration: 3FT Hon
Entry Requirements: *GCE:* AAB. *SQAH:* AAAAB. *SQAAH:* AAB. *IB:* 33. *OCR ND:* D *OCR NED:* D1

K84 KINGSTON UNIVERSITY
STUDENT INFORMATION & ADVICE CENTRE
COOPER HOUSE
40-46 SURBITON ROAD
KINGSTON UPON THAMES KT1 2HX
t: 0844 8552177 f: 020 8547 7080
e: aps@kingston.ac.uk
// www.kingston.ac.uk

C800 BSc Psychology
Duration: 3FT Hon
Entry Requirements: *GCE:* 260. *IB:* 30.

L14 LANCASTER UNIVERSITY
THE UNIVERSITY
LANCASTER
LANCASHIRE LA1 4YW
t: 01524 592029 f: 01524 846243
e: ugadmissions@lancaster.ac.uk
// www.lancs.ac.uk

C802 BA Psychology
Duration: 3FT Hon
Entry Requirements: *GCE:* AAB. *SQAH:* ABBBB. *SQAAH:* AAB. *IB:* 35.

C800 BSc Psychology
Duration: 3FT Hon
Entry Requirements: *GCE:* AAB. *SQAH:* ABBBB. *SQAAH:* AAB. *IB:* 35.

L23 UNIVERSITY OF LEEDS
THE UNIVERSITY OF LEEDS
WOODHOUSE LANE
LEEDS LS2 9JT
t: 0113 343 3999
e: admissions@leeds.ac.uk
// www.leeds.ac.uk

C800 BSc Psychology
Duration: 3FT Hon
Entry Requirements: *GCE:* AAB. *SQAAH:* AAB. *IB:* 35. *BTEC SubDip:* D*. *BTEC Dip:* D*D. *BTEC ExtDip:* D*DD.

L24 LEEDS TRINITY UNIVERSITY COLLEGE
BROWNBERRIE LANE
HORSFORTH
LEEDS LS18 5HD
t: 0113 283 7150 f: 0113 283 7222
e: enquiries@leedstrinity.ac.uk
// www.leedstrinity.ac.uk

C800 BSc Psychology
Duration: 3FT Hon
Entry Requirements: *GCE:* 280. *IB:* 25. *OCR ND:* D *OCR NED:* M2

L27 LEEDS METROPOLITAN UNIVERSITY
COURSE ENQUIRIES OFFICE
CITY CAMPUS
LEEDS LS1 3HE
t: 0113 81 23113 f: 0113 81 23129
// www.leedsmet.ac.uk

C800 BSc Psychology
Duration: 3FT Hon
Entry Requirements: *GCE:* 260. *IB:* 24.

L34 UNIVERSITY OF LEICESTER
UNIVERSITY ROAD
LEICESTER LE1 7RH
t: 0116 252 5281 f: 0116 252 2447
e: admissions@le.ac.uk
// www.le.ac.uk

C800 BSc Psychology
Duration: 3FT Hon
Entry Requirements: *GCE:* AAB. *SQAH:* AAAAB-AAABB. *SQAAH:* AAB. *IB:* 34.

L39 UNIVERSITY OF LINCOLN
ADMISSIONS
BRAYFORD POOL
LINCOLN LN6 7TS
t: 01522 886097 f: 01522 886146
e: admissions@lincoln.ac.uk
// www.lincoln.ac.uk

C800 BSc Psychology
Duration: 3FT Hon
Entry Requirements: *GCE:* 300.

L41 THE UNIVERSITY OF LIVERPOOL
THE FOUNDATION BUILDING
BROWNLOW HILL
LIVERPOOL L69 7ZX
t: 0151 794 2000 f: 0151 708 6502
e: ugrecruitment@liv.ac.uk
// www.liv.ac.uk

C800 BSc Psychology
Duration: 3FT Hon
Entry Requirements: *GCE:* AAB. *SQAAH:* AAB. *IB:* 35.

C801 BSc Psychology (2+2, Wirral, mature applicants only)
Duration: 4FT Hon
Entry Requirements: Contact the institution for details.

L46 LIVERPOOL HOPE UNIVERSITY
HOPE PARK
LIVERPOOL L16 9JD
t: 0151 291 3331 f: 0151 291 3434
e: administration@hope.ac.uk
// www.hope.ac.uk

C800 BSc Psychology
Duration: 3FT Hon
Entry Requirements: *GCE:* 300-320. *IB:* 25.

L68 LONDON METROPOLITAN UNIVERSITY
166-220 HOLLOWAY ROAD
LONDON N7 8DB
t: 020 7133 4200
e: admissions@londonmet.ac.uk
// www.londonmet.ac.uk

C800 BSc Psychology
Duration: 3FT Hon
Entry Requirements: *GCE:* 300. *IB:* 28.

L75 LONDON SOUTH BANK UNIVERSITY
ADMISSIONS AND RECRUITMENT CENTRE
90 LONDON ROAD
LONDON SE1 6LN
t: 0800 923 8888 f: 020 7815 8273
e: course.enquiry@lsbu.ac.uk
// www.lsbu.ac.uk

C800 BSc Psychology
Duration: 3FT Hon
Entry Requirements: *GCE:* 260. *IB:* 24.

L79 LOUGHBOROUGH UNIVERSITY
LOUGHBOROUGH
LEICESTERSHIRE LE11 3TU
t: 01509 223522 f: 01509 223905
e: admissions@lboro.ac.uk
// www.lboro.ac.uk

C800 BSc Psychology
Duration: 3FT Hon
Entry Requirements: *GCE:* AAB-ABB. *SQAH:* BBBBB. *SQAAH:* AB.
IB: 34. *BTEC ExtDip:* DDD.

C801 BSc Psychology
Duration: 4SW Hon
Entry Requirements: *GCE:* AAB-ABB. *SQAH:* BBBBB. *SQAAH:* AB.
IB: 34. *BTEC ExtDip:* DDD.

M20 THE UNIVERSITY OF MANCHESTER
RUTHERFORD BUILDING
OXFORD ROAD
MANCHESTER M13 9PL
t: 0161 275 2077 f: 0161 275 2106
e: ug-admissions@manchester.ac.uk
// www.manchester.ac.uk

C800 BSc Psychology
Duration: 3FT Hon
Entry Requirements: *GCE:* AAB. *SQAH:* AAAABB. *SQAAH:* AAB. *IB:*
35. Interview required.

M40 THE MANCHESTER METROPOLITAN UNIVERSITY
ADMISSIONS OFFICE
ALL SAINTS (GMS)
ALL SAINTS
MANCHESTER M15 6BH
t: 0161 247 2000
// www.mmu.ac.uk

C800 BSc Psychology
Duration: 3FT Hon
Entry Requirements: *GCE:* BBB. *SQAH:* AABBB. *SQAAH:* BBC. *IB:*
29. *OCR NED:* D2

C801 BSc Psychology (Foundation)
Duration: 4FT Hon
Entry Requirements: *GCE:* 200. *IB:* 25. *BTEC Dip:* DM. *BTEC*
ExtDip: MMP.

M80 MIDDLESEX UNIVERSITY
MIDDLESEX UNIVERSITY
THE BURROUGHS
LONDON NW4 4BT
t: 020 8411 5555 f: 020 8411 5649
e: enquiries@mdx.ac.uk
// www.mdx.ac.uk

C800 BSc Psychology
Duration: 3FT/4SW Hon
Entry Requirements: *GCE:* 200-300. *IB:* 28.

N21 NEWCASTLE UNIVERSITY
KING'S GATE
NEWCASTLE UPON TYNE NE1 7RU
t: 01912083333
// www.ncl.ac.uk

C800 BSc Psychology
Duration: 3FT Hon
Entry Requirements: *GCE:* AAA-ABB. *SQAH:* AAAAA-AABBB. *IB:*
34.

N31 NEWHAM COLLEGE OF FURTHER EDUCATION
EAST HAM CAMPUS
HIGH STREET SOUTH
LONDON E6 6ER
t: 020 8257 4000 f: 020 8257 4325
e: admissions@newham.ac.uk
// www.newham.ac.uk

C800 BSc Psychology
Duration: 3FT Hon
Entry Requirements: Contact the institution for details.

N36 NEWMAN UNIVERSITY COLLEGE, BIRMINGHAM
GENNERS LANE
BARTLEY GREEN
BIRMINGHAM B32 3NT
t: 0121 476 1181 f: 0121 476 1196
e: Admissions@newman.ac.uk
// www.newman.ac.uk

C800 BSc Psychology
Duration: 3FT Hon
Entry Requirements: *Foundation:* Distinction. *GCE:* 280. *IB:* 25. *BTEC ExtDip:* DMM. *OCR ND:* M2 *OCR NED:* M2

N37 UNIVERSITY OF WALES, NEWPORT
ADMISSIONS
LODGE ROAD
CAERLEON
NEWPORT NP18 3QT
t: 01633 432030 f: 01633 432850
e: admissions@newport.ac.uk
// www.newport.ac.uk

C801 BSc Psychology
Duration: 3FT Hon
Entry Requirements: *GCE:* 240. *IB:* 24. Interview required.

N38 UNIVERSITY OF NORTHAMPTON
PARK CAMPUS
BOUGHTON GREEN ROAD
NORTHAMPTON NN2 7AL
t: 0800 358 2232 f: 01604 722083
e: admissions@northampton.ac.uk
// www.northampton.ac.uk

C800 BSc Psychology
Duration: 3FT Hon
Entry Requirements: *GCE:* 280-320. *SQAH:* AABB. *IB:* 26. *BTEC Dip:* DD. *BTEC ExtDip:* DMM. *OCR ND:* D *OCR NED:* M2

N77 NORTHUMBRIA UNIVERSITY
TRINITY BUILDING
NORTHUMBERLAND ROAD
NEWCASTLE UPON TYNE NE1 8ST
t: 0191 243 7420 f: 0191 227 4561
e: er.admissions@northumbria.ac.uk
// www.northumbria.ac.uk

C800 BSc Psychology
Duration: 3FT Hon
Entry Requirements: *GCE:* 320. *SQAH:* BBBBC. *SQAAH:* BBC. *IB:* 26. *OCR ND:* D *OCR NED:* M2

N84 THE UNIVERSITY OF NOTTINGHAM
THE ADMISSIONS OFFICE
THE UNIVERSITY OF NOTTINGHAM
UNIVERSITY PARK
NOTTINGHAM NG7 2RD
t: 0115 951 5151 f: 0115 951 4668
// www.nottingham.ac.uk

C800 BSc Psychology
Duration: 3FT Hon
Entry Requirements: *GCE:* AAB. *SQAAH:* AAB. *IB:* 34.

N91 NOTTINGHAM TRENT UNIVERSITY
DRYDEN BUILDING
BURTON STREET
NOTTINGHAM NG1 4BU
t: +44 (0) 115 848 4200 f: +44 (0) 115 848 8869
e: applications@ntu.ac.uk
// www.ntu.ac.uk

C800 BSc Psychology
Duration: 3FT Hon
Entry Requirements: *GCE:* 320. *OCR NED:* D2

O66 OXFORD BROOKES UNIVERSITY
ADMISSIONS OFFICE
HEADINGTON CAMPUS
GIPSY LANE
OXFORD OX3 0BP
t: 01865 483040 f: 01865 483983
e: admissions@brookes.ac.uk
// www.brookes.ac.uk

C800 BSc Psychology
Duration: 3FT Hon
Entry Requirements: *GCE:* ABB.

P60 PLYMOUTH UNIVERSITY
DRAKE CIRCUS
PLYMOUTH PL4 8AA
t: 01752 585858 f: 01752 588055
e: admissions@plymouth.ac.uk
// www.plymouth.ac.uk

C800 BSc Psychology
Duration: 3FT Hon
Entry Requirements: *GCE:* 320. *IB:* 28.

P80 UNIVERSITY OF PORTSMOUTH
ACADEMIC REGISTRY
UNIVERSITY HOUSE
WINSTON CHURCHILL AVENUE
PORTSMOUTH PO1 2UP
t: 023 9284 8484 f: 023 9284 3082
e: admissions@port.ac.uk
// www.port.ac.uk

C800 BSc Psychology
Duration: 3FT Hon
Entry Requirements: *GCE:* 320. *IB:* 27. *BTEC ExtDip:* DDM.

Q25 QUEEN MARGARET UNIVERSITY, EDINBURGH
QUEEN MARGARET UNIVERSITY DRIVE
EDINBURGH EH21 6UU
t: 0131474 0000 f: 0131 474 0001
e: admissions@qmu.ac.uk
// www.qmu.ac.uk

C800 BSc Psychology
Duration: 4FT Hon
Entry Requirements: *GCE:* 260. *IB:* 28.

Q50 QUEEN MARY, UNIVERSITY OF LONDON
QUEEN MARY, UNIVERSITY OF LONDON
MILE END ROAD
LONDON E1 4NS
t: 020 7882 5555 f: 020 7882 5500
e: admissions@qmul.ac.uk
// www.qmul.ac.uk

C800 BSc Psychology
Duration: 3FT Hon
Entry Requirements: *GCE:* AAB. *SQAAH:* AAB. *IB:* 34.

Q75 QUEEN'S UNIVERSITY BELFAST
UNIVERSITY ROAD
BELFAST BT7 1NN
t: 028 9097 3838 f: 028 9097 5151
e: admissions@qub.ac.uk
// www.qub.ac.uk

C800 BSc Psychology
Duration: 3FT Hon
Entry Requirements: *GCE:* ABB-BBBb. *SQAH:* ABBBB. *SQAAH:* ABB. *IB:* 33.

R12 THE UNIVERSITY OF READING
THE UNIVERSITY OF READING
PO BOX 217
READING RG6 6AH
t: 0118 378 8619 f: 0118 378 8924
e: student.recruitment@reading.ac.uk
// www.reading.ac.uk

C800 BSc Psychology
Duration: 3FT Hon
Entry Requirements: *GCE:* AAB. *SQAH:* AAABB. *SQAAH:* AAB. *BTEC Dip:* DD. *BTEC ExtDip:* DDD. Interview required.

C805 BSc Psychology, Childhood and Ageing
Duration: 3FT Hon
Entry Requirements: *GCE:* AAB. *SQAH:* AAABB. *SQAAH:* AAB. *BTEC Dip:* DD. *BTEC ExtDip:* DDD. Interview required.

C806 BSc Psychology, Mental and Physical Health
Duration: 3FT Hon
Entry Requirements: *GCE:* AAB. *SQAH:* AAABB. *SQAAH:* AAB. *BTEC Dip:* DD. *BTEC ExtDip:* DDD. Interview required.

R18 REGENT'S COLLEGE, LONDON (INCORPORATING REGENT'S BUSINESS SCHOOL, LONDON)
INNER CIRCLE, REGENT'S COLLEGE
REGENT'S PARK
LONDON NW1 4NS
t: +44(0)20 7487 7505 f: +44(0)20 7487 7425
e: exrel@regents.ac.uk
// www.regents.ac.uk/

C801 BSc Psychology
Duration: 3FT Hon
Entry Requirements: Contact the institution for details.

C802 BSc Psychology (with Integrated Foundation)
Duration: 4FT Hon
Entry Requirements: Contact the institution for details.

C800 Foundation Psychology (Foundation)
Duration: 1FT FYr
Entry Requirements: Contact the institution for details.

R48 ROEHAMPTON UNIVERSITY
ROEHAMPTON LANE
LONDON SW15 5PU
t: 020 8392 3232 f: 020 8392 3470
e: enquiries@roehampton.ac.uk
// www.roehampton.ac.uk

C800 BSc Psychology
Duration: 3FT Hon
Entry Requirements: *GCE:* 300. *IB:* 26. *BTEC ExtDip:* DDM. *OCR NED:* D2 Interview required.

R72 ROYAL HOLLOWAY, UNIVERSITY OF LONDON
ROYAL HOLLOWAY, UNIVERSITY OF LONDON
EGHAM
SURREY TW20 0EX
t: 01784 414944 f: 01784 473662
e: Admissions@rhul.ac.uk
// www.rhul.ac.uk

C804 BSc Applied Psychology
Duration: 3FT Hon
Entry Requirements: Contact the institution for details.

C800 BSc Psychology
Duration: 3FT Hon
Entry Requirements: *GCE:* 340. *IB:* 35.

C807 BSc Psychology, Clinical & Cognitive Neuroscience
Duration: 3FT Hon
Entry Requirements: Contact the institution for details.

C806 BSc Psychology, Clinical Psychology & Mental Health
Duration: 3FT Hon
Entry Requirements: Contact the institution for details.

C805 BSc Psychology, Development & Development Disorders
Duration: 3FT Hon
Entry Requirements: Contact the institution for details.

C808 BSc Science Foundation - Option: Psychology
Duration: 4FT Hon
Entry Requirements: Contact the institution for details.

S03 THE UNIVERSITY OF SALFORD
SALFORD M5 4WT
t: 0161 295 4545 f: 0161 295 4646
e: ug-admissions@salford.ac.uk
// www.salford.ac.uk

C802 BSc Psychology
Duration: 3FT Hon
Entry Requirements: *GCE:* 300. *IB:* 27. *OCR NED:* M1

S18 THE UNIVERSITY OF SHEFFIELD
THE UNIVERSITY OF SHEFFIELD
LEVEL 2, ARTS TOWER
WESTERN BANK
SHEFFIELD S10 2TN
t: 0114 222 8030 f: 0114 222 8032
// www.sheffield.ac.uk

C802 BA Psychology
Duration: 3FT Hon
Entry Requirements: *GCE:* AAB. *SQAH:* AAABB. *SQAAH:* AB. *IB:* 35. *BTEC ExtDip:* DDD.

C800 BSc Psychology
Duration: 3FT Hon
Entry Requirements: *GCE:* AAB. *SQAH:* AAABB. *SQAAH:* AB. *IB:* 35. *BTEC ExtDip:* DDD.

S21 SHEFFIELD HALLAM UNIVERSITY
CITY CAMPUS
HOWARD STREET
SHEFFIELD S1 1WB
t: 0114 225 5555 f: 0114 225 2167
e: admissions@shu.ac.uk
// www.shu.ac.uk

C800 BSc Psychology
Duration: 3FT Hon
Entry Requirements: *GCE:* 300.

S27 UNIVERSITY OF SOUTHAMPTON
HIGHFIELD
SOUTHAMPTON SO17 1BJ
t: 023 8059 4732 f: 023 8059 3037
e: admissions@soton.ac.uk
// www.southampton.ac.uk

C800 BSc Psychology
Duration: 3FT Hon   CRB Check: Required
Entry Requirements: *GCE:* AAB. *IB:* 34.

S30 SOUTHAMPTON SOLENT UNIVERSITY
EAST PARK TERRACE
SOUTHAMPTON
HAMPSHIRE SO14 0RT
t: +44 (0) 23 8031 9039 f: + 44 (0)23 8022 2259
e: admissions@solent.ac.uk
// www.solent.ac.uk/

C800 BSc Psychology
Duration: 3FT Hon
Entry Requirements: *Foundation:* Distinction. *GCE:* 240. *SQAAH:* AA-CCD. *IB:* 24. *BTEC ExtDip:* MMM. *OCR ND:* D *OCR NED:* M3

S36 UNIVERSITY OF ST ANDREWS
ST KATHARINE'S WEST
16 THE SCORES
ST ANDREWS
FIFE KY16 9AX
t: 01334 462150 f: 01334 463330
e: admissions@st-andrews.ac.uk
// www.st-andrews.ac.uk

C800 BSc Psychology
Duration: 4FT Hon
Entry Requirements: *GCE:* AAA. *SQAH:* AAAB. *IB:* 36.

C802 MA Psychology
Duration: 4FT Hon
Entry Requirements: *GCE:* AAA. *SQAH:* AAAB. *IB:* 36.

S64 ST MARY'S UNIVERSITY COLLEGE, TWICKENHAM
WALDEGRAVE ROAD
STRAWBERRY HILL
MIDDLESEX TW1 4SX
t: 020 8240 4029 f: 020 8240 2361
e: admit@smuc.ac.uk
// www.smuc.ac.uk

C800 BSc Psychology
Duration: 3FT Hon
Entry Requirements: *GCE:* 240. *SQAH:* BBBC. *IB:* 28. *OCR ND:* D *OCR NED:* M3 Interview required.

S72 STAFFORDSHIRE UNIVERSITY
COLLEGE ROAD
STOKE ON TRENT ST4 2DE
t: 01782 292753 f: 01782 292740
e: admissions@staffs.ac.uk
// www.staffs.ac.uk

C800 BSc Psychology
Duration: 3FT Hon
Entry Requirements: *GCE:* 200-280. *IB:* 24.

C801 BSc Psychology (with Foundation Year)
Duration: 4FT Hon
Entry Requirements: Interview required.

S75 THE UNIVERSITY OF STIRLING
STUDENT RECRUITMENT & ADMISSIONS SERVICE
UNIVERSITY OF STIRLING
STIRLING
SCOTLAND FK9 4LA
t: 01786 467044 f: 01786 466800
e: admissions@stir.ac.uk
// www.stir.ac.uk

C801 BA Psychology
Duration: 4FT Hon
Entry Requirements: *GCE:* BBC. *SQAH:* BBBB. *SQAAH:* AAA-CCC. *IB:* 32. *BTEC ExtDip:* DMM.

C800 BSc Psychology
Duration: 4FT Hon
Entry Requirements: *GCE:* BBC. *SQAH:* BBBB. *SQAAH:* AAA-CCC. *IB:* 32. *BTEC ExtDip:* DMM.

S78 THE UNIVERSITY OF STRATHCLYDE
GLASGOW G1 1XQ
t: 0141 552 4400 f: 0141 552 0775
// www.strath.ac.uk

C800 BA Psychology
Duration: 4FT Hon
Entry Requirements: *GCE:* ABB. *SQAH:* AAABB-AAAB. *IB:* 34.

S84 UNIVERSITY OF SUNDERLAND
STUDENT HELPLINE
THE STUDENT GATEWAY
CHESTER ROAD
SUNDERLAND SR1 3SD
t: 0191 515 3000 f: 0191 515 3805
e: student.helpline@sunderland.ac.uk
// www.sunderland.ac.uk

C800 BSc Psychology
Duration: 3FT Hon
Entry Requirements: *GCE:* 260. *IB:* 24. *OCR ND:* D

C801 BSc Psychology with Foundation Year
Duration: 4FT Hon
Entry Requirements: *GCE:* 100-360. *SQAH:* CC.

S85 UNIVERSITY OF SURREY
STAG HILL
GUILDFORD
SURREY GU2 7XH
t: +44(0)1483 689305 f: +44(0)1483 689388
e: ugteam@surrey.ac.uk
// www.surrey.ac.uk

C800 BSc Psychology (4 years)
Duration: 4SW Hon
Entry Requirements: *GCE:* AAA-AAB. *SQAH:* AABBB.

S90 UNIVERSITY OF SUSSEX
UNDERGRADUATE ADMISSIONS
SUSSEX HOUSE
UNIVERSITY OF SUSSEX
BRIGHTON BN1 9RH
t: 01273 678416 f: 01273 678545
e: ug.applicants@sussex.ac.uk
// www.sussex.ac.uk

C800 BSc Psychology
Duration: 3FT Hon
Entry Requirements: *GCE:* AAB. *SQAH:* AAABB. *IB:* 35. *BTEC SubDip:* D. *BTEC Dip:* DD. *BTEC ExtDip:* DDD. *OCR ND:* D *OCR NED:* D1

S93 SWANSEA UNIVERSITY
SINGLETON PARK
SWANSEA SA2 8PP
t: 01792 295111 f: 01792 295110
e: admissions@swansea.ac.uk
// www.swansea.ac.uk

C800 BSc Psychology
Duration: 3FT Hon
Entry Requirements: *GCE:* AAB. *IB:* 34.

T20 TEESSIDE UNIVERSITY
MIDDLESBROUGH TS1 3BA
t: 01642 218121 f: 01642 384201
e: registry@tees.ac.uk
// www.tees.ac.uk

C800 BSc Psychology
Duration: 3FT Hon
Entry Requirements: *GCE:* 260.

T80 UNIVERSITY OF WALES TRINITY SAINT DAVID
COLLEGE ROAD
CARMARTHEN SA31 3EP
t: 01267 676767 f: 01267 676766
e: registry@trinitysaintdavid.ac.uk
// www.tsd.ac.uk

C800 BSc Psychology
Duration: 3FT Hon
Entry Requirements: *GCE:* 180-360. *IB:* 26. Interview required.

T85 TRURO AND PENWITH COLLEGE
TRURO COLLEGE
COLLEGE ROAD
TRURO
CORNWALL TR1 3XX
t: 01872 267122 f: 01872 267526
e: heinfo@trurocollege.ac.uk
// www.truro-penwith.ac.uk

008C HND Applied Psychology
Duration: 2FT HND
Entry Requirements: *GCE:* 60. *IB:* 24. *BTEC Dip:* MP. *BTEC ExtDip:* PPP. Interview required.

U40 UNIVERSITY OF THE WEST OF SCOTLAND
PAISLEY
RENFREWSHIRE
SCOTLAND PA1 2BE
t: 0141 848 3727 f: 0141 848 3623
e: admissions@uws.ac.uk
// www.uws.ac.uk

C800 BSc Psychology
Duration: 3FT/4FT Ord/Hon
Entry Requirements: *GCE:* CD. *SQAH:* BBC-BCCC.

U80 UNIVERSITY COLLEGE LONDON (UNIVERSITY OF LONDON)
GOWER STREET
LONDON WC1E 6BT
t: 020 7679 3000 f: 020 7679 3001
// www.ucl.ac.uk

C800 BSc Psychology
Duration: 3FT Hon
Entry Requirements: *GCE:* A*AAe-AAAe. *SQAAH:* AAA. Interview required.

W05 THE UNIVERSITY OF WEST LONDON
ST MARY'S ROAD
EALING
LONDON W5 5RF
t: 0800 036 8888 f: 020 8566 1353
e: learning.advice@uwl.ac.uk
// www.uwl.ac.uk

C800 BSc Psychology
Duration: 3FT Hon
Entry Requirements: *GCE:* 200. *IB:* 28. Interview required.

C801 BSc Psychology with Foundation Year
Duration: 4FT Hon
Entry Requirements: *GCE:* 120. *IB:* 24. Interview required.

W20 THE UNIVERSITY OF WARWICK
COVENTRY CV4 8UW
t: 024 7652 3723 f: 024 7652 4649
e: ugadmissions@warwick.ac.uk
// www.warwick.ac.uk

C800 BSc Psychology
Duration: 3FT Hon
Entry Requirements: *GCE:* AAA. *IB:* 38.

W50 UNIVERSITY OF WESTMINSTER
2ND FLOOR, CAVENDISH HOUSE
101 NEW CAVENDISH STREET,
LONDON W1W 6XH
t: 020 7915 5511
e: course-enquiries@westminster.ac.uk
// www.westminster.ac.uk

C801 BSc Psychology
Duration: 3FT/4SW Hon
Entry Requirements: *GCE:* ABB. *SQAH:* BBBBB. *SQAAH:* BBB. *IB:* 32. Interview required.

W75 UNIVERSITY OF WOLVERHAMPTON
ADMISSIONS UNIT
MX207, CAMP STREET
WOLVERHAMPTON
WEST MIDLANDS WV1 1AD
t: 01902 321000 f: 01902 321896
e: admissions@wlv.ac.uk
// www.wlv.ac.uk

C800 BSc Psychology
Duration: 3FT Hon
Entry Requirements: *GCE:* 220. *IB:* 24. *BTEC Dip:* DD. *BTEC ExtDip:* MMM.

W76 UNIVERSITY OF WINCHESTER
WINCHESTER
HANTS SO22 4NR
t: 01962 827234 f: 01962 827288
e: course.enquiries@winchester.ac.uk
// www.winchester.ac.uk

C801 BSc Psychological Science
Duration: 3FT Hon
Entry Requirements: *Foundation:* Distinction. *GCE:* 260-300. *IB:* 25. *OCR ND:* D *OCR NED:* M2

C800 BSc Psychology
Duration: 3FT Hon
Entry Requirements: *Foundation:* Distinction. *GCE:* 260-300. *IB:* 26. *OCR ND:* D Interview required.

W80 UNIVERSITY OF WORCESTER
HENWICK GROVE
WORCESTER WR2 6AJ
t: 01905 855111 f: 01905 855377
e: admissions@worc.ac.uk
// www.worcester.ac.uk

C800 BSc Psychology
Duration: 3FT Hon
Entry Requirements: *GCE:* 280. *IB:* 25. *OCR ND:* D *OCR NED:* M3

Y50 THE UNIVERSITY OF YORK
STUDENT RECRUITMENT AND ADMISSIONS
UNIVERSITY OF YORK
HESLINGTON
YORK YO10 5DD
t: 01904 324000 f: 01904 323538
e: ug-admissions@york.ac.uk
// www.york.ac.uk

C800 BSc Psychology
Duration: 3FT Hon
Entry Requirements: *GCE:* AAA-AAB. *SQAH:* AAAAA-AAAAB. *SQAAH:* AA-AB. *IB:* 36. *BTEC ExtDip:* DDD. Admissions Test required.

Y75 YORK ST JOHN UNIVERSITY
LORD MAYOR'S WALK
YORK YO31 7EX
t: 01904 876598 f: 01904 876940/876921
e: admissions@yorksj.ac.uk
// w3.yorksj.ac.uk

C800 BSc Psychology
Duration: 3FT Hon
Entry Requirements: *Foundation:* Pass. *GCE:* 260. *IB:* 24.

C802 BSc Psychology (for international applicants only)
Duration: 4FT Hon
Entry Requirements: *Foundation:* Pass. *GCE:* 260. *IB:* 24.

APPLIED PSYCHOLOGY

A40 ABERYSTWYTH UNIVERSITY
ABERYSTWYTH UNIVERSITY, WELCOME CENTRE
PENGLAIS CAMPUS
ABERYSTWYTH
CEREDIGION SY23 3FB
t: 01970 622021 f: 01970 627410
e: ug-admissions@aber.ac.uk
// www.aber.ac.uk

M9C8 BScEcon Criminology with Applied Psychology
Duration: 3FT Hon
Entry Requirements: *GCE:* 300. *IB:* 28.

B22 UNIVERSITY OF BEDFORDSHIRE
PARK SQUARE
LUTON
BEDS LU1 3JU
t: 0844 8482234 f: 01582 489323
e: admissions@beds.ac.uk
// www.beds.ac.uk

C810 BSc Applied Psychology
Duration: 4SW Hon
Entry Requirements: *GCE:* 160-240. *IB:* 30.

B24 BIRKBECK, UNIVERSITY OF LONDON
MALET STREET
LONDON WC1E 7HX
t: 020 7631 6316
e: webform: www.bbk.ac.uk/ask
// www.bbk.ac.uk/ask

C815 BSc Business Psychology
Duration: 3FT Hon
Entry Requirements: *IB:* 26. Interview required. Admissions Test required.

B40 BLACKBURN COLLEGE
FEILDEN STREET
BLACKBURN BB2 1LH
t: 01254 292594 f: 01254 679647
e: he-admissions@blackburn.ac.uk
// www.blackburn.ac.uk

C810 BSc Applied Psychology
Duration: 3FT Hon
Entry Requirements: *GCE:* 200.

B44 UNIVERSITY OF BOLTON
DEANE ROAD
BOLTON BL3 5AB
t: 01204 903903 f: 01204 399074
e: enquiries@bolton.ac.uk
// www.bolton.ac.uk

CF84 BSc Criminological & Forensic Psychology
Duration: 3FT Hon
Entry Requirements: *GCE:* 300. Interview required.

B72 UNIVERSITY OF BRIGHTON
MITHRAS HOUSE 211
LEWES ROAD
BRIGHTON BN2 4AT
t: 01273 644644 f: 01273 642607
e: admissions@brighton.ac.uk
// www.brighton.ac.uk

MC98 BA Applied Psychology and Criminology
Duration: 3FT Hon
Entry Requirements: *GCE:* BBB. *IB:* 30.

CL83 BA Applied Psychology and Sociology
Duration: 3FT Hon
Entry Requirements: *GCE:* BBB. *IB:* 32.

B94 BUCKINGHAMSHIRE NEW UNIVERSITY
QUEEN ALEXANDRA ROAD
HIGH WYCOMBE
BUCKINGHAMSHIRE HP11 2JZ
t: 0800 0565 660 f: 01494 605 023
e: admissions@bucks.ac.uk
// bucks.ac.uk

L4C8 BSc Police Studies with Criminological Psychology
Duration: 3FT Hon
Entry Requirements: *GCE:* 240-280. *IB:* 25. *OCR ND:* D *OCR NED:* M2

C813 BSc Sports Psychology
Duration: 3FT Hon
Entry Requirements: *GCE:* 240-280. *IB:* 25. *OCR ND:* D *OCR NED:* M2

C15 CARDIFF UNIVERSITY
PO BOX 927
30-36 NEWPORT ROAD
CARDIFF CF24 0DE
t: 029 2087 9999 f: 029 2087 6138
e: admissions@cardiff.ac.uk
// www.cardiff.ac.uk

C810 BSc Psychology with Professional Placement
Duration: 4SW Hon
Entry Requirements: *GCE:* AAA-AAB. *SQAH:* AAAAB. *SQAAH:* AA. *IB:* 35. Interview required.

C99 UNIVERSITY OF CUMBRIA
FUSEHILL STREET
CARLISLE
CUMBRIA CA1 2HH
t: 01228 616234 f: 01228 616235
// www.cumbria.ac.uk

C810 BSc Applied Psychology
Duration: 3FT Hon
Entry Requirements: *Foundation:* Pass. *GCE:* 160. *IB:* 30. *OCR ND:* M2 *OCR NED:* P2

D86 DURHAM UNIVERSITY
DURHAM UNIVERSITY
UNIVERSITY OFFICE
DURHAM DH1 3HP
t: 0191 334 2000 f: 0191 334 6055
e: admissions@durham.ac.uk
// www.durham.ac.uk

C817 BSc Psychology (Applied)
Duration: 3FT Hon
Entry Requirements: *GCE:* ABB. *SQAH:* AABBB. *SQAAH:* ABB. *IB:* 34.

C818 BSc Psychology (Applied) with Foundation
Duration: 4FT Hon
Entry Requirements: Contact the institution for details.

E28 UNIVERSITY OF EAST LONDON
DOCKLANDS CAMPUS
UNIVERSITY WAY
LONDON E16 2RD
t: 020 8223 3333 f: 020 8223 2978
e: study@uel.ac.uk
// www.uel.ac.uk

C810 BSc Critical Psychology
Duration: 3FT Hon
Entry Requirements: *GCE:* 240. *IB:* 24.

C816 BSc Forensic Psychology
Duration: 3FT Hon
Entry Requirements: *GCE:* 240. *IB:* 24.

E42 EDGE HILL UNIVERSITY
ORMSKIRK
LANCASHIRE L39 4QP
t: 01695 657000 f: 01695 584355
e: study@edgehill.ac.uk
// www.edgehill.ac.uk

C812 BSc Educational Psychology
Duration: 3FT Hon   CRB Check: Required
Entry Requirements: *GCE:* 280. *IB:* 26. *OCR ND:* D *OCR NED:* M2

C813 BSc Sport & Exercise Psychology
Duration: 3FT Hon
Entry Requirements: *GCE:* 280. *IB:* 26. *OCR ND:* D *OCR NED:* M2

E59 EDINBURGH NAPIER UNIVERSITY
CRAIGLOCKHART CAMPUS
EDINBURGH EH14 1DJ
t: +44 (0)8452 60 60 40 f: 0131 455 6464
e: info@napier.ac.uk
// www.napier.ac.uk

CC68 BSc Sport and Exercise Science (Sport Psychology)
Duration: 3FT/4FT Ord/Hon
Entry Requirements: *GCE:* 260.

E84 UNIVERSITY OF EXETER
LAVER BUILDING
NORTH PARK ROAD
EXETER
DEVON EX4 4QE
t: 01392 723044 f: 01392 722479
e: admissions@exeter.ac.uk
// www.exeter.ac.uk

C810 BSc Applied Psychology (Clinical)
Duration: 3FT Hon   CRB Check: Required
Entry Requirements: *GCE:* AAA-AAB. *SQAH:* AAAAB-AAABB.
SQAAH: AAB-ABB. *BTEC ExtDip:* DDM.   Interview required.

G14 UNIVERSITY OF GLAMORGAN, CARDIFF AND PONTYPRIDD
ENQUIRIES AND ADMISSIONS UNIT
PONTYPRIDD CF37 1DL
t: 08456 434030 f: 01443 654050
e: enquiries@glam.ac.uk
// www.glam.ac.uk

C810 BSc Applied Psychology
Duration: 3FT Hon
Entry Requirements: *GCE:* BBB.

G50 THE UNIVERSITY OF GLOUCESTERSHIRE
PARK CAMPUS
THE PARK
CHELTENHAM GL50 2RH
t: 01242 714501 f: 01242 714869
e: admissions@glos.ac.uk
// www.glos.ac.uk

X155 BSc Sports Education
Duration: 2FT Hon   CRB Check: Required
Entry Requirements: Contact the institution for details.

G70 UNIVERSITY OF GREENWICH
GREENWICH CAMPUS
OLD ROYAL NAVAL COLLEGE
PARK ROW
LONDON SE10 9LS
t: 020 8331 9000 f: 020 8331 8145
e: courseinfo@gre.ac.uk
// www.gre.ac.uk

C815 BA Business Psychology
Duration: 3FT Hon
Entry Requirements: *GCE:* 280. *IB:* 24.

H24 HERIOT-WATT UNIVERSITY, EDINBURGH
EDINBURGH CAMPUS
EDINBURGH EH14 4AS
t: 0131 449 5111 f: 0131 451 3630
e: ugadmissions@hw.ac.uk
// www.hw.ac.uk

C810 BSc Psychology (Applied)
Duration: 4FT Hon
Entry Requirements: *GCE:* BBB. *SQAH:* BBBBC. *SQAAH:* BB. *IB:* 27.

K12 KEELE UNIVERSITY
KEELE UNIVERSITY
STAFFORDSHIRE ST5 5BG
t: 01782 734005 f: 01782 632343
e: undergraduate@keele.ac.uk
// www.keele.ac.uk

NC48 BSc Accounting and Applied Psychology
Duration: 4FT Hon
Entry Requirements: *GCE:* ABB.

C811 BSc Applied Psychology (Major with 2nd subject)
Duration: 4FT Hon
Entry Requirements: *GCE:* BBC.

CT8R BSc Applied Psychology and American Studies
Duration: 4FT Deg
Entry Requirements: *GCE:* BBB.

CF87 BSc Applied Psychology and Applied Environmental Science
Duration: 4FT Deg
Entry Requirements: *GCE:* BBC.

CC8R BSc Applied Psychology and Biochemistry
Duration: 4FT Deg
Entry Requirements: *GCE:* BBC.

CC8C BSc Applied Psychology and Biology
Duration: 4FT Deg
Entry Requirements: *GCE:* BBC.

CN8F BSc Applied Psychology and Business Management
Duration: 4FT Deg
Entry Requirements: *GCE:* ABB.

CF8C BSc Applied Psychology and Chemistry
Duration: 4FT Deg
Entry Requirements: *GCE:* BBC.

CG8K BSc Applied Psychology and Computer Science
Duration: 4FT Deg
Entry Requirements: *GCE:* BBC.

CGV4 BSc Applied Psychology and Creative Computing
Duration: 4FT Hon
Entry Requirements: *GCE:* BBC.

CM8Y BSc Applied Psychology and Criminology
Duration: 4FT Deg
Entry Requirements: *GCE:* BBC.

CL8C BSc Applied Psychology and Economics
Duration: 4FT Deg
Entry Requirements: *GCE:* ABB.

CX8H BSc Applied Psychology and Educational Studies
Duration: 4FT Deg
Entry Requirements: *GCE:* BBC.

CQ8H BSc Applied Psychology and English
Duration: 4FT Deg
Entry Requirements: *GCE:* BBB.

CF84 BSc Applied Psychology and Forensic Science
Duration: 4FT Deg
Entry Requirements: *GCE:* BBC.

CF8P BSc Applied Psychology and Geology
Duration: 4FT Deg
Entry Requirements: *GCE:* BBC.

CV8C BSc Applied Psychology and History
Duration: 4FT Deg
Entry Requirements: *GCE:* BBB.

CC8D BSc Applied Psychology and Human Biology
Duration: 4FT Deg
Entry Requirements: *GCE:* BBC.

CN8P BSc Applied Psychology and Human Resource Management
Duration: 4FT Deg
Entry Requirements: *GCE:* ABB.

CG85 BSc Applied Psychology and Information Systems
Duration: 4FT Deg
Entry Requirements: *GCE:* BBC.

CN81 BSc Applied Psychology and International Business
Duration: 4FT Hon
Entry Requirements: *GCE:* ABB.

CN8M BSc Applied Psychology and Marketing
Duration: 4FT Deg
Entry Requirements: *GCE:* ABB.

CG8C BSc Applied Psychology and Mathematics
Duration: 4FT Deg
Entry Requirements: *GCE:* BBC.

CP83 BSc Applied Psychology and Media, Communications and Culture
Duration: 4FT Deg
Entry Requirements: *GCE:* BBC.

CF8D BSc Applied Psychology and Medicinal Chemistry
Duration: 4FT Deg
Entry Requirements: *GCE:* BBC.

CW8H BSc Applied Psychology and Music
Duration: 4FT Deg
Entry Requirements: *GCE:* BBC.

CJ89 BSc Applied Psychology and Music Technology
Duration: 4FT Deg
Entry Requirements: *GCE:* BBC.

CB81 BSc Applied Psychology and Neuroscience
Duration: 4FT Deg
Entry Requirements: *GCE:* BBC.

CV8M BSc Applied Psychology and Philosophy
Duration: 4FT Deg
Entry Requirements: *GCE:* BBB.

CL8F BSc Applied Psychology and Politics
Duration: 4FT Deg
Entry Requirements: *GCE:* BBB.

CG87 BSc Applied Psychology and Smart Systems
Duration: 4FT Hon
Entry Requirements: *GCE:* BBC.

CL8H BSc Applied Psychology and Sociology
Duration: 4FT Deg
Entry Requirements: *GCE:* BBC.

C810 BSc Applied Psychology with Science Foundation Year
Duration: 5FT Hon
Entry Requirements: *GCE:* 160.

K24 THE UNIVERSITY OF KENT
RECRUITMENT & ADMISSIONS OFFICE
REGISTRY
UNIVERSITY OF KENT
CANTERBURY, KENT CT2 7NZ
t: 01227 827272 f: 01227 827077
e: information@kent.ac.uk
// www.kent.ac.uk

C850 BSc Applied Psychology (4-year sandwich)
Duration: 4SW Hon
Entry Requirements: *GCE:* AAA. *SQAH:* AAAAA. *SQAAH:* AAA. *IB:* 33. *OCR ND:* D *OCR NED:* D1

C823 BSc Applied Psychology with Clinical Psychology (4-year sandwich)
Duration: 4SW Hon
Entry Requirements: *GCE:* AAA. *SQAH:* AAAAA. *SQAAH:* AAA. *IB:* 33. *OCR ND:* D *OCR NED:* D1

L24 LEEDS TRINITY UNIVERSITY COLLEGE
BROWNBERRIE LANE
HORSFORTH
LEEDS LS18 5HD
t: 0113 283 7150 f: 0113 283 7222
e: enquiries@leedstrinity.ac.uk
// www.leedstrinity.ac.uk

CF84 BSc Forensic Psychology
Duration: 3FT Hon
Entry Requirements: *GCE:* 280. *IB:* 25. *OCR ND:* D *OCR NED:* M2

L34 UNIVERSITY OF LEICESTER
UNIVERSITY ROAD
LEICESTER LE1 7RH
t: 0116 252 5281 f: 0116 252 2447
e: admissions@le.ac.uk
// www.le.ac.uk

C810 BSc Applied Psychology
Duration: 3FT Hon
Entry Requirements: Contact the institution for details.

L39 UNIVERSITY OF LINCOLN
ADMISSIONS
BRAYFORD POOL
LINCOLN LN6 7TS
t: 01522 886097 f: 01522 886146
e: admissions@lincoln.ac.uk
// www.lincoln.ac.uk

C890 BSc Psychology with Forensic Psychology
Duration: 3FT Hon
Entry Requirements: *GCE:* 300.

L51 LIVERPOOL JOHN MOORES UNIVERSITY
KINGSWAY HOUSE
HATTON GARDEN
LIVERPOOL L3 2AJ
t: 0151 231 5090 f: 0151 904 6368
e: courses@ljmu.ac.uk
// www.ljmu.ac.uk

C870 BSc Applied Psychology
Duration: 3FT Hon
Entry Requirements: *GCE:* 260-300. *IB:* 25.

CM82 BSc Forensic Psychology and Criminal Justice
Duration: 3FT Hon
Entry Requirements: *GCE:* 300. *IB:* 29.

N36 NEWMAN UNIVERSITY COLLEGE, BIRMINGHAM
GENNERS LANE
BARTLEY GREEN
BIRMINGHAM B32 3NT
t: 0121 476 1181 f: 0121 476 1196
e: Admissions@newman.ac.uk
// www.newman.ac.uk

CW81 BA Applied Psychology and Art & Design
Duration: 3FT Hon
Entry Requirements: *Foundation:* Distinction. *GCE:* 260. *IB:* 24. *BTEC ExtDip:* DMM. *OCR ND:* M2 *OCR NED:* M2

CB89 BA Applied Psychology and Counselling Studies
Duration: 3FT Hon
Entry Requirements: *Foundation:* Distinction. *GCE:* 260. *IB:* 24. *BTEC ExtDip:* DMM. *OCR ND:* M2 *OCR NED:* M2

CV85 BA Applied Psychology and Philosophy, Religion & Ethics
Duration: 3FT Hon
Entry Requirements: *Foundation:* Distinction. *GCE:* 260. *IB:* 24. *BTEC ExtDip:* DMM. *OCR ND:* M2 *OCR NED:* M2

WC48 BA Drama and Applied Psychology
Duration: 3FT Hon
Entry Requirements: *Foundation:* Distinction. *GCE:* 260. *IB:* 24. *BTEC ExtDip:* DMM. *OCR ND:* M2 *OCR NED:* M2

W4C8 BA Drama with Applied Psychology
Duration: 3FT Hon
Entry Requirements: *Foundation:* Distinction. *GCE:* 260. *IB:* 24. *BTEC ExtDip:* DMM. *OCR ND:* M2 *OCR NED:* M2

QC38 BA English and Applied Psychology
Duration: 3FT Hon
Entry Requirements: *Foundation:* Distinction. *GCE:* 260. *IB:* 24. *BTEC ExtDip:* DMM. *OCR ND:* M2 *OCR NED:* M2

Q3C8 BA English with Applied Psychology
Duration: 3FT Hon
Entry Requirements: *Foundation:* Distinction. *GCE:* 260. *IB:* 24. *BTEC ExtDip:* DMM. *OCR ND:* M2 *OCR NED:* M2

VC18 BA History and Applied Psychology
Duration: 3FT Hon
Entry Requirements: *Foundation:* Distinction. *GCE:* 260. *IB:* 24. *BTEC ExtDip:* DMM. *OCR ND:* M2 *OCR NED:* M2

V1C8 BA History with Applied Psychology
Duration: 3FT Hon
Entry Requirements: *Foundation:* Distinction. *GCE:* 260. *IB:* 24. *BTEC ExtDip:* DMM. *OCR ND:* M2 *OCR NED:* M2

GC58 BA IT and Applied Psychology
Duration: 3FT Hon
Entry Requirements: *Foundation:* Distinction. *GCE:* 260. *IB:* 24. *BTEC ExtDip:* DMM. *OCR ND:* M2 *OCR NED:* M2

NC28 BA Management & Business and Applied Psychology
Duration: 3FT Hon
Entry Requirements: *Foundation:* Distinction. *GCE:* 260. *IB:* 24. *BTEC ExtDip:* DMM. *OCR ND:* M2 *OCR NED:* M2

N2C8 BA Management & Business with Applied Psychology
Duration: 3FT Hon
Entry Requirements: *Foundation:* Distinction. *GCE:* 260. *IB:* 24. *BTEC ExtDip:* DMM. *OCR ND:* M2 *OCR NED:* M2

PC38 BA Media & Communication and Applied Psychology
Duration: 3FT Hon
Entry Requirements: *Foundation:* Distinction. *GCE:* 260. *IB:* 24. *BTEC ExtDip:* DMM. *OCR ND:* M2 *OCR NED:* M2

CX83 BA Sports Studies and Applied Psychology
Duration: 3FT Hon
Entry Requirements: *Foundation:* Distinction. *GCE:* 260. *IB:* 24. *BTEC ExtDip:* DMM. *OCR ND:* M2 *OCR NED:* M2

CV86 BA Theology and Applied Psychology
Duration: 3FT Hon
Entry Requirements: *Foundation:* Distinction. *GCE:* 260. *IB:* 24. *BTEC ExtDip:* DMM. *OCR ND:* M2 *OCR NED:* M2

V6C8 BA Theology with Applied Psychology
Duration: 3FT Hon
Entry Requirements: *Foundation:* Distinction. *GCE:* 260. *IB:* 24. *BTEC ExtDip:* DMM. *OCR ND:* M2 *OCR NED:* M2

LC58 BA Working with Children Young People & Families and Applied Psychology
Duration: 3FT Hon
Entry Requirements: *Foundation:* Distinction. *GCE:* 260. *IB:* 24. *BTEC ExtDip:* DMM. *OCR ND:* M2 *OCR NED:* M2

L5C8 BA Working with Children Young People & Families with Applied Psychology
Duration: 3FT Hon
Entry Requirements: *Foundation:* Distinction. *GCE:* 260. *IB:* 24. *BTEC ExtDip:* DMM. *OCR ND:* M2 *OCR NED:* M2

G5C8 BSc IT with Applied Psychology
Duration: 3FT Hon
Entry Requirements: *Foundation:* Distinction. *GCE:* 260. *IB:* 24. *BTEC ExtDip:* DMM. *OCR ND:* M2 *OCR NED:* M2

C6C8 BSc Sports Studies with Applied Psychology
Duration: 3FT Hon
Entry Requirements: *Foundation:* Distinction. *GCE:* 280. *IB:* 25. *BTEC ExtDip:* DMM. *OCR ND:* M2 *OCR NED:* M2

N38 UNIVERSITY OF NORTHAMPTON
PARK CAMPUS
BOUGHTON GREEN ROAD
NORTHAMPTON NN2 7AL
t: 0800 358 2232 f: 01604 722083
e: admissions@northampton.ac.uk
// www.northampton.ac.uk

C891 BSc Developmental and Educational Psychology
Duration: 3FT Hon
Entry Requirements: *GCE:* 300-320. *SQAH:* AAAB-AABB. *IB:* 26. *BTEC Dip:* DD. *BTEC ExtDip:* DMM. *OCR ND:* D *OCR NED:* M2

CC86 BSc Sport & Exercise Psychology
Duration: 3FT Hon
Entry Requirements: *GCE:* 280-320. *SQAH:* AABB. *IB:* 26. *BTEC Dip:* DD. *BTEC ExtDip:* DMM. *OCR ND:* D *OCR NED:* M2

N91 NOTTINGHAM TRENT UNIVERSITY
DRYDEN BUILDING
BURTON STREET
NOTTINGHAM NG1 4BU
t: +44 (0) 115 848 4200 f: +44 (0) 115 848 8869
e: applications@ntu.ac.uk
// www.ntu.ac.uk

CX8J BA Early Years, Psychology and Education
Duration: 3FT Hon   CRB Check: Required
Entry Requirements: *GCE:* 280. *BTEC Dip:* D*D*. *BTEC ExtDip:* DMM. *OCR NED:* M2

P60 PLYMOUTH UNIVERSITY
DRAKE CIRCUS
PLYMOUTH PL4 8AA
t: 01752 585858 f: 01752 588055
e: admissions@plymouth.ac.uk
// www.plymouth.ac.uk

C817 BSc Psychological Studies
Duration: 1FT Hon
Entry Requirements: Contact the institution for details.

P80 UNIVERSITY OF PORTSMOUTH
ACADEMIC REGISTRY
UNIVERSITY HOUSE
WINSTON CHURCHILL AVENUE
PORTSMOUTH PO1 2UP
t: 023 9284 8484 f: 023 9284 3082
e: admissions@port.ac.uk
// www.port.ac.uk

C810 BSc Forensic Psychology
Duration: 3FT Hon
Entry Requirements: *GCE:* 320. *IB:* 27. *BTEC ExtDip:* DDM.

R12 THE UNIVERSITY OF READING
THE UNIVERSITY OF READING
PO BOX 217
READING RG6 6AH
t: 0118 378 8619 f: 0118 378 8924
e: student.recruitment@reading.ac.uk
// www.reading.ac.uk

NC58 BSc Consumer Behaviour and Marketing with Industrial Training
Duration: 4FT Hon
Entry Requirements: *GCE:* 320.

S30 SOUTHAMPTON SOLENT UNIVERSITY
EAST PARK TERRACE
SOUTHAMPTON
HAMPSHIRE SO14 0RT
t: +44 (0) 23 8031 9039 f: + 44 (0)23 8022 2259
e: admissions@solent.ac.uk
// www.solent.ac.uk/

C812 BSc Psychology (Education)
Duration: 3FT Hon
Entry Requirements: *Foundation:* Distinction. *GCE:* 240. *SQAAH:* AA-CCD. *IB:* 24. *BTEC ExtDip:* MMM. *OCR ND:* D *OCR NED:* M3

U20 UNIVERSITY OF ULSTER
COLERAINE
CO. LONDONDERRY
NORTHERN IRELAND BT52 1SA
t: 028 7012 4221 f: 028 7012 4908
e: online@ulster.ac.uk
// www.ulster.ac.uk

C815 BSc Psychology
Duration: 3FT Hon
Entry Requirements: *GCE:* 280-300.

W75 UNIVERSITY OF WOLVERHAMPTON
ADMISSIONS UNIT
MX207, CAMP STREET
WOLVERHAMPTON
WEST MIDLANDS WV1 1AD
t: 01902 321000 f: 01902 321896
e: admissions@wlv.ac.uk
// www.wlv.ac.uk

C816 BSc Psychology (Criminal Behaviour)
Duration: 3FT Hon
Entry Requirements: *GCE:* 220. *IB:* 24. *BTEC Dip:* DD. *BTEC ExtDip:* MMM.

C811 BSc Psychology (Occupational)
Duration: 3FT Hon
Entry Requirements: Contact the institution for details.

W80 UNIVERSITY OF WORCESTER
HENWICK GROVE
WORCESTER WR2 6AJ
t: 01905 855111 f: 01905 855377
e: admissions@worc.ac.uk
// www.worcester.ac.uk

C815 BSc Business Psychology
Duration: 3FT Hon
Entry Requirements: *GCE:* 280. *IB:* 24. *OCR ND:* D *OCR NED:* M3

C816 BSc Forensic Psychology
Duration: 3FT Hon
Entry Requirements: *GCE:* 280. *IB:* 25. *OCR ND:* D *OCR NED:* M3

CLINICAL AND HEALTH PSYCHOLOGY

A30 UNIVERSITY OF ABERTAY DUNDEE
BELL STREET
DUNDEE DD1 1HG
t: 01382 308080 f: 01382 308081
e: sro@abertay.ac.uk
// www.abertay.ac.uk

C843 BSc Psychology and Counselling
Duration: 4FT Hon
Entry Requirements: *GCE:* CC. *SQAH:* BBB. *IB:* 26.

A60 ANGLIA RUSKIN UNIVERSITY
BISHOP HALL LANE
CHELMSFORD
ESSEX CM1 1SQ
t: 0845 271 3333 f: 01245 251789
e: answers@anglia.ac.uk
// www.anglia.ac.uk

C842 BSc Abnormal and Clinical Psychology
Duration: 3FT Hon
Entry Requirements: *GCE:* 240. *SQAH:* BBBC. *SQAAH:* BB. *IB:* 30.

B06 BANGOR UNIVERSITY
BANGOR UNIVERSITY
BANGOR
GWYNEDD LL57 2DG
t: 01248 388484 f: 01248 370451
e: admissions@bangor.ac.uk
// www.bangor.ac.uk

C880 BSc Psychology with Clinical & Health Psychology
Duration: 3FT Hon
Entry Requirements: *GCE:* 280-320. *IB:* 28.

C801 BSc Psychology with Neuropsychology
Duration: 3FT Hon
Entry Requirements: *GCE:* 280-320. *IB:* 28.

B22 UNIVERSITY OF BEDFORDSHIRE
PARK SQUARE
LUTON
BEDS LU1 3JU
t: 0844 8482234 f: 01582 489323
e: admissions@beds.ac.uk
// www.beds.ac.uk

C841 BSc Health Psychology
Duration: 3FT Hon
Entry Requirements: *GCE:* 160-240. *IB:* 30.

C10 CANTERBURY CHRIST CHURCH UNIVERSITY
NORTH HOLMES ROAD
CANTERBURY
KENT CT1 1QU
t: 01227 782900 f: 01227 782888
e: admissions@canterbury.ac.uk
// www.canterbury.ac.uk

G5CV BA Business Computing with Sport & Exercise Psychology
Duration: 3FT Hon
Entry Requirements: *GCE:* 240. *IB:* 24.

C30 UNIVERSITY OF CENTRAL LANCASHIRE
PRESTON
LANCS PR1 2HE
t: 01772 201201 f: 01772 894954
e: uadmissions@uclan.ac.uk
// www.uclan.ac.uk

BC98 BA Counselling and Psychotherapy Studies
Duration: 3FT Hon
Entry Requirements: *GCE:* 240. *IB:* 28. *OCR ND:* D *OCR NED:* M3

C841 BSc Health Psychology
Duration: 3FT Hon
Entry Requirements: *Foundation:* Distinction. *GCE:* 260-300. *SQAH:* BBBBC-BBCCC. *IB:* 30. *OCR NED:* M2

C85 COVENTRY UNIVERSITY
THE STUDENT CENTRE
COVENTRY UNIVERSITY
1 GULSON RD
COVENTRY CV1 2JH
t: 024 7615 2222 f: 024 7615 2223
e: studentenquiries@coventry.ac.uk
// www.coventry.ac.uk

C841 BSc Sport Psychology
Duration: 3FT/4SW Hon
Entry Requirements: *GCE:* BBB. *SQAH:* BBBBC. *IB:* 28. *BTEC ExtDip:* DDM. *OCR NED:* M1

E42 EDGE HILL UNIVERSITY
ORMSKIRK
LANCASHIRE L39 4QP
t: 01695 657000 f: 01695 584355
e: study@edgehill.ac.uk
// www.edgehill.ac.uk

C841 BSc Health Psychology
Duration: 3FT Hon
Entry Requirements: *GCE:* 280. *IB:* 26. *OCR ND:* D *OCR NED:* M2

H14 HAVERING COLLEGE OF FURTHER AND HIGHER EDUCATION
ARDLEIGH GREEN ROAD
HORNCHURCH
ESSEX RM11 2LL
t: 01708 462793 f: 01708 462736
e: HE@havering-college.ac.uk
// www.havering-college.ac.uk

BCY8 BA Integrative Counselling and Psychotherapy
Duration: 1.5FT Hon
Entry Requirements: Interview required.

K24 THE UNIVERSITY OF KENT
RECRUITMENT & ADMISSIONS OFFICE
REGISTRY
UNIVERSITY OF KENT
CANTERBURY, KENT CT2 7NZ
t: 01227 827272 f: 01227 827077
e: information@kent.ac.uk
// www.kent.ac.uk

C822 BSc Psychology with Clinical Psychology
Duration: 3FT Hon
Entry Requirements: *GCE:* AAB. *SQAH:* AAAAB. *SQAAH:* AAB. *IB:* 33. *OCR ND:* D *OCR NED:* D1

L39 UNIVERSITY OF LINCOLN
ADMISSIONS
BRAYFORD POOL
LINCOLN LN6 7TS
t: 01522 886097 f: 01522 886146
e: admissions@lincoln.ac.uk
// www.lincoln.ac.uk

C840 BSc Psychology with Clinical Psychology
Duration: 3FT Hon
Entry Requirements: *GCE:* 300.

L46 LIVERPOOL HOPE UNIVERSITY
HOPE PARK
LIVERPOOL L16 9JD
t: 0151 291 3331 f: 0151 291 3434
e: administration@hope.ac.uk
// www.hope.ac.uk

CV68 BA Psychology and World Religions
Duration: 3FT Hon
Entry Requirements: *GCE:* 300-320. *IB:* 25.

CC8P BSc Psychology and Sport & Exercise Science
Duration: 3FT Hon
Entry Requirements: *GCE:* 300-320. *IB:* 25.

L75 LONDON SOUTH BANK UNIVERSITY
ADMISSIONS AND RECRUITMENT CENTRE
90 LONDON ROAD
LONDON SE1 6LN
t: 0800 923 8888 f: 020 7815 8273
e: course.enquiry@lsbu.ac.uk
// www.lsbu.ac.uk

C840 BSc Psychology (Clinical)
Duration: 3FT Hon
Entry Requirements: *GCE:* 260. *IB:* 24.

M40 THE MANCHESTER METROPOLITAN UNIVERSITY
ADMISSIONS OFFICE
ALL SAINTS (GMS)
ALL SAINTS
MANCHESTER M15 6BH
t: 0161 247 2000
// www.mmu.ac.uk

C841 BSc Psychology of Sport and Exercise
Duration: 3FT Hon
Entry Requirements: *GCE:* 280. *IB:* 28. *BTEC Dip:* D*D*. *BTEC ExtDip:* DMM.

C842 BSc Psychology of Sport and Exercise (Foundation)
Duration: 4FT Hon
Entry Requirements: *GCE:* 160. *IB:* 24. *BTEC Dip:* MM. *BTEC ExtDip:* MPP.

N49 NESCOT, SURREY
REIGATE ROAD
EWELL
EPSOM
SURREY KT17 3DS
t: 020 8394 3038 f: 020 8394 3030
e: info@nescot.ac.uk
// www.nescot.ac.uk

C848 DipHE Psychodynamic Counselling
Duration: 2FT Dip
Entry Requirements: Contact the institution for details.

R48 ROEHAMPTON UNIVERSITY
ROEHAMPTON LANE
LONDON SW15 5PU
t: 020 8392 3232 f: 020 8392 3470
e: enquiries@roehampton.ac.uk
// www.roehampton.ac.uk

C845 BSc Psychology & Counselling
Duration: 3FT Hon
Entry Requirements: *GCE:* 300. *IB:* 26. *BTEC ExtDip:* DDM. *OCR NED:* D2 Interview required.

S03 THE UNIVERSITY OF SALFORD
SALFORD M5 4WT
t: 0161 295 4545 f: 0161 295 4646
e: ug-admissions@salford.ac.uk
// www.salford.ac.uk

B9C8 BSc Counselling and Psychotherapy (Professional Practice)
Duration: 3FT Hon
Entry Requirements: Contact the institution for details.

S30 SOUTHAMPTON SOLENT UNIVERSITY
EAST PARK TERRACE
SOUTHAMPTON
HAMPSHIRE SO14 0RT
t: +44 (0) 23 8031 9039 f: + 44 (0)23 8022 2259
e: admissions@solent.ac.uk
// www.solent.ac.uk/

C890 BSc Psychology (Health Psychology)
Duration: 3FT Hon
Entry Requirements: *Foundation:* Distinction. *GCE:* 240. *SQAAH:* AA-CCD. *IB:* 24. *BTEC ExtDip:* MMM. *OCR ND:* D *OCR NED:* M3

W75 UNIVERSITY OF WOLVERHAMPTON
ADMISSIONS UNIT
MX207, CAMP STREET
WOLVERHAMPTON
WEST MIDLANDS WV1 1AD
t: 01902 321000 f: 01902 321896
e: admissions@wlv.ac.uk
// www.wlv.ac.uk

C841 BSc Psychology (Health)
Duration: 3FT Hon
Entry Requirements: Contact the institution for details.

C813 BSc Psychology (Counselling Psychology)
Duration: 3FT Hon
Entry Requirements: *GCE:* 220. *IB:* 24. *BTEC Dip:* DD. *BTEC ExtDip:* MMM.

W80 UNIVERSITY OF WORCESTER
HENWICK GROVE
WORCESTER WR2 6AJ
t: 01905 855111 f: 01905 855377
e: admissions@worc.ac.uk
// www.worcester.ac.uk

C843 BSc Counselling Psychology
Duration: 3FT Hon
Entry Requirements: *GCE:* 280. *IB:* 25. *OCR ND:* D *OCR NED:* M3

COGNITIVE PSYCHOLOGY

D65 UNIVERSITY OF DUNDEE
NETHERGATE
DUNDEE DD1 4HN
t: 01382 383838 f: 01382 388150
e: contactus@dundee.ac.uk
// www.dundee.ac.uk/admissions/undergraduate/

GC48 BSc Computing and Cognitive Science
Duration: 4FT Hon
Entry Requirements: *GCE:* BCC. *SQAH:* BBBB. *IB:* 30.

E56 THE UNIVERSITY OF EDINBURGH
STUDENT RECRUITMENT & ADMISSIONS
57 GEORGE SQUARE
EDINBURGH EH8 9JU
t: 0131 650 4360 f: 0131 651 1236
e: sra.enquiries@ed.ac.uk
// www.ed.ac.uk/studying/undergraduate/

C859 BSc Cognitive Science
Duration: 4FT Hon
Entry Requirements: *GCE:* AAA-ABB. *SQAH:* AAAA-ABBB.

C851 MA Cognitive Science (Humanities)
Duration: 4FT Hon
Entry Requirements: *GCE:* AAA-BBB. *SQAH:* AAAA-BBBB. *IB:* 34.

N31 NEWHAM COLLEGE OF FURTHER EDUCATION
EAST HAM CAMPUS
HIGH STREET SOUTH
LONDON E6 6ER
t: 020 8257 4000 f: 020 8257 4325
e: admissions@newham.ac.uk
// www.newham.ac.uk

BC9V BSc Counselling Studies (Cognitive Behaviour Therapy)
Duration: 3FT Hon
Entry Requirements: Contact the institution for details.

P80 UNIVERSITY OF PORTSMOUTH
ACADEMIC REGISTRY
UNIVERSITY HOUSE
WINSTON CHURCHILL AVENUE
PORTSMOUTH PO1 2UP
t: 023 9284 8484 f: 023 9284 3082
e: admissions@port.ac.uk
// www.port.ac.uk

BC68 FdSc Speech, Language and Communication Science
Duration: 2FT Fdg   CRB Check: Required
Entry Requirements: *GCE:* 160. *IB:* 25. *BTEC Dip:* MM. *BTEC ExtDip:* MPP. Interview required.

EXPERIMENTAL PSYCHOLOGY

B32 THE UNIVERSITY OF BIRMINGHAM
EDGBASTON
BIRMINGHAM B15 2TT
t: 0121 415 8900 f: 0121 414 7159
e: admissions@bham.ac.uk
// www.birmingham.ac.uk

C890 MSci Psychology and Psychological Research
Duration: 4FT Hon
Entry Requirements: *GCE:* AAA. *SQAH:* AAAAB-AAABB. *SQAAH:* AA. *IB:* 36.

H60 THE UNIVERSITY OF HUDDERSFIELD
QUEENSGATE
HUDDERSFIELD HD1 3DH
t: 01484 473969 f: 01484 472765
e: admissionsandrecords@hud.ac.uk
// www.hud.ac.uk

C830 BSc Behavioural Sciences
Duration: 3FT Hon
Entry Requirements: *GCE:* 280.

O33 OXFORD UNIVERSITY
UNDERGRADUATE ADMISSIONS OFFICE
UNIVERSITY OF OXFORD
WELLINGTON SQUARE
OXFORD OX1 2JD
t: 01865 288000 f: 01865 270212
e: undergraduate.admissions@admin.ox.ac.uk
// www.admissions.ox.ac.uk

C830 BA Experimental Psychology
Duration: 3FT Hon
Entry Requirements: *GCE:* AAA. *SQAH:* AAAAA-AAAAB. *SQAAH:* AAB. Interview required. Admissions Test required.

SOCIAL PSYCHOLOGY

B22 UNIVERSITY OF BEDFORDSHIRE
PARK SQUARE
LUTON
BEDS LU1 3JU
t: 0844 8482234 f: 01582 489323
e: admissions@beds.ac.uk
// www.beds.ac.uk

C880 FdA Psychology and Criminal Behaviour
Duration: 2FT Fdg
Entry Requirements: Contact the institution for details.

B56 THE UNIVERSITY OF BRADFORD
RICHMOND ROAD
BRADFORD
WEST YORKSHIRE BD7 1DP
t: 0800 073 1225 f: 01274 235585
e: course-enquiries@bradford.ac.uk
// www.bradford.ac.uk

CN82 BA Psychology and Management
Duration: 3FT Hon
Entry Requirements: *GCE:* 240. *IB:* 24.

E28 UNIVERSITY OF EAST LONDON
DOCKLANDS CAMPUS
UNIVERSITY WAY
LONDON E16 2RD
t: 020 8223 3333 f: 020 8223 2978
e: study@uel.ac.uk
// www.uel.ac.uk

LC18 BA Business Economics and Psychosocial Studies
Duration: 3FT Hon
Entry Requirements: *GCE:* 240.

P9C8 BA Communication Studies with Psychosocial Studies
Duration: 3FT Hon
Entry Requirements: *GCE:* 240. *IB:* 24.

XC38 BA Early Childhood Studies/Psychosocial Studies
Duration: 3FT Hon
Entry Requirements: *GCE:* 240. *IB:* 24.

W1C8 BA Fine Art with Psychosocial Studies
Duration: 3FT Hon
Entry Requirements: *GCE:* 240. *IB:* 24.

CB8X BA Health Services Management/Psychosocial Studies
Duration: 3FT Hon
Entry Requirements: *GCE:* 240. *IB:* 24.

N6CV BA Human Resource Management with Psychosocial Studies
Duration: 3FT Hon
Entry Requirements: *GCE:* 240. *IB:* 24.

NC68 BA Human Resource Management/Psychosocial Studies
Duration: 3FT Hon
Entry Requirements: *GCE:* 240. *IB:* 24.

C881 BA Psychosocial Studies
Duration: 3FT Hon
Entry Requirements: *GCE:* 240. *IB:* 24.

C880 BA Psychosocial Studies (Extended Degree)
Duration: 4FT Hon
Entry Requirements: *GCE:* 80. *IB:* 24.

C8W8 BA Psychosocial Studies with Creative and Professional Writing
Duration: 3FT Hon
Entry Requirements: *GCE:* 240. *IB:* 24.

C8L6 BA Psychosocial Studies with Cultural Studies
Duration: 3FT Hon
Entry Requirements: *GCE:* 240. *IB:* 24.

C8V1 BA Psychosocial Studies with History
Duration: 3FT Hon
Entry Requirements: *GCE:* 240. *IB:* 24.

C882 BA Psychosocial Studies with Professional Studies
Duration: 4FT Hon
Entry Requirements: *GCE:* 240. *IB:* 24.

C883 BA Psychosocial Studies with Professional Studies (Extended Degree)
Duration: 4FT Hon
Entry Requirements: *GCE:* 80.

C8C6 BA Psychosocial Studies with Sports Development
Duration: 3FT Hon
Entry Requirements: *GCE:* 240. *IB:* 24.

CB89 BA Psychosocial Studies/Health Promotion
Duration: 3FT Hon
Entry Requirements: *GCE:* 240. *IB:* 24.

CB8Y BA Psychosocial Studies/Public Health
Duration: 3FT Hon
Entry Requirements: *GCE:* 240. *IB:* 24.

LC9V BA Psychosocial Studies/Third World Development
Duration: 3FT Hon
Entry Requirements: *GCE:* 240. *IB:* 24.

L3C8 BA Sociology (Professional Development) with Psychosocial Studies
Duration: 3FT Hon
Entry Requirements: *GCE:* 240. *IB:* 24.

XC18 BA Special Needs and Inclusive Education/Psychosocial Studies
Duration: 3FT Hon
Entry Requirements: *GCE:* 240. *IB:* 24.

GC58 BA/BSc Business Information Systems/Psychosocial Studies
Duration: 3FT Hon
Entry Requirements: *GCE:* 240. *IB:* 24.

LC38 BA/BSc Sociology (Professional Development)/Psychosocial Studies
Duration: 3FT Hon
Entry Requirements: *GCE:* 240. *IB:* 24.

G4CV BSc Computer Networks with Psychosocial Studies
Duration: 3FT Hon
Entry Requirements: *GCE:* 240. *IB:* 24.

I1C8 BSc Computing with Psychosocial Studies
Duration: 3FT Hon
Entry Requirements: *GCE:* 240. *IB:* 24.

B9CW BSc Health Promotion with Psychosocial Studies
Duration: 3FT Hon
Entry Requirements: *GCE:* 240. *IB:* 24.

CC18 BSc Human Biology with Psychosocial Studies
Duration: 3FT Hon
Entry Requirements: *GCE:* 240. *IB:* 24.

B9CB BSc Public Health with Psychosocial Studies
Duration: 3FT Hon
Entry Requirements: *GCE:* 240. *IB:* 24.

C6CW BSc Sports Development with Psychosocial Studies
Duration: 3FT Hon
Entry Requirements: *GCE:* 240. *IB:* 24.

E70 THE UNIVERSITY OF ESSEX
WIVENHOE PARK
COLCHESTER
ESSEX CO4 3SQ
t: 01206 873666 f: 01206 874477
e: admit@essex.ac.uk
// www.essex.ac.uk

L3C8 BA Criminology with Social Psychology
Duration: 3FT Hon
Entry Requirements: *GCE:* ABB-BBB. *SQAH:* AAAB-AABB.

LHC8 BA Criminology with Social Psychology (Including Year Abroad)
Duration: 4FT Hon
Entry Requirements: *GCE:* ABB-BBB. *SQAH:* AAAB-AABB.

LJC8 BA Sociology with Psychosocial Studies
Duration: 3FT Hon
Entry Requirements: *GCE:* ABB-BBB. *SQAH:* AAAB-AABB.

CL83 BSc Social Psychology and Sociology
Duration: 3FT Hon
Entry Requirements: *SQAH:* AABB. *IB:* 32. *BTEC ExtDip:* DDM.
Interview required.

G70 UNIVERSITY OF GREENWICH
GREENWICH CAMPUS
OLD ROYAL NAVAL COLLEGE
PARK ROW
LONDON SE10 9LS
t: 020 8331 9000 f: 020 8331 8145
e: courseinfo@gre.ac.uk
// www.gre.ac.uk

MC98 BSc Criminology and Criminal Psychology
Duration: 3FT Hon
Entry Requirements: *GCE:* 280. *IB:* 24.

K24 THE UNIVERSITY OF KENT
RECRUITMENT & ADMISSIONS OFFICE
REGISTRY
UNIVERSITY OF KENT
CANTERBURY, KENT CT2 7NZ
t: 01227 827272 f: 01227 827077
e: information@kent.ac.uk
// www.kent.ac.uk

C881 BSc Psychology with a year in Europe (4 years)
Duration: 4FT Hon
Entry Requirements: *GCE:* AAB. *SQAH:* AAABB. *SQAAH:* AAB. *IB:* 33. *OCR ND:* D *OCR NED:* D1

C882 BSc Social Psychology
Duration: 3FT Hon
Entry Requirements: *GCE:* AAB. *SQAH:* AAAAB. *SQAAH:* AAB. *IB:* 33. *OCR ND:* D *OCR NED:* D1

L27 LEEDS METROPOLITAN UNIVERSITY
COURSE ENQUIRIES OFFICE
CITY CAMPUS
LEEDS LS1 3HE
t: 0113 81 23113 f: 0113 81 23129
// www.leedsmet.ac.uk

C880 BA Psychology & Society
Duration: 3FT Hon
Entry Requirements: *GCE:* 240.

L79 LOUGHBOROUGH UNIVERSITY
LOUGHBOROUGH
LEICESTERSHIRE LE11 3TU
t: 01509 223522 f: 01509 223905
e: admissions@lboro.ac.uk
// www.lboro.ac.uk

C880 BSc Social Psychology
Duration: 3FT Hon
Entry Requirements: *GCE:* AAB-ABB. *SQAAH:* AB. *IB:* 34. *BTEC ExtDip:* DDM.

N36 NEWMAN UNIVERSITY COLLEGE, BIRMINGHAM
GENNERS LANE
BARTLEY GREEN
BIRMINGHAM B32 3NT
t: 0121 476 1181 f: 0121 476 1196
e: Admissions@newman.ac.uk
// www.newman.ac.uk

C8G5 BSc Psychology with IT
Duration: 3FT Hon
Entry Requirements: *Foundation:* Distinction. *GCE:* 280. *IB:* 25. *BTEC ExtDip:* DMM. *OCR ND:* M2 *OCR NED:* M2

N82 NORWICH CITY COLLEGE OF FURTHER AND HIGHER EDUCATION (AN ASSOCIATE COLLEGE OF UEA)
IPSWICH ROAD
NORWICH
NORFOLK NR2 2LJ
t: 01603 773012 f: 01603 773301
e: he_office@ccn.ac.uk
// www.ccn.ac.uk

QC38 BA English and Psychology in Society
Duration: 3FT Hon
Entry Requirements: *GCE:* 160.

C880 BSc Psychology and Sociology
Duration: 3FT Hon
Entry Requirements: Contact the institution for details.

P56 UNIVERSITY CENTRE PETERBOROUGH
PARK CRESCENT
PETERBOROUGH PE1 4DZ
t: 0845 1965750 f: 01733 767986
e: UCPenquiries@anglia.ac.uk
// www.anglia.ac.uk/ucp

C880 BA Psychosocial Studies
Duration: 3FT Hon
Entry Requirements: *GCE:* 200. Interview required.

R20 RICHMOND, THE AMERICAN INTERNATIONAL UNIVERSITY IN LONDON
QUEENS ROAD
RICHMOND
SURREY TW10 6JP
t: 020 8332 9000 f: 020 8332 1596
e: enroll@richmond.ac.uk
// www.richmond.ac.uk

C880 BA Social Sciences: Psychology
Duration: 3FT/4FT Hon
Entry Requirements: *GCE:* 260. *IB:* 33.

S82 UNIVERSITY CAMPUS SUFFOLK (UCS)
WATERFRONT BUILDING
NEPTUNE QUAY
IPSWICH
SUFFOLK IP4 1QJ
t: 01473 338833 f: 01473 339900
e: info@ucs.ac.uk
// www.ucs.ac.uk

CL8H BSc Psychology and Criminology
Duration: 3FT Hon
Entry Requirements: *GCE:* 240-280. *IB:* 28. *BTEC ExtDip:* DMM.

U20 UNIVERSITY OF ULSTER
COLERAINE
CO. LONDONDERRY
NORTHERN IRELAND BT52 1SA
t: 028 7012 4221 f: 028 7012 4908
e: online@ulster.ac.uk
// www.ulster.ac.uk

C880 BSc Social Psychology
Duration: 3FT Hon
Entry Requirements: *GCE:* 280-300.

W35 COLLEGE OF WEST ANGLIA
MAIN CAMPUS
TENNYSON AVENUE
KING'S LYNN
NORFOLK PE30 2QW
t: 01553 761144 f: 01553 770115
e: enquiries@col-westanglia.ac.uk
// www.col-westanglia.ac.uk

C880 BA Psychosocial Studies
Duration: 3FT Hon
Entry Requirements: *GCE:* 80-160.

W76 UNIVERSITY OF WINCHESTER
WINCHESTER
HANTS SO22 4NR
t: 01962 827234 f: 01962 827288
e: course.enquiries@winchester.ac.uk
// www.winchester.ac.uk

C880 BSc Social Psychology
Duration: 3FT Hon
Entry Requirements: *Foundation:* Distinction. *GCE:* 260-300. *IB:* 25. *OCR ND:* D *OCR NED:* M2

SPORT PSYCHOLOGY

A30 UNIVERSITY OF ABERTAY DUNDEE
BELL STREET
DUNDEE DD1 1HG
t: 01382 308080 f: 01382 308081
e: sro@abertay.ac.uk
// www.abertay.ac.uk

CC68 BSc Sport and Psychology
Duration: 4FT Hon   CRB Check: Required
Entry Requirements: *GCE:* DDD. *SQAH:* BBB. *IB:* 26. Interview required.

B06 BANGOR UNIVERSITY
BANGOR UNIVERSITY
BANGOR
GWYNEDD LL57 2DG
t: 01248 388484 f: 01248 370451
e: admissions@bangor.ac.uk
// www.bangor.ac.uk

C6CV BSc Sport Science with Psychology
Duration: 3FT Hon
Entry Requirements: *GCE:* 260-300. *IB:* 28.

C680 BSc Sport and Exercise Psychology
Duration: 3FT Hon
Entry Requirements: Contact the institution for details.

B38 BISHOP GROSSETESTE UNIVERSITY COLLEGE LINCOLN
BISHOP GROSSETESTE UNIVERSITY COLLEGE
LINCOLN LN1 3DY
t: 01522 583658 f: 01522 530243
e: admissions@bishopg.ac.uk
// www.bishopg.ac.uk/courses

CC86 BA Psychology and Sport
Duration: 3FT Hon   CRB Check: Required
Entry Requirements: Contact the institution for details.

B50 BOURNEMOUTH UNIVERSITY
TALBOT CAMPUS
FERN BARROW
POOLE
DORSET BH12 5BB
t: 01202 524111
// www.bournemouth.ac.uk

CX81 BSc Sport Psychology and Coaching Sciences
Duration: 4SW Hon
Entry Requirements: *GCE:* 320. *IB:* 32. *BTEC SubDip:* D. *BTEC Dip:* DD. *BTEC ExtDip:* DDM.

C10 CANTERBURY CHRIST CHURCH UNIVERSITY
NORTH HOLMES ROAD
CANTERBURY
KENT CT1 1QU
t: 01227 782900 f: 01227 782888
e: admissions@canterbury.ac.uk
// www.canterbury.ac.uk

CM89 BA Applied Criminology and Sport & Exercise Psychology
Duration: 3FT Hon
Entry Requirements: *GCE:* 240. *IB:* 24.

GC5V BA Business Computing and Sport & Exercise Psychology
Duration: 3FT Hon
Entry Requirements: *GCE:* 240. *IB:* 24.

GCK8 BA Internet Computing and Sport & Exercise Psychology
Duration: 3FT Hon
Entry Requirements: *GCE:* 240. *IB:* 24.

C8GM BA Sport & Exercise Psychology with Business Computing
Duration: 3FT Hon
Entry Requirements: Contact the institution for details.

C8GA BA Sport & Exercise Psychology with Internet Computing
Duration: 3FT Hon
Entry Requirements: Contact the institution for details.

M9CV BA/BSc Applied Criminology with Sport & Exercise Psychology
Duration: 3FT Hon
Entry Requirements: *GCE:* 240. *IB:* 24.

X3CV BA/BSc Early Childhood Studies with Sport & Exercise Psychology
Duration: 3FT Hon   CRB Check: Required
Entry Requirements: *GCE:* 240. *IB:* 24.

V1CV BA/BSc History with Sport & Exercise Psychology
Duration: 3FT Hon
Entry Requirements: *GCE:* 240. *IB:* 24.

MC28 BA/BSc Legal Studies and Sport & Exercise Psychology
Duration: 3FT Hon
Entry Requirements: *GCE:* 240. *IB:* 24.

M2C8 BA/BSc Legal Studies with Sport & Exercise Psychology
Duration: 3FT Hon
Entry Requirements: *GCE:* 240. *IB:* 24.

CC86 BA/BSc Psychology and Sport & Exercise Science
Duration: 3FT Hon
Entry Requirements: *GCE:* 260. *IB:* 24.

C8C6 BA/BSc Psychology with Sport & Exercise Science
Duration: 3FT Hon
Entry Requirements: *GCE:* 260. *IB:* 24.

C8M9 BA/BSc Sport & Exercise Psychology with Applied Criminology
Duration: 3FT Hon
Entry Requirements: Contact the institution for details.

C8WC BA/BSc Sport & Exercise Psychology with Art
Duration: 3FT Hon
Entry Requirements: Contact the institution for details.

C8XH BA/BSc Sport & Exercise Psychology with Early Childhood Studies
Duration: 3FT Hon
Entry Requirements: Contact the institution for details.

C8VC BA/BSc Sport & Exercise Psychology with History
Duration: 3FT Hon
Entry Requirements: Contact the institution for details.

C8M2 BA/BSc Sport & Exercise Psychology with Legal Studies
Duration: 3FT Hon
Entry Requirements: Contact the institution for details.

GC48 BSc Computing and Sport & Exercise Psychology
Duration: 3FT Hon
Entry Requirements: *GCE:* 240. *IB:* 24.

G4C8 BSc Computing with Sport & Exercise Psychology
Duration: 3FT Hon
Entry Requirements: *GCE:* 240. *IB:* 24.

C813 BSc Psychology (Sport and Exercise)
Duration: 3FT Hon **CRB Check:** Required
Entry Requirements: *GCE:* 260. *IB:* 24. Interview required.

C8G4 BSc Sport & Exercise Psychology with Computing
Duration: 3FT Hon
Entry Requirements: Contact the institution for details.

CX83 BSc/BA Sport & Exercise Psychology and Early Childhood Studies
Duration: 3FT Hon **CRB Check:** Required
Entry Requirements: *GCE:* 240. *IB:* 24.

VC18 BSc/BA Sport & Exercise Psychology and History
Duration: 3FT Hon
Entry Requirements: *GCE:* 240. *IB:* 24.

C6C8 BSc/BA Sport & Exercise Science with Psychology
Duration: 3FT Hon
Entry Requirements: *GCE:* 260. *IB:* 24.

C30 UNIVERSITY OF CENTRAL LANCASHIRE
PRESTON
LANCS PR1 2HE
t: 01772 201201 f: 01772 894954
e: uadmissions@uclan.ac.uk
// www.uclan.ac.uk

C8C6 BSc Sport Psychology
Duration: 3FT Hon
Entry Requirements: *Foundation:* Distinction. *GCE:* 260-300.
SQAH: BBBBC-BBCCC. *IB:* 30. *OCR NED:* M2

C55 UNIVERSITY OF CHESTER
PARKGATE ROAD
CHESTER CH1 4BJ
t: 01244 511000 f: 01244 511300
e: enquiries@chester.ac.uk
// www.chester.ac.uk

CC68 BSc Sport & Exercise Sciences and Psychology
Duration: 3FT Hon
Entry Requirements: *Foundation:* Pass. *GCE:* 260-300. *SQAH:* BBBB. *IB:* 28.

C58 UNIVERSITY OF CHICHESTER
BISHOP OTTER CAMPUS
COLLEGE LANE
CHICHESTER
WEST SUSSEX PO19 6PE
t: 01243 816002 f: 01243 816161
e: admissions@chi.ac.uk
// www.chiuni.ac.uk

C841 BSc Sport & Exercise Psychology
Duration: 3FT Hon
Entry Requirements: *GCE:* BCD-CCC. *SQAH:* CCC. *IB:* 30. *BTEC Dip:* DD. *BTEC ExtDip:* DMM.

D39 UNIVERSITY OF DERBY
KEDLESTON ROAD
DERBY DE22 1GB
t: 01332 591167 f: 01332 597724
e: askadmissions@derby.ac.uk
// www.derby.ac.uk

CC6W BA/BSc Sports Coaching and Sports Psychology
Duration: 3FT Hon
Entry Requirements: *Foundation:* Distinction. *GCE:* 260-280. *IB:* 28. *BTEC Dip:* D*D*. *BTEC ExtDip:* DMM. *OCR NED:* M2

CCPW BA/BSc Sports Development and Sports Psychology
Duration: 3FT Hon
Entry Requirements: *Foundation:* Distinction. *GCE:* 260-280. *IB:* 28. *BTEC Dip:* D*D*. *BTEC ExtDip:* DMM. *OCR NED:* M2

CCQ8 BA/BSc Sports Massage & Exercise Therapy and Sports Psychology
Duration: 3FT Hon
Entry Requirements: *Foundation:* Distinction. *GCE:* 260-280. *IB:* 28. *BTEC Dip:* D*D*. *BTEC ExtDip:* DMM. *OCR NED:* M2

E28 UNIVERSITY OF EAST LONDON
DOCKLANDS CAMPUS
UNIVERSITY WAY
LONDON E16 2RD
t: 020 8223 3333 f: 020 8223 2978
e: study@uel.ac.uk
// www.uel.ac.uk

C6CV BSc Sports & Exercise Science with Psychology
Duration: 3FT Hon
Entry Requirements: *GCE:* 240. *IB:* 24.

C6C8 BSc Sports Coaching with Psychology
Duration: 3FT Hon
Entry Requirements: *GCE:* 240. *IB:* 24.

C9C8 BSc Sports Development with Psychology
Duration: 3FT Hon
Entry Requirements: *GCE:* 240. *IB:* 24.

E84 UNIVERSITY OF EXETER
LAVER BUILDING
NORTH PARK ROAD
EXETER
DEVON EX4 4QE
t: 01392 723044 f: 01392 722479
e: admissions@exeter.ac.uk
// www.exeter.ac.uk

C8C6 BSc Psychology with Sport & Exercise Science
Duration: 3FT Hon
Entry Requirements: *GCE:* AAA-AAB. *SQAH:* AAAAB-AAABB. *SQAAH:* AAB-ABB. *BTEC ExtDip:* DDM.

G14 UNIVERSITY OF GLAMORGAN, CARDIFF AND PONTYPRIDD
ENQUIRIES AND ADMISSIONS UNIT
PONTYPRIDD CF37 1DL
t: 08456 434030 f: 01443 654050
e: enquiries@glam.ac.uk
// www.glam.ac.uk

C601 BSc Sport Psychology
Duration: 3FT/4SW Hon
Entry Requirements: *GCE:* BBC. *IB:* 25. *BTEC SubDip:* M. *BTEC Dip:* D*D*. *BTEC ExtDip:* DMM.

H36 UNIVERSITY OF HERTFORDSHIRE
UNIVERSITY ADMISSIONS SERVICE
COLLEGE LANE
HATFIELD
HERTS AL10 9AB
t: 01707 284800
// www.herts.ac.uk

C8C6 BSc Psychology/Sports Studies
Duration: 3FT/4SW Hon
Entry Requirements: *GCE:* 320.

C6C8 BSc Sports Studies/Psychology
Duration: 3FT/4SW Hon
Entry Requirements: *GCE:* 320.

H72 THE UNIVERSITY OF HULL
THE UNIVERSITY OF HULL
COTTINGHAM ROAD
HULL HU6 7RX
t: 01482 466100 f: 01482 442290
e: admissions@hull.ac.uk
// www.hull.ac.uk

C8C6 BSc Psychology with Sports Science
Duration: 3FT Hon
Entry Requirements: *GCE:* 280. *IB:* 32. *BTEC ExtDip:* DMM.

L24 LEEDS TRINITY UNIVERSITY COLLEGE
BROWNBERRIE LANE
HORSFORTH
LEEDS LS18 5HD
t: 0113 283 7150 f: 0113 283 7222
e: enquiries@leedstrinity.ac.uk
// www.leedstrinity.ac.uk

C600 BSc Sport and Exercise Sciences (Sport Psychology)
Duration: 3FT Hon
Entry Requirements: Contact the institution for details.

L46 LIVERPOOL HOPE UNIVERSITY
HOPE PARK
LIVERPOOL L16 9JD
t: 0151 291 3331 f: 0151 291 3434
e: administration@hope.ac.uk
// www.hope.ac.uk

CC86 BSc Psychology and Sport Studies
Duration: 3FT Hon
Entry Requirements: *GCE:* 300-320. *IB:* 25.

C891 BSc Sport Psychology
Duration: 3FT Hon
Entry Requirements: *GCE:* 300-320. *IB:* 25.

L51 LIVERPOOL JOHN MOORES UNIVERSITY
KINGSWAY HOUSE
HATTON GARDEN
LIVERPOOL L3 2AJ
t: 0151 231 5090 f: 0151 904 6368
e: courses@ljmu.ac.uk
// www.ljmu.ac.uk

C890 BSc Applied Sport Psychology
Duration: 3FT Hon
Entry Requirements: *GCE:* 280-320. *IB:* 25.

L68 LONDON METROPOLITAN UNIVERSITY
166-220 HOLLOWAY ROAD
LONDON N7 8DB
t: 020 7133 4200
e: admissions@londonmet.ac.uk
// www.londonmet.ac.uk

XC18 BSc Sport Psychology and Coaching
Duration: 3FT Hon
Entry Requirements: *GCE:* 220. *IB:* 28.

M40 THE MANCHESTER METROPOLITAN UNIVERSITY
ADMISSIONS OFFICE
ALL SAINTS (GMS)
ALL SAINTS
MANCHESTER M15 6BH
t: 0161 247 2000
// www.mmu.ac.uk

CC68 BSc Psychology/Sport
Duration: 3FT Hon
Entry Requirements: *GCE:* 280. *IB:* 28. *BTEC Dip:* D*D*. *BTEC ExtDip:* DMM.

N36 NEWMAN UNIVERSITY COLLEGE, BIRMINGHAM
GENNERS LANE
BARTLEY GREEN
BIRMINGHAM B32 3NT
t: 0121 476 1181 f: 0121 476 1196
e: Admissions@newman.ac.uk
// www.newman.ac.uk

C8C6 BSc Psychology with Sports Studies
Duration: 3FT Hon
Entry Requirements: *Foundation:* Distinction. *GCE:* 280. *IB:* 25. *BTEC ExtDip:* DMM. *OCR ND:* M2 *OCR NED:* M2

N37 UNIVERSITY OF WALES, NEWPORT
ADMISSIONS
LODGE ROAD
CAERLEON
NEWPORT NP18 3QT
t: 01633 432030 f: 01633 432850
e: admissions@newport.ac.uk
// www.newport.ac.uk

C6C8 BSc Sports Studies with Psychology
Duration: 3FT Hon   CRB Check: Required
Entry Requirements: *GCE:* 240. *IB:* 24. Interview required.

N38 UNIVERSITY OF NORTHAMPTON
PARK CAMPUS
BOUGHTON GREEN ROAD
NORTHAMPTON NN2 7AL
t: 0800 358 2232 f: 01604 722083
e: admissions@northampton.ac.uk
// www.northampton.ac.uk

C8C6 BA Psychology/Sport Studies
Duration: 3FT Hon
Entry Requirements: *GCE:* 260-280. *SQAH:* AAA-BBBB. *IB:* 24. *BTEC Dip:* DD. *BTEC ExtDip:* DMM. *OCR ND:* D *OCR NED:* M2

C6C8 BA Sport Studies/Psychology
Duration: 3FT Hon
Entry Requirements: *GCE:* 260-280. *SQAH:* AAA-BBBB. *IB:* 24. *BTEC Dip:* DD. *BTEC ExtDip:* DMM. *OCR ND:* D *OCR NED:* M2

N77 NORTHUMBRIA UNIVERSITY
TRINITY BUILDING
NORTHUMBERLAND ROAD
NEWCASTLE UPON TYNE NE1 8ST
t: 0191 243 7420 f: 0191 227 4561
e: er.admissions@northumbria.ac.uk
// www.northumbria.ac.uk

C8C6 BSc Psychology with Sport Science
Duration: 3FT Hon
Entry Requirements: *GCE:* 300. *SQAH:* BBBBC. *SQAAH:* BBC. *IB:* 26. *OCR ND:* D *OCR NED:* M2

N91 NOTTINGHAM TRENT UNIVERSITY
DRYDEN BUILDING
BURTON STREET
NOTTINGHAM NG1 4BU
t: +44 (0) 115 848 4200 f: +44 (0) 115 848 8869
e: applications@ntu.ac.uk
// www.ntu.ac.uk

XC3V BA Sport and Leisure, Psychology and Education
Duration: 3FT Hon   CRB Check: Required
Entry Requirements: *GCE:* 280. *BTEC Dip:* D*D*. *BTEC ExtDip:* DMM. *OCR NED:* M2

O66 OXFORD BROOKES UNIVERSITY
ADMISSIONS OFFICE
HEADINGTON CAMPUS
GIPSY LANE
OXFORD OX3 0BP
t: 01865 483040 f: 01865 483983
e: admissions@brookes.ac.uk
// www.brookes.ac.uk

CC86 BA/BSc Sport, Coaching and Physical Education/Psychology
Duration: 3FT Hon
Entry Requirements: Contact the institution for details.

R48 ROEHAMPTON UNIVERSITY
ROEHAMPTON LANE
LONDON SW15 5PU
t: 020 8392 3232 f: 020 8392 3470
e: enquiries@roehampton.ac.uk
// www.roehampton.ac.uk

C813 BSc Sport Psychology
Duration: 3FT Hon
Entry Requirements: *Foundation:* Distinction. *GCE:* 280. *IB:* 25. *BTEC Dip:* D*D*. *BTEC ExtDip:* DMM. *OCR NED:* M2 Interview required.

S64 ST MARY'S UNIVERSITY COLLEGE, TWICKENHAM
WALDEGRAVE ROAD
STRAWBERRY HILL
MIDDLESEX TW1 4SX
t: 020 8240 4029 f: 020 8240 2361
e: admit@smuc.ac.uk
// www.smuc.ac.uk

CC86 BSc Psychology and Sport Science
Duration: 3FT Hon
Entry Requirements: *GCE:* 240. *SQAH:* BBBC. *IB:* 28. *OCR ND:* D
OCR NED: M3 Interview required.

S72 STAFFORDSHIRE UNIVERSITY
COLLEGE ROAD
STOKE ON TRENT ST4 2DE
t: 01782 292753 f: 01782 292740
e: admissions@staffs.ac.uk
// www.staffs.ac.uk

C810 BSc Sport and Exercise Psychology
Duration: 3FT Hon
Entry Requirements: *GCE:* 200-280. *IB:* 24.

S75 THE UNIVERSITY OF STIRLING
STUDENT RECRUITMENT & ADMISSIONS SERVICE
UNIVERSITY OF STIRLING
STIRLING
SCOTLAND FK9 4LA
t: 01786 467044 f: 01786 466800
e: admissions@stir.ac.uk
// www.stir.ac.uk

CC68 BA Psychology and Sports Studies
Duration: 4FT Hon
Entry Requirements: *GCE:* BBC. *SQAH:* BBBB. *SQAAH:* AAA-CCC.
IB: 32. *BTEC ExtDip:* DMM.

S84 UNIVERSITY OF SUNDERLAND
STUDENT HELPLINE
THE STUDENT GATEWAY
CHESTER ROAD
SUNDERLAND SR1 3SD
t: 0191 515 3000 f: 0191 515 3805
e: student.helpline@sunderland.ac.uk
// www.sunderland.ac.uk

C8C6 BSc Psychology with Sport
Duration: 3FT Hon
Entry Requirements: *GCE:* 260-360. *OCR ND:* D *OCR NED:* M3

C6C8 BSc Sport with Psychology
Duration: 3FT Hon
Entry Requirements: *GCE:* 260-360. *OCR ND:* D *OCR NED:* M3

W76 UNIVERSITY OF WINCHESTER
WINCHESTER
HANTS SO22 4NR
t: 01962 827234 f: 01962 827288
e: course.enquiries@winchester.ac.uk
// www.winchester.ac.uk

CN8V BA Psychology and Sports Management
Duration: 3FT Hon
Entry Requirements: *Foundation:* Distinction. *GCE:* 260-300. *IB:* 24. *OCR ND:* D

CL8H BA Psychology and Sports Studies
Duration: 3FT Hon
Entry Requirements: *Foundation:* Merit. *GCE:* 260-300. *IB:* 24.

W80 UNIVERSITY OF WORCESTER
HENWICK GROVE
WORCESTER WR2 6AJ
t: 01905 855111 f: 01905 855377
e: admissions@worc.ac.uk
// www.worcester.ac.uk

C813 BSc Sport & Exercise Psychology
Duration: 3FT Hon
Entry Requirements: *GCE:* 280. *IB:* 25. *OCR ND:* D *OCR NED:* M3

LANGUAGE COMBINATIONS

A20 THE UNIVERSITY OF ABERDEEN
UNIVERSITY OFFICE
KING'S COLLEGE
ABERDEEN AB24 3FX
t: +44 (0) 1224 273504 f: +44 (0) 1224 272034
e: sras@abdn.ac.uk
// www.abdn.ac.uk/sras

CCR1 BSc Behavioural Studies with French
Duration: 4FT Hon
Entry Requirements: Contact the institution for details.

C1Q5 BSc Behavioural Studies with Gaelic
Duration: 4FT Hon
Entry Requirements: Contact the institution for details.

C1R2 BSc Behavioural Studies with German
Duration: 4FT Hon
Entry Requirements: Contact the institution for details.

C8R1 BSc Psychology with French
Duration: 4FT Hon
Entry Requirements: *GCE:* 240. *SQAH:* BBBB. *SQAAH:* BCC. *IB:* 28.

C8QN BSc Psychology with Gaelic
Duration: 4FT Hon
Entry Requirements: *GCE:* 240. *SQAH:* BBBB. *SQAAH:* BCC. *IB:* 28.

C8R2 BSc Psychology with German
Duration: 4FT Hon
Entry Requirements: *GCE:* 240. *SQAH:* BBBB. *SQAAH:* BCC. *IB:* 28.

C1R1 MA Behavioural Studies with French
Duration: 4FT Hon
Entry Requirements: Contact the institution for details.

CCQ5 MA Behavioural Studies with Gaelic
Duration: 4FT Hon
Entry Requirements: Contact the institution for details.

CCR2 MA Behavioural Studies with German
Duration: 4FT Hon
Entry Requirements: Contact the institution for details.

C8RC MA Psychology with French
Duration: 4FT Hon
Entry Requirements: *GCE:* BBB. *SQAH:* BBBB. *IB:* 30.

C8QM MA Psychology with Gaelic
Duration: 4FT Hon
Entry Requirements: *GCE:* BBB. *SQAH:* BBBB. *IB:* 30.

C8RF MA Psychology with German
Duration: 4FT Hon
Entry Requirements: *GCE:* BBB. *SQAH:* BBBB. *IB:* 30.

A40 ABERYSTWYTH UNIVERSITY
ABERYSTWYTH UNIVERSITY, WELCOME CENTRE
PENGLAIS CAMPUS
ABERYSTWYTH
CEREDIGION SY23 3FB
t: 01970 622021 f: 01970 627410
e: ug-admissions@aber.ac.uk
// www.aber.ac.uk

CQ83 BA Psychology/English Literature
Duration: 3FT Hon
Entry Requirements: *GCE:* 300. *IB:* 28.

A80 ASTON UNIVERSITY, BIRMINGHAM
ASTON TRIANGLE
BIRMINGHAM B4 7ET
t: 0121 204 4444 f: 0121 204 3696
e: admissions@aston.ac.uk   (automatic response)
// www.aston.ac.uk/prospective-students/ug

CQ83 BSc Psychology and English Language
Duration: 4SW Hon
Entry Requirements: *GCE:* AAB-ABB. *SQAH:* AABBB. *SQAAH:* AAB-ABB. *IB:* 33. *BTEC ExtDip:* DDD. *OCR ND:* D *OCR NED:* D1

B06 BANGOR UNIVERSITY
BANGOR UNIVERSITY
BANGOR
GWYNEDD LL57 2DG
t: 01248 388484 f: 01248 370451
e: admissions@bangor.ac.uk
// www.bangor.ac.uk

CQ83 BA English Language and Psychology
Duration: 3FT Hon
Entry Requirements: *GCE:* 260-300. *IB:* 28.

R1C8 BA French with Psychology (4 years)
Duration: 4FT Hon
Entry Requirements: *GCE:* 240-280. *IB:* 28.

R2C8 BA German with Psychology (4 years)
Duration: 4FT Hon
Entry Requirements: *GCE:* 240-280. *IB:* 28.

CQ81 BA Psychology/Linguistics
Duration: 3FT Hon
Entry Requirements: *GCE:* 260-300. *IB:* 28.

C8X9 BSc Psychology with Child Language Development
Duration: 3FT Hon
Entry Requirements: *GCE:* 280-320. *IB:* 28.

B20 BATH SPA UNIVERSITY
NEWTON PARK
NEWTON ST LOE
BATH BA2 9BN
t: 01225 875875 f: 01225 875444
e: enquiries@bathspa.ac.uk
// www.bathspa.ac.uk/clearing

QC38 BA/BSc English Literature/Psychology
Duration: 3FT Hon
Entry Requirements: *GCE:* 220-280. *IB:* 24.

CQ83 DipHE English Literature/Psychology
Duration: 2FT Dip
Entry Requirements: *GCE:* 220-280. *IB:* 24.

B25 BIRMINGHAM CITY UNIVERSITY
PERRY BARR
BIRMINGHAM B42 2SU
t: 0121 331 5595 f: 0121 331 7994
// www.bcu.ac.uk

QC38 BA English and Psychology
Duration: 3FT Hon
Entry Requirements: *GCE:* 280. *IB:* 25.

B32 THE UNIVERSITY OF BIRMINGHAM
EDGBASTON
BIRMINGHAM B15 2TT
t: 0121 415 8900 f: 0121 414 7159
e: admissions@bham.ac.uk
// www.birmingham.ac.uk

R9C8 BA Modern Languages with Psychology (4 years)
Duration: 4FT Hon
Entry Requirements: *GCE:* ABB. *SQAH:* AAABB. *SQAAH:* AB. *IB:* 32.

B90 THE UNIVERSITY OF BUCKINGHAM
YEOMANRY HOUSE
HUNTER STREET
BUCKINGHAM MK18 1EG
t: 01280 820313 f: 01280 822245
e: info@buckingham.ac.uk
// www.buckingham.ac.uk

Q3C8 BA English Literature with Psychology
Duration: 2FT Hon
Entry Requirements: *GCE:* BBB. *SQAH:* ABBB. *SQAAH:* BBB. *IB:* 34. *OCR NED:* M2

C8Q2 BSc Psychology with English Literature
Duration: 2FT Hon
Entry Requirements: *GCE:* BBB. *SQAH:* ABBB. *SQAAH:* BBB. *IB:* 34.

C8R1 BSc Psychology with French
Duration: 2FT Hon
Entry Requirements: *GCE:* BBB. *SQAH:* ABBB. *SQAAH:* BBB. *IB:* 34.

C8R4 BSc Psychology with Spanish
Duration: 2FT Hon
Entry Requirements: *GCE:* BBB. *SQAH:* ABBB. *SQAAH:* BBB. *IB:* 34.

C10 CANTERBURY CHRIST CHURCH UNIVERSITY
NORTH HOLMES ROAD
CANTERBURY
KENT CT1 1QU
t: 01227 782900 f: 01227 782888
e: admissions@canterbury.ac.uk
// www.canterbury.ac.uk

QC3V BA English Language & Communication and Psychology
Duration: 3FT Hon
Entry Requirements: *GCE:* 260. *IB:* 24.

Q3CA BA English Language & Communication with Psychology
Duration: 3FT Hon
Entry Requirements: *GCE:* 260. *IB:* 24.

C8QJ BA Psychology with English Language & Communication
Duration: 3FT Hon
Entry Requirements: *GCE:* 260. *IB:* 24.

CQ83 BA/BSc English Literature and Psychology
Duration: 3FT Hon
Entry Requirements: *GCE:* 260. *IB:* 24.

Q3C8 BA/BSc English Literature with Psychology
Duration: 3FT Hon
Entry Requirements: *GCE:* 260. *IB:* 24.

C8Q3 BA/BSc Psychology with English Literature
Duration: 3FT Hon
Entry Requirements: *GCE:* 260. *IB:* 24.

C55 UNIVERSITY OF CHESTER
PARKGATE ROAD
CHESTER CH1 4BJ
t: 01244 511000 f: 01244 511300
e: enquiries@chester.ac.uk
// www.chester.ac.uk

QC3V BA English Language and Psychology
Duration: 3FT Hon
Entry Requirements: *Foundation:* Merit. *GCE:* 260-300. *SQAH:* BBBB. *IB:* 28.

QC38 BA English and Psychology
Duration: 3FT Hon
Entry Requirements: *Foundation:* Merit. *GCE:* 260-300. *SQAH:* BBBB. *IB:* 28.

CR81 BA Psychology and French
Duration: 4FT Hon
Entry Requirements: *GCE:* 260-300. *SQAH:* BBBB. *IB:* 28.

CR82 BA Psychology and German
Duration: 4FT Hon
Entry Requirements: *GCE:* 260-300. *SQAH:* BBBB. *IB:* 26.

CR84 BA Psychology and Spanish
Duration: 4FT Hon
Entry Requirements: *GCE:* 260-300. *SQAH:* BBBB. *IB:* 28.

D39 UNIVERSITY OF DERBY
KEDLESTON ROAD
DERBY DE22 1GB
t: 01332 591167 f: 01332 597724
e: askadmissions@derby.ac.uk
// www.derby.ac.uk

CQ83 BA English and Psychology
Duration: 3FT Hon
Entry Requirements: *Foundation:* Distinction. *GCE:* 260-300. *IB:* 28. *BTEC Dip:* D*D*. *BTEC ExtDip:* DMM. *OCR NED:* M2

D65 UNIVERSITY OF DUNDEE
NETHERGATE
DUNDEE DD1 4HN
t: 01382 383838 f: 01382 388150
e: contactus@dundee.ac.uk
// www.dundee.ac.uk/admissions/
undergraduate/

C8RA BSc Psychology with French
Duration: 4FT Hon
Entry Requirements: *GCE:* BCC. *SQAH:* ABBB. *IB:* 30.

C8RG BSc Psychology with German
Duration: 4FT Hon
Entry Requirements: *GCE:* BCC. *SQAH:* ABBB. *IB:* 30.

C8RL BSc Psychology with Spanish
Duration: 4FT Hon
Entry Requirements: *GCE:* BCC. *SQAH:* ABBB. *IB:* 30.

CT87 MA American Studies and Psychology
Duration: 4FT Hon
Entry Requirements: *GCE:* BCC. *SQAH:* ABBB. *IB:* 30.

CQ83 MA English and Psychology
Duration: 4FT Hon
Entry Requirements: *GCE:* BCC. *SQAH:* ABBB. *IB:* 30.

CR88 MA European Studies and Psychology
Duration: 4FT Hon
Entry Requirements: *GCE:* BCC. *SQAH:* ABBB. *IB:* 30.

C8R1 MA Psychology with French
Duration: 4FT Hon
Entry Requirements: *GCE:* BCC. *SQAH:* ABBB. *IB:* 30.

C8R2 MA Psychology with German
Duration: 4FT Hon
Entry Requirements: *GCE:* BCC. *SQAH:* ABBB. *IB:* 30.

C8R4 MA Psychology with Spanish
Duration: 4FT Hon
Entry Requirements: *GCE:* BCC. *SQAH:* ABBB. *IB:* 30.

E28 UNIVERSITY OF EAST LONDON
DOCKLANDS CAMPUS
UNIVERSITY WAY
LONDON E16 2RD
t: 020 8223 3333 f: 020 8223 2978
e: study@uel.ac.uk
// www.uel.ac.uk

Q3CV BA English Literature with Psychology
Duration: 3FT Hon
Entry Requirements: *GCE:* 240. *IB:* 24.

E56 THE UNIVERSITY OF EDINBURGH
STUDENT RECRUITMENT & ADMISSIONS
57 GEORGE SQUARE
EDINBURGH EH8 9JU
t: 0131 650 4360 f: 0131 651 1236
e: sra.enquiries@ed.ac.uk
// www.ed.ac.uk/studying/undergraduate/

CQ81 MA Psychology and Linguistics
Duration: 4FT Hon
Entry Requirements: *GCE:* AAA-BBB. *SQAH:* AAAA-BBBB. *IB:* 34.

G28 UNIVERSITY OF GLASGOW
71 SOUTHPARK AVENUE
UNIVERSITY OF GLASGOW
GLASGOW G12 8QQ
t: 0141 330 6062 f: 0141 330 2961
e: student.recruitment@glasgow.ac.uk
// www.glasgow.ac.uk

CQV5 MA Celtic Civilisation/Psychology
Duration: 4FT Hon
Entry Requirements: *GCE:* ABB. *SQAH:* AAAB-ABBB. *IB:* 36.

CQ85 MA Celtic Studies/Psychology
Duration: 4FT Hon
Entry Requirements: *GCE:* ABB. *SQAH:* AAAB-ABBB. *IB:* 36.

CQ88 MA Classics/Psychology
Duration: 4FT Hon
Entry Requirements: *GCE:* ABB. *SQAH:* AAAB-ABBB. *IB:* 36.

QC88 MA Classics/Psychology
Duration: 4FT Hon
Entry Requirements: *GCE:* ABB. *SQAH:* AAAA-AABB. *IB:* 36.

CQ8J MA English Language/Psychology
Duration: 4FT Hon
Entry Requirements: *GCE:* ABB. *SQAH:* AAAB-ABBB. *IB:* 36.

CQ8H MA English Literature/Psychology
Duration: 4FT Hon
Entry Requirements: *GCE:* ABB. *SQAH:* AAAB-ABBB. *IB:* 36.

CR81 MA French/Psychology
Duration: 5FT Hon
Entry Requirements: *GCE:* ABB. *SQAH:* AAAB-ABBB. *IB:* 36.

QC58 MA Gaelic/Psychology
Duration: 4FT Hon
Entry Requirements: *GCE:* ABB. *SQAH:* AAAB-ABBB. *IB:* 36.

CR82 MA German/Psychology
Duration: 5FT Hon
Entry Requirements: *GCE:* ABB. *SQAH:* AAAB-ABBB. *IB:* 36.

C8R1 MA Psychology with French Language
Duration: 5FT Hon
Entry Requirements: *GCE:* ABB. *SQAH:* AAAA-AABB. *IB:* 36.

Q5C8 MA Psychology with Gaelic Language
Duration: 4FT Hon
Entry Requirements: *GCE:* ABB. *SQAH:* AAAA-AABB. *IB:* 36.

C8R2 MA Psychology with German Language
Duration: 5FT Hon
Entry Requirements: *GCE:* ABB. *SQAH:* AAAA-AABB. *IB:* 36.

C8R3 MA Psychology with Italian Language
Duration: 5FT Hon
Entry Requirements: *GCE:* ABB. *SQAH:* AAAA-AABB. *IB:* 36.

C8R7 MA Psychology with Russian Language
Duration: 5FT Hon
Entry Requirements: *GCE:* ABB. *SQAH:* AAAA-AABB. *IB:* 36.

CR87 MA Psychology/Russian
Duration: 5FT Hon
Entry Requirements: *GCE:* ABB. *SQAH:* AAAB-ABBB. *IB:* 36.

CQ82 MA Psychology/Scottish Literature
Duration: 4FT Hon
Entry Requirements: *GCE:* ABB. *SQAH:* AAAB-ABBB. *IB:* 36.

H36 UNIVERSITY OF HERTFORDSHIRE
UNIVERSITY ADMISSIONS SERVICE
COLLEGE LANE
HATFIELD
HERTS AL10 9AB
t: 01707 284800
// www.herts.ac.uk

Q1C8 BSc English Language & Communication/Psychology
Duration: 3FT/4SW Hon
Entry Requirements: Contact the institution for details.

C8Q1 BSc Psychology/English Language & Communication
Duration: 3FT/4SW Hon
Entry Requirements: *GCE:* 320.

K12 KEELE UNIVERSITY
KEELE UNIVERSITY
STAFFORDSHIRE ST5 5BG
t: 01782 734005 f: 01782 632343
e: undergraduate@keele.ac.uk
// www.keele.ac.uk

CTW7 BSc American Studies and Psychology
Duration: 3FT Hon
Entry Requirements: *GCE:* BBB.

CQ83 BSc English and Psychology
Duration: 3FT Hon
Entry Requirements: *GCE:* BBB.

K84 KINGSTON UNIVERSITY
STUDENT INFORMATION & ADVICE CENTRE
COOPER HOUSE
40-46 SURBITON ROAD
KINGSTON UPON THAMES KT1 2HX
t: 0844 8552177 f: 020 8547 7080
e: aps@kingston.ac.uk
// www.kingston.ac.uk

Q3C8 BA English Language & Communication with Psychology
Duration: 3FT Hon
Entry Requirements: *GCE:* 240-360. *IB:* 30.

QC38 BA English Language & Communications and Psychology
Duration: 3FT Hon
Entry Requirements: *GCE:* 240-360. *IB:* 30.

C8Q3 BA Psychology with English Language & Communication
Duration: 3FT Hon
Entry Requirements: *GCE:* 240-360. *IB:* 30.

C8R1 BSc Psychology with French
Duration: 3FT Hon
Entry Requirements: *GCE:* 240-360. *IB:* 24.

C8R4 BSc Psychology with Spanish
Duration: 3FT Hon
Entry Requirements: *GCE:* 240-360.

L14 LANCASTER UNIVERSITY
THE UNIVERSITY
LANCASTER
LANCASHIRE LA1 4YW
t: 01524 592029 f: 01524 846243
e: ugadmissions@lancaster.ac.uk
// www.lancs.ac.uk

CR81 BA French Studies and Psychology
Duration: 4SW Hon
Entry Requirements: *GCE:* AAB. *SQAH:* ABBBB. *SQAAH:* AAB. *IB:* 35.

CR82 BA German Studies and Psychology
Duration: 4SW Hon
Entry Requirements: *GCE:* AAB. *SQAH:* ABBBB. *SQAAH:* AAB. *IB:* 35.

CQ81 BA Linguistics and Psychology
Duration: 3FT Hon
Entry Requirements: *GCE:* AAB. *SQAH:* ABBBB. *SQAAH:* AAB. *IB:* 35.

CR84 BA Spanish Studies and Psychology
Duration: 4SW Hon
Entry Requirements: *GCE:* AAB. *SQAH:* ABBBB. *SQAAH:* AAB. *IB:* 35.

L46 LIVERPOOL HOPE UNIVERSITY
HOPE PARK
LIVERPOOL L16 9JD
t: 0151 291 3331 f: 0151 291 3434
e: administration@hope.ac.uk
// www.hope.ac.uk

CQ83 BA English Language and Psychology
Duration: 3FT Hon
Entry Requirements: *GCE:* 300-320. *IB:* 25.

Q2C8 BA English Literature and Psychology
Duration: 3FT Hon
Entry Requirements: *GCE:* 300-320. *IB:* 25.

M40 THE MANCHESTER METROPOLITAN UNIVERSITY
ADMISSIONS OFFICE
ALL SAINTS (GMS)
ALL SAINTS
MANCHESTER M15 6BH
t: 0161 247 2000
// www.mmu.ac.uk

QC38 BA/BSc English/Psychology
Duration: 3FT Hon
Entry Requirements: *GCE:* 280. *IB:* 28.

N31 NEWHAM COLLEGE OF FURTHER EDUCATION
EAST HAM CAMPUS
HIGH STREET SOUTH
LONDON E6 6ER
t: 020 8257 4000 f: 020 8257 4325
e: admissions@newham.ac.uk
// www.newham.ac.uk

QC38 BA English and Psychology
Duration: 3FT Hon
Entry Requirements: Contact the institution for details.

N36 NEWMAN UNIVERSITY COLLEGE, BIRMINGHAM
GENNERS LANE
BARTLEY GREEN
BIRMINGHAM B32 3NT
t: 0121 476 1181 f: 0121 476 1196
e: Admissions@newman.ac.uk
// www.newman.ac.uk

C8Q3 BA Psychology with English Literature
Duration: 3FT Hon
Entry Requirements: *Foundation:* Distinction. *GCE:* 280. *IB:* 25. *BTEC ExtDip:* DMM. *OCR ND:* M2 *OCR NED:* M2

CVQ3 BSc Psychology with English Language
Duration: 3FT Hon
Entry Requirements: *Foundation:* Distinction. *GCE:* 280. *IB:* 25. *BTEC ExtDip:* DMM. *OCR ND:* M2 *OCR NED:* M2

N38 UNIVERSITY OF NORTHAMPTON
PARK CAMPUS
BOUGHTON GREEN ROAD
NORTHAMPTON NN2 7AL
t: 0800 358 2232 f: 01604 722083
e: admissions@northampton.ac.uk
// www.northampton.ac.uk

Q3C8 BA English/Psychology
Duration: 3FT Hon
Entry Requirements: *GCE:* 260-280. *SQAH:* AAA-BBBB. *IB:* 24. *BTEC Dip:* DD. *BTEC ExtDip:* DMM. *OCR ND:* D *OCR NED:* M2

R1C8 BA French/Psychology
Duration: 3FT Hon
Entry Requirements: *GCE:* 260-280. *SQAH:* AAA-BBBB. *IB:* 24. *BTEC Dip:* DD. *BTEC ExtDip:* DMM. *OCR ND:* D *OCR NED:* M2

C8Q3 BA Psychology/English
Duration: 3FT Hon
Entry Requirements: *GCE:* 260-280. *SQAH:* AAA-BBBB. *IB:* 24. *BTEC Dip:* DD. *BTEC ExtDip:* DMM. *OCR ND:* D *OCR NED:* M2

C8R1 BA Psychology/French
Duration: 3FT Hon
Entry Requirements: *GCE:* 260-280. *SQAH:* AAA-BBBB. *IB:* 24. *BTEC Dip:* DD. *BTEC ExtDip:* DMM. *OCR ND:* D *OCR NED:* M2

O33 OXFORD UNIVERSITY
UNDERGRADUATE ADMISSIONS OFFICE
UNIVERSITY OF OXFORD
WELLINGTON SQUARE
OXFORD OX1 2JD
t: 01865 288000 f: 01865 270212
e: undergraduate.admissions@admin.ox.ac.uk
// www.admissions.ox.ac.uk

CQ81 BA Psychology and Linguistics
Duration: 3FT Hon
Entry Requirements: Interview required. Admissions Test required.

O66 OXFORD BROOKES UNIVERSITY
ADMISSIONS OFFICE
HEADINGTON CAMPUS
GIPSY LANE
OXFORD OX3 0BP
t: 01865 483040 f: 01865 483983
e: admissions@brookes.ac.uk
// www.brookes.ac.uk

QC38 BA/BSc English/Psychology
Duration: 3FT Hon
Entry Requirements: *GCE:* BBB.

P80 UNIVERSITY OF PORTSMOUTH
ACADEMIC REGISTRY
UNIVERSITY HOUSE
WINSTON CHURCHILL AVENUE
PORTSMOUTH PO1 2UP
t: 023 9284 8484 f: 023 9284 3082
e: admissions@port.ac.uk
// www.port.ac.uk

Q3C8 BA English with Psychology
Duration: 3FT Hon
Entry Requirements: *GCE:* 240-300. *BTEC Dip:* DD. *BTEC ExtDip:* DMM.

S18 THE UNIVERSITY OF SHEFFIELD
THE UNIVERSITY OF SHEFFIELD
LEVEL 2, ARTS TOWER
WESTERN BANK
SHEFFIELD S10 2TN
t: 0114 222 8030 f: 0114 222 8032
// www.sheffield.ac.uk

QC18 BSc Human Communication Sciences
Duration: 3FT Hon   CRB Check: Required
Entry Requirements: *GCE:* ABB. *SQAH:* AAABB. *IB:* 33. *BTEC ExtDip:* DDM.

S36 UNIVERSITY OF ST ANDREWS
ST KATHARINE'S WEST
16 THE SCORES
ST ANDREWS
FIFE KY16 9AX
t: 01334 462150 f: 01334 463330
e: admissions@st-andrews.ac.uk
// www.st-andrews.ac.uk

CQ83 MA English and Psychology
Duration: 4FT Hon
Entry Requirements: *GCE:* AAA. *SQAH:* AAAB. *IB:* 36.

CR81 MA French and Psychology
Duration: 4FT Hon
Entry Requirements: *GCE:* AAA. *SQAH:* AAAB. *IB:* 36.

CR8C MA French and Psychology (year abroad)
Duration: 5FT Hon
Entry Requirements: *GCE:* AAA. *SQAH:* AAAB. *IB:* 36.

CR82 MA German and Psychology
Duration: 4FT Hon
Entry Requirements: *GCE:* AAA. *SQAH:* AAAB. *IB:* 36.

CR8F MA German and Psychology (year abroad)
Duration: 5FT Hon
Entry Requirements: *GCE:* AAA. *SQAH:* AAAB. *IB:* 36.

RC38 MA Italian and Psychology
Duration: 4FT Hon
Entry Requirements: *GCE:* AAA. *SQAH:* AAAB. *IB:* 36.

CR83 MA Italian and Psychology (year abroad)
Duration: 5FT Hon
Entry Requirements: *GCE:* AAA. *SQAH:* AAAB. *IB:* 36.

S64 ST MARY'S UNIVERSITY COLLEGE, TWICKENHAM
WALDEGRAVE ROAD
STRAWBERRY HILL
MIDDLESEX TW1 4SX
t: 020 8240 4029 f: 020 8240 2361
e: admit@smuc.ac.uk
// www.smuc.ac.uk

QC38 BA/BSc English and Psychology
Duration: 3FT Hon
Entry Requirements: *GCE:* 240. *SQAH:* BBBC. *IB:* 28. *OCR ND:* D *OCR NED:* M3 Interview required.

S75 THE UNIVERSITY OF STIRLING
STUDENT RECRUITMENT & ADMISSIONS SERVICE
UNIVERSITY OF STIRLING
STIRLING
SCOTLAND FK9 4LA
t: 01786 467044 f: 01786 466800
e: admissions@stir.ac.uk
// www.stir.ac.uk

QC38 BA English Studies and Psychology
Duration: 4FT Hon
Entry Requirements: *GCE:* BBC. *SQAH:* BBBB. *SQAAH:* AAA-CCC.
IB: 32. *BTEC ExtDip:* DMM.

CR89 BA Psychology and European Language
Duration: 4FT Hon
Entry Requirements: *GCE:* BBC. *SQAH:* BBBB. *SQAAH:* AAA-CCC.
IB: 32. *BTEC ExtDip:* DMM.

S78 THE UNIVERSITY OF STRATHCLYDE
GLASGOW G1 1XQ
t: 0141 552 4400 f: 0141 552 0775
// www.strath.ac.uk

QC38 BA English and Psychology
Duration: 4FT Hon
Entry Requirements: *GCE:* ABB. *SQAH:* AAABB-AAAB. *IB:* 34.

RC18 BA French and Psychology
Duration: 5FT Hon
Entry Requirements: *GCE:* ABB. *SQAH:* AAABB-AAAB. *IB:* 34.

RC38 BA Italian and Psychology
Duration: 5FT Hon
Entry Requirements: *GCE:* ABB. *SQAH:* AAABB-AAAB. *IB:* 34.

CR84 BA Psychology and Spanish
Duration: 5FT Hon
Entry Requirements: *GCE:* ABB. *SQAH:* AAABB-AAAB. *IB:* 34.

S82 UNIVERSITY CAMPUS SUFFOLK (UCS)
WATERFRONT BUILDING
NEPTUNE QUAY
IPSWICH
SUFFOLK IP4 1QJ
t: 01473 338833 f: 01473 339900
e: info@ucs.ac.uk
// www.ucs.ac.uk

CQ83 BA English and Psychology
Duration: 3FT Hon
Entry Requirements: *GCE:* 280. *IB:* 28. *BTEC ExtDip:* DMM.

S84 UNIVERSITY OF SUNDERLAND
STUDENT HELPLINE
THE STUDENT GATEWAY
CHESTER ROAD
SUNDERLAND SR1 3SD
t: 0191 515 3000 f: 0191 515 3805
e: student.helpline@sunderland.ac.uk
// www.sunderland.ac.uk

Q1C8 BA English Language & Linguistics with Psychology
Duration: 3FT Hon
Entry Requirements: *GCE:* 260-360. *OCR ND:* D *OCR NED:* M3

Q3C8 BA English with Psychology
Duration: 3FT Hon
Entry Requirements: *GCE:* 260-360. *IB:* 31. *OCR ND:* D *OCR NED:* M3

RC18 BA Modern Foreign Languages (French) and Psychology
Duration: 3FT Hon
Entry Requirements: *GCE:* 260-360. *IB:* 31. *OCR ND:* D *OCR NED:* M3

CR82 BA Modern Foreign Languages (German) and Psychology
Duration: 3FT Hon
Entry Requirements: *GCE:* 260-360. *IB:* 31. *OCR ND:* D *OCR NED:* M3

CR84 BA Modern Foreign Languages (Spanish) and Psychology
Duration: 3FT Hon
Entry Requirements: *GCE:* 260-360. *IB:* 31. *OCR ND:* D *OCR NED:* M3

C8R1 BA Psychology with Modern Foreign Languages (French)
Duration: 3FT Hon
Entry Requirements: *GCE:* 260-360. *OCR ND:* D *OCR NED:* M3

C8R2 BA Psychology with Modern Foreign Languages (German)
Duration: 3FT Hon
Entry Requirements: *GCE:* 260-360. *OCR ND:* D *OCR NED:* M3

C8R4 BA Psychology with Modern Foreign Languages (Spanish)
Duration: 3FT Hon
Entry Requirements: *GCE:* 260-360. *OCR ND:* D *OCR NED:* M3

QC38 BA/BSc English and Psychology
Duration: 3FT Hon
Entry Requirements: *GCE:* 260-360. *IB:* 31. *OCR ND:* D *OCR NED:* M3

CQ81 BA/BSc Psychology and English Language/Linguistics
Duration: 3FT Hon
Entry Requirements: *GCE:* 260-360. *IB:* 32. *OCR ND:* D *OCR NED:* M3

C8Q1 BSc Psychology with English Language/Linguistics
Duration: 3FT Hon
Entry Requirements: *GCE:* 260-360. *IB:* 32. *OCR ND:* D *OCR NED:* M3

C8Q3 BSc Psychology with English Studies
Duration: 3FT Hon
Entry Requirements: *GCE:* 260-360. *IB:* 32. *OCR ND:* D *OCR NED:* M3

S90 UNIVERSITY OF SUSSEX
UNDERGRADUATE ADMISSIONS
SUSSEX HOUSE
UNIVERSITY OF SUSSEX
BRIGHTON BN1 9RH
t: 01273 678416 f: 01273 678545
e: ug.applicants@sussex.ac.uk
// www.sussex.ac.uk

C8T7 BSc Psychology with American Studies
Duration: 4FT Hon
Entry Requirements: *GCE:* AAB. *SQAH:* AAABB. *IB:* 35. *BTEC SubDip:* D. *BTEC Dip:* DD. *BTEC ExtDip:* DDD. *OCR ND:* D *OCR NED:* D1

U20 UNIVERSITY OF ULSTER
COLERAINE
CO. LONDONDERRY
NORTHERN IRELAND BT52 1SA
t: 028 7012 4221 f: 028 7012 4908
e: online@ulster.ac.uk
// www.ulster.ac.uk

Q3C8 BA English with Psychology
Duration: 3FT Hon
Entry Requirements: *GCE:* 280. *IB:* 24.

R1C8 BA French with Psychology
Duration: 3FT Hon
Entry Requirements: *GCE:* 260. *IB:* 24.

R2C8 BA German with Psychology
Duration: 3FT Hon
Entry Requirements: *GCE:* 260. *IB:* 24.

R4C8 BA Spanish with Psychology
Duration: 4SW Hon
Entry Requirements: *GCE:* 260. *IB:* 24.

W76 UNIVERSITY OF WINCHESTER
WINCHESTER
HANTS SO22 4NR
t: 01962 827234 f: 01962 827288
e: course.enquiries@winchester.ac.uk
// www.winchester.ac.uk

TC78 BA American Studies and Psychology
Duration: 3FT Hon
Entry Requirements: *Foundation:* Distinction. *GCE:* 260-300. *IB:* 25. *OCR ND:* D *OCR NED:* M2

QC38 BA English Language Studies and Psychology
Duration: 3FT Hon
Entry Requirements: *Foundation:* Distinction. *GCE:* 260-300. *IB:* 25. *OCR ND:* D *OCR NED:* M2

CQ83 BA English and Psychology
Duration: 3FT Hon
Entry Requirements: *Foundation:* Distinction. *GCE:* 260-300. *IB:* 25. *OCR ND:* D *OCR NED:* M2

PSYCHOLOGY COMBINATIONS

A20 THE UNIVERSITY OF ABERDEEN
UNIVERSITY OFFICE
KING'S COLLEGE
ABERDEEN AB24 3FX
t: +44 (0) 1224 273504 f: +44 (0) 1224 272034
e: sras@abdn.ac.uk
// www.abdn.ac.uk/sras

CG84 BSc Behavioural Studies and Computing Science
Duration: 4FT Hon
Entry Requirements: *GCE:* BBB. *SQAH:* BBBB. *IB:* 30.

GC48 BSc Computing Science and Psychology
Duration: 4FT Hon
Entry Requirements: *GCE:* 240. *SQAH:* BBBB. *SQAAH:* BCC. *IB:* 28.

B170 BSc Neuroscience with Psychology
Duration: 4FT Hon
Entry Requirements: *GCE:* 240. *SQAH:* BBBB. *SQAAH:* BCC. *IB:* 28.

LC68 MA Anthropology and Psychology
Duration: 4FT Hon
Entry Requirements: *GCE:* BBB. *SQAH:* BBBB. *IB:* 30.

CV15 MA Behavioural Studies and Philosophy
Duration: 4FT Hon
Entry Requirements: Contact the institution for details.

CL13 MA Behavioural Studies and Sociology
Duration: 4FT Hon
Entry Requirements: Contact the institution for details.

LC18 MA Economics and Psychology
Duration: 4FT Hon
Entry Requirements: *GCE:* BBB. *SQAH:* BBBB. *IB:* 30.

CM89 MA Legal Studies and Psychology
Duration: 4FT Hon
Entry Requirements: *GCE:* BBB. *SQAH:* BBBB. *IB:* 30.

CN28 MA Management Studies and Psychology
Duration: 4FT Hon
Entry Requirements: *GCE:* BBB. *SQAH:* BBBB. *IB:* 30.

VC58 MA Philosophy and Psychology
Duration: 4FT Hon
Entry Requirements: *GCE:* BBB. *SQAH:* BBBB. *IB:* 30.

LC38 MA Psychology and Sociology
Duration: 4FT Hon
Entry Requirements: *GCE:* BBB. *SQAH:* BBBB. *IB:* 30.

B1C8 MSci Neuroscience with Psychology with Industrial Placement
Duration: 5FT Hon
Entry Requirements: *GCE:* ABB. *SQAH:* AABB. *IB:* 32.

A40 ABERYSTWYTH UNIVERSITY
ABERYSTWYTH UNIVERSITY, WELCOME CENTRE
PENGLAIS CAMPUS
ABERYSTWYTH
CEREDIGION SY23 3FB
t: 01970 622021 f: 01970 627410
e: ug-admissions@aber.ac.uk
// www.aber.ac.uk

CX83 BSc Psychology/Education
Duration: 3FT Hon
Entry Requirements: *GCE:* 280. *IB:* 28.

CM89 BScEcon Psychology/Criminology
Duration: 3FT Hon
Entry Requirements: *GCE:* 300. *IB:* 30.

CN85 BScEcon Psychology/Marketing
Duration: 3FT Hon
Entry Requirements: *GCE:* 280. *IB:* 28.

A60 ANGLIA RUSKIN UNIVERSITY
BISHOP HALL LANE
CHELMSFORD
ESSEX CM1 1SQ
t: 0845 271 3333 f: 01245 251789
e: answers@anglia.ac.uk
// www.anglia.ac.uk

CL8H BSc Psychology and Criminology
Duration: 3FT Hon
Entry Requirements: *GCE:* 220. *SQAH:* AABC. *SQAAH:* AB. *IB:* 30.

A80 ASTON UNIVERSITY, BIRMINGHAM
ASTON TRIANGLE
BIRMINGHAM B4 7ET
t: 0121 204 4444 f: 0121 204 3696
e: admissions@aston.ac.uk (automatic response)
// www.aston.ac.uk/prospective-students/ug

CN81 BSc Psychology and Business
Duration: 4SW Hon
Entry Requirements: *GCE:* AAB-ABB. *SQAH:* AABBB. *SQAAH:* AAB. *IB:* 33.

B06 BANGOR UNIVERSITY
BANGOR UNIVERSITY
BANGOR
GWYNEDD LL57 2DG
t: 01248 388484 f: 01248 370451
e: admissions@bangor.ac.uk
// www.bangor.ac.uk

XC38 BA Astudiaethau Plentyndod/Seicoleg
Duration: 3FT Hon
Entry Requirements: *GCE:* 260-300. *IB:* 28.

CXV3 BA Childhood Studies/Psychology
Duration: 3FT Hon
Entry Requirements: *GCE:* 260-300. *IB:* 28.

MC98 BA Criminology & Criminal Justice and Psychology
Duration: 3FT Hon
Entry Requirements: *GCE:* 260-300. *IB:* 28.

CL84 BA Social Policy/Psychology
Duration: 3FT Hon
Entry Requirements: *GCE:* 260-300. *IB:* 28.

CL83 BA Sociology/Psychology
Duration: 3FT Hon
Entry Requirements: *GCE:* 260-300. *IB:* 28.

B20 BATH SPA UNIVERSITY
NEWTON PARK
NEWTON ST LOE
BATH BA2 9BN
t: 01225 875875 f: 01225 875444
e: enquiries@bathspa.ac.uk
// www.bathspa.ac.uk/clearing

NC18 BA/BSc Business & Management/Psychology
Duration: 3FT Hon
Entry Requirements: *GCE:* 220-280. *IB:* 24.

WC88 BA/BSc Creative Writing/Psychology
Duration: 3FT Hon
Entry Requirements: *GCE:* 220-280. *IB:* 24.

WC58 BA/BSc Dance/Psychology
Duration: 3FT Hon
Entry Requirements: *GCE:* 220-280. *IB:* 24. Interview required.

CW8L BA/BSc Drama Studies/Psychology
Duration: 3FT Hon
Entry Requirements: *GCE:* 220-280. *IB:* 24.

XC38 BA/BSc Education/Psychology
Duration: 3FT Hon CRB Check: Required
Entry Requirements: *GCE:* 220-280. *IB:* 24.

WC68 BA/BSc Film & Screen Studies/Psychology
Duration: 3FT Hon
Entry Requirements: *GCE:* 220-280. *IB:* 24.

VC18 BA/BSc History/Psychology
Duration: 3FT Hon
Entry Requirements: *GCE:* 220-280. *IB:* 24.

PC98 BA/BSc Media Communications/Psychology
Duration: 3FT Hon
Entry Requirements: *GCE:* 220-280. *IB:* 24.

WC38 BA/BSc Music/Psychology
Duration: 3FT Hon
Entry Requirements: *GCE:* 220-280. *IB:* 24. Interview required.

VC58 BA/BSc Philosophy & Ethics/Psychology
Duration: 3FT Hon
Entry Requirements: *GCE:* 220-280. *IB:* 24.

CV86 BA/BSc Psychology/Study of Religions
Duration: 3FT Hon
Entry Requirements: *GCE:* 220-280. *IB:* 24.

CC18 BSc Biology/Psychology
Duration: 3FT Hon
Entry Requirements: *GCE:* 220-280. *IB:* 24.

XC18 BSc Education/Psychology
Duration: 3FT Hon CRB Check: Required
Entry Requirements: *GCE:* 220-280. *IB:* 24.

FC88 BSc Geography/Psychology
Duration: 3FT Hon
Entry Requirements: *GCE:* 220-280. *IB:* 24.

LC48 BSc Health Studies/Psychology
Duration: 3FT Hon
Entry Requirements: *GCE:* 220-280. *IB:* 24.

CL83 BSc Psychology/Sociology
Duration: 3FT Hon
Entry Requirements: *GCE:* 220-280. *IB:* 24.

CC81 DipHE Biology/Psychology
Duration: 2FT Dip
Entry Requirements: *GCE:* 220-280. *IB:* 24.

CN81 DipHE Business & Management/Psychology
Duration: 2FT Dip
Entry Requirements: *GCE:* 220-280. *IB:* 24.

CW85 DipHE Dance/Psychology
Duration: 2FT Dip
Entry Requirements: *GCE:* 220-280. *IB:* 24. Interview required.

CW8K DipHE Drama Studies/Psychology
Duration: 2FT Dip
Entry Requirements: *GCE:* 220-280. *IB:* 24.

CX83 DipHE Education/Psychology
Duration: 2FT Dip
Entry Requirements: *GCE:* 220-280. *IB:* 24.

WC6V DipHE Film & Screen Studies/Psychology
Duration: 2FT Dip
Entry Requirements: *GCE:* 220-280. *IB:* 24.

CF88 DipHE Geography/Psychology
Duration: 2FT Dip
Entry Requirements: *GCE:* 220-280. *IB:* 24.

CL84 DipHE Health Studies/Psychology
Duration: 2FT Dip
Entry Requirements: *GCE:* 220-280. *IB:* 24.

CV81 DipHE History/Psychology
Duration: 2FT Dip
Entry Requirements: *GCE:* 220-280. *IB:* 24.

CP89 DipHE Media Communications/Psychology
Duration: 2FT Dip
Entry Requirements: *GCE:* 220-280. *IB:* 24.

CW83 DipHE Music/Psychology
Duration: 2FT Dip
Entry Requirements: *GCE:* 220-280. *IB:* 24.

58CV DipHE Philosophy & Ethics/Psychology
Duration: 2FT Dip
Entry Requirements: *GCE:* 220-280.

LC38 DipHE Psychology/Sociology
Duration: 2FT Dip
Entry Requirements: *GCE:* 220-280. *IB:* 24.

VC68 DipHE Psychology/Study of Religions
Duration: 2FT Dip
Entry Requirements: *GCE:* 220-280. *IB:* 24.

B22 UNIVERSITY OF BEDFORDSHIRE
PARK SQUARE
LUTON
BEDS LU1 3JU
t: 0844 8482234 f: 01582 489323
e: admissions@beds.ac.uk
// www.beds.ac.uk

CL83 BSc Psychology and Criminal Behaviour
Duration: 3FT Hon
Entry Requirements: *GCE:* 200.

CM89 BSc Psychology and Criminology
Duration: 3FT Hon
Entry Requirements: *GCE:* 160-240. *SQAH:* BBC. *SQAAH:* BBC.
IB: 30.

CB89 BSc Psychology, Counselling and Therapies
Duration: 3FT Hon
Entry Requirements: *GCE:* 200.

CL8H FdA Psychology and Crime
Duration: 2FT Fdg
Entry Requirements: Contact the institution for details.

B25 BIRMINGHAM CITY UNIVERSITY
PERRY BARR
BIRMINGHAM B42 2SU
t: 0121 331 5595 f: 0121 331 7994
// www.bcu.ac.uk

MC98 BA Criminology and Psychology
Duration: 3FT Hon
Entry Requirements: *GCE:* 280. *IB:* 26.

LC38 BA Sociology and Psychology
Duration: 3FT Hon
Entry Requirements: *GCE:* 280. *IB:* 26. *OCR NED:* M2

B38 BISHOP GROSSETESTE UNIVERSITY COLLEGE LINCOLN
BISHOP GROSSETESTE UNIVERSITY COLLEGE
LINCOLN LN1 3DY
t: 01522 583658 f: 01522 530243
e: admissions@bishopg.ac.uk
// www.bishopg.ac.uk/courses

CW84 BA Applied Drama with Psychology
Duration: 3FT Hon   CRB Check: Required
Entry Requirements: Contact the institution for details.

C8L5 BA Early Childhood Studies with Psychology
Duration: 3FT Hon   CRB Check: Required
Entry Requirements: Contact the institution for details.

C8XH BA Education Studies and Psychology
Duration: 3FT Hon   CRB Check: Required
Entry Requirements: Contact the institution for details.

CVXH BA Education Studies with Psychology
Duration: 3FT Hon   CRB Check: Required
Entry Requirements: Contact the institution for details.

C8W4 BA Psychology and Applied Drama
Duration: 3FT Hon   CRB Check: Required
Entry Requirements: Contact the institution for details.

C8X3 BA Psychology and Early Childhood Studies
Duration: 3FT Hon   CRB Check: Required
Entry Requirements: Contact the institution for details.

CV81 BA Psychology and History
Duration: 3FT Hon   CRB Check: Required
Entry Requirements: Contact the institution for details.

CX83 BA Psychology and Special Educational Needs and Inclusion
Duration: 3FT Hon   CRB Check: Required
Entry Requirements: Contact the institution for details.

B44 UNIVERSITY OF BOLTON
DEANE ROAD
BOLTON BL3 5AB
t: 01204 903903 f: 01204 399074
e: enquiries@bolton.ac.uk
// www.bolton.ac.uk

CB89 BSc Counselling & Psychology
Duration: 3FT Hon
Entry Requirements: *GCE:* 300. Interview required.

B54 BPP UNIVERSITY COLLEGE OF PROFESSIONAL STUDIES LIMITED
142-144 UXBRIDGE ROAD
LONDON W12 8AW
t: 02031 312 298
e: admissions@bpp.com
// undergraduate.bpp.com/

MC18 LLB Law with Psychology
Duration: 3FT Hon
Entry Requirements: Contact the institution for details.

MCC8 LLB Law with Psychology (Accelerated)
Duration: 2FT Hon
Entry Requirements: Contact the institution for details.

B56 THE UNIVERSITY OF BRADFORD
RICHMOND ROAD
BRADFORD
WEST YORKSHIRE BD7 1DP
t: 0800 073 1225 f: 01274 235585
e: course-enquiries@bradford.ac.uk
// www.bradford.ac.uk

LC38 BA Sociology and Psychology
Duration: 3FT Hon
Entry Requirements: GCE: 240. IB: 24.

CL83 BSc Psychology and Crime
Duration: 3FT Hon
Entry Requirements: GCE: 240. IB: 24.

C8B9 BSc Psychology with Counselling
Duration: 3FT Hon
Entry Requirements: GCE: 260. IB: 24.

B60 BRADFORD COLLEGE: AN ASSOCIATE COLLEGE OF LEEDS METROPOLITAN UNIVERSITY
GREAT HORTON ROAD
BRADFORD
WEST YORKSHIRE BD7 1AY
t: 01274 433008 f: 01274 431652
e: heregistry@bradfordcollege.ac.uk
// www.bradfordcollege.ac.uk/
university-centre

CL85 BA Counselling and Psychology in Community Settings
Duration: 3FT Hon   CRB Check: Required
Entry Requirements: GCE: 200. Interview required.

B78 UNIVERSITY OF BRISTOL
UNDERGRADUATE ADMISSIONS OFFICE
SENATE HOUSE
TYNDALL AVENUE
BRISTOL BS8 1TH
t: 0117 928 9000 f: 0117 331 7391
e: ug-admissions@bristol.ac.uk
// www.bristol.ac.uk

VC58 BSc Psychology and Philosophy
Duration: 3FT Hon
Entry Requirements: GCE: A*AA-AAB. SQAH: AAAAA-AAABB. SQAAH: AA.

B80 UNIVERSITY OF THE WEST OF ENGLAND, BRISTOL
FRENCHAY CAMPUS
COLDHARBOUR LANE
BRISTOL BS16 1QY
t: +44 (0)117 32 83333 f: +44 (0)117 32 82810
e: admissions@uwe.ac.uk
// www.uwe.ac.uk

M9C8 BSc (Hons) Criminology with Psychology
Duration: 3FT Hon
Entry Requirements: GCE: 320.

C8M9 BSc (Hons) Psychology with Criminology
Duration: 3FT/4SW Hon
Entry Requirements: GCE: 340.

C8M1 BSc (Hons) Psychology with Law
Duration: 3FT Hon
Entry Requirements: GCE: 340.

C8L3 BSc (Hons) Psychology with Sociology
Duration: 3FT/4SW Hon
Entry Requirements: GCE: 340.

L3C8 BSc (Hons) Sociology with Psychology
Duration: 3FT Hon
Entry Requirements: GCE: 280.

M1C8 LLB (Hons) Law with Psychology
Duration: 3FT Hon
Entry Requirements: Contact the institution for details.

B84 BRUNEL UNIVERSITY
UXBRIDGE
MIDDLESEX UB8 3PH
t: 01895 265265 f: 01895 269790
e: admissions@brunel.ac.uk
// www.brunel.ac.uk

LC68 BSc Psychology and Anthropology
Duration: 3FT Hon
Entry Requirements: *GCE:* AAB. *SQAAH:* AAB. *IB:* 35. *BTEC SubDip:* D. *BTEC Dip:* D*D. *BTEC ExtDip:* D*D*D.

LC6V BSc Psychology and Anthropology (4 year thin SW)
Duration: 4SW Hon
Entry Requirements: *GCE:* AAB. *SQAAH:* AAB. *IB:* 35. *BTEC SubDip:* D. *BTEC Dip:* D*D. *BTEC ExtDip:* D*D*D.

CL8H BSc Psychology and Sociology
Duration: 3FT Hon
Entry Requirements: *GCE:* AAB. *SQAAH:* AAB. *IB:* 35. *BTEC SubDip:* D. *BTEC Dip:* D*D. *BTEC ExtDip:* D*D*D.

CL83 BSc Psychology and Sociology (4 year Thin SW)
Duration: 4SW Hon
Entry Requirements: *GCE:* AAB. *SQAAH:* AAB. *IB:* 35. *BTEC SubDip:* D. *BTEC Dip:* D*D. *BTEC ExtDip:* D*D*D.

B90 THE UNIVERSITY OF BUCKINGHAM
YEOMANRY HOUSE
HUNTER STREET
BUCKINGHAM MK18 1EG
t: 01280 820313 f: 01280 822245
e: info@buckingham.ac.uk
// www.buckingham.ac.uk

N5C8 BSc Marketing with Psychology
Duration: 2FT Hon
Entry Requirements: *GCE:* BBB-BBC. *SQAH:* ABBB-BBBB. *SQAAH:* BBB-BBC. *IB:* 34.

C8G5 BSc Psychology with Applied Computing
Duration: 2FT Hon
Entry Requirements: *GCE:* BBB. *SQAH:* ABBB. *SQAAH:* BBB. *IB:* 34.

C8N1 BSc Psychology with Business & Management
Duration: 2FT Hon
Entry Requirements: *GCE:* BBB. *SQAH:* ABBB. *SQAAH:* BBB. *IB:* 34.

C8N5 BSc Psychology with Marketing
Duration: 2FT Hon
Entry Requirements: *GCE:* BBB. *SQAH:* ABBB. *SQAAH:* BBB. *IB:* 34.

C8P3 BSc Psychology with Media Communications
Duration: 2FT Hon
Entry Requirements: *GCE:* BBB. *SQAH:* ABBB. *SQAAH:* BBB. *IB:* 34.

B94 BUCKINGHAMSHIRE NEW UNIVERSITY
QUEEN ALEXANDRA ROAD
HIGH WYCOMBE
BUCKINGHAMSHIRE HP11 2JZ
t: 0800 0565 660 f: 01494 605 023
e: admissions@bucks.ac.uk
// bucks.ac.uk

CM89 BSc Psychology and Criminology
Duration: 3FT Hon
Entry Requirements: *GCE:* 240-280. *IB:* 25. *OCR ND:* D *OCR NED:* M2

CL83 BSc Psychology and Sociology
Duration: 3FT Hon
Entry Requirements: *GCE:* 240-280. *IB:* 25. *OCR ND:* D *OCR NED:* M2

C10 CANTERBURY CHRIST CHURCH UNIVERSITY
NORTH HOLMES ROAD
CANTERBURY
KENT CT1 1QU
t: 01227 782900 f: 01227 782888
e: admissions@canterbury.ac.uk
// www.canterbury.ac.uk

MC98 BA Applied Criminology and Psychology
Duration: 3FT Hon
Entry Requirements: *GCE:* 260. *IB:* 24.

M9C8 BA Applied Criminology with Psychology
Duration: 3FT Hon
Entry Requirements: *GCE:* 260. *IB:* 24.

M9CW BA Applied Criminology with Psychology 'International Only'
Duration: 4FT Hon
Entry Requirements: *GCE:* 260. *IB:* 24.

GC58 BA Business Computing and Psychology
Duration: 3FT Hon
Entry Requirements: *GCE:* 260. *IB:* 24.

G5C8 BA Business Computing with Psychology
Duration: 3FT Hon
Entry Requirements: *GCE:* 260. *IB:* 24.

GC4W BA Internet Computing and Psychology
Duration: 3FT Hon
Entry Requirements: *GCE:* 260. *IB:* 24.

G4CW BA Internet Computing with Psychology
Duration: 3FT Hon
Entry Requirements: *GCE:* 260. *IB:* 24.

LC28 BA Politics & Governance and Psychology
Duration: 3FT Hon
Entry Requirements: *GCE:* 260. *IB:* 24.

L2CV BA Politics & Governance with Psychology
Duration: 3FT Hon
Entry Requirements: *GCE:* 260. *IB:* 24.

C8G5 BA Psychology with Business Computing
Duration: 3FT Hon
Entry Requirements: *GCE:* 260. *IB:* 24.

C8GL BA Psychology with Internet Computing
Duration: 3FT Hon
Entry Requirements: *GCE:* 260. *IB:* 24.

C8LG BA Psychology with Politics & Governance
Duration: 3FT Hon
Entry Requirements: *GCE:* 260. *IB:* 24.

NC18 BA/BSc Business Studies and Psychology
Duration: 3FT Hon
Entry Requirements: *GCE:* 260. *IB:* 24.

GC4V BA/BSc Computing and Psychology
Duration: 3FT Hon
Entry Requirements: *GCE:* 260. *IB:* 24.

XC38 BA/BSc Early Childhood Studies and Psychology
Duration: 3FT Hon   CRB Check: Required
Entry Requirements: *GCE:* 260. *IB:* 24.

XC3V BA/BSc Education Studies and Psychology
Duration: 3FT Hon   CRB Check: Required
Entry Requirements: *GCE:* 260. *IB:* 24.

X3CW BA/BSc Education Studies with Psychology
Duration: 3FT Hon   CRB Check: Required
Entry Requirements: *GCE:* 260. *IB:* 24.

W6C8 BA/BSc Film, Radio & Television Studies with Psychology
Duration: 3FT Hon
Entry Requirements: *GCE:* 260. *IB:* 24.

CW81 BA/BSc Fine & Applied Arts and Psychology
Duration: 3FT Hon
Entry Requirements: *GCE:* 260. *IB:* 24.

W1C8 BA/BSc Fine & Applied Arts with Psychology
Duration: 3FT Hon
Entry Requirements: *GCE:* 260. *IB:* 24.

BC98 BA/BSc Health Studies and Psychology
Duration: 3FT Hon
Entry Requirements: *GCE:* 260. *IB:* 24.

NC58 BA/BSc Marketing and Psychology
Duration: 3FT Hon
Entry Requirements: *GCE:* 260. *IB:* 24.

CP83 BA/BSc Media and Communications and Psychology
Duration: 3FT Hon
Entry Requirements: *GCE:* 260. *IB:* 24.

P3C8 BA/BSc Media and Communications with Psychology
Duration: 3FT Hon
Entry Requirements: *GCE:* 260. *IB:* 24.

CW83 BA/BSc Music and Psychology
Duration: 3FT Hon
Entry Requirements: *GCE:* 260. *IB:* 24.

W3C8 BA/BSc Music with Psychology
Duration: 3FT Hon
Entry Requirements: *GCE:* 260. *IB:* 24.

CW86 BA/BSc Psychology and Film, Radio & Television Studies
Duration: 3FT Hon
Entry Requirements: *GCE:* 260. *IB:* 24.

C8MX BA/BSc Psychology with Applied Criminology
Duration: 3FT Hon
Entry Requirements: *GCE:* 260. *IB:* 24.

C8C1 BA/BSc Psychology with Biosciences
Duration: 3FT Hon
Entry Requirements: *GCE:* 260. *IB:* 24.

C8N1 BA/BSc Psychology with Business Studies
Duration: 3FT Hon
Entry Requirements: *GCE:* 260. *IB:* 24.

C8GK BA/BSc Psychology with Computing
Duration: 3FT Hon
Entry Requirements: *GCE:* 260. *IB:* 24.

C8X3 BA/BSc Psychology with Early Childhood Studies
Duration: 3FT Hon   CRB Check: Required
Entry Requirements: *GCE:* 260. *IB:* 24.

C8XJ BA/BSc Psychology with Education Studies
Duration: 3FT Hon   CRB Check: Required
Entry Requirements: *GCE:* 260. *IB:* 24.

C8W6 BA/BSc Psychology with Film, Radio & Television Studies
Duration: 3FT Hon
Entry Requirements: *GCE:* 260. *IB:* 24.

C8W1 BA/BSc Psychology with Fine & Applied Arts
Duration: 3FT Hon
Entry Requirements: *GCE:* 260. *IB:* 24.

C8FK BA/BSc Psychology with Forensic Investigation
Duration: 3FT Hon
Entry Requirements: *GCE:* 260. *IB:* 24.

C8V1 BA/BSc Psychology with History
Duration: 3FT Hon
Entry Requirements: *GCE:* 260. *IB:* 24.

C8N5 BA/BSc Psychology with Marketing
Duration: 3FT Hon
Entry Requirements: *GCE:* 260. *IB:* 24.

C8P3 BA/BSc Psychology with Media and Communications
Duration: 3FT Hon
Entry Requirements: *GCE:* 260. *IB:* 24.

C8W3 BA/BSc Psychology with Music
Duration: 3FT Hon
Entry Requirements: *GCE:* 260. *IB:* 24.

C8N8 BA/BSc Psychology with Tourism & Leisure Studies
Duration: 3FT Hon
Entry Requirements: *GCE:* 260. *IB:* 24.

N8C8 BA/BSc Tourism & Leisure Studies with Psychology
Duration: 3FT Hon
Entry Requirements: *GCE:* 260. *IB:* 24.

CC18 BSc Biosciences and Psychology
Duration: 3FT Hon
Entry Requirements: *GCE:* 260. *IB:* 24.

N1C8 BSc Business Studies with Psychology
Duration: 3FT Hon
Entry Requirements: *GCE:* 260. *IB:* 24.

B9C8 BSc Health Studies with Psychology
Duration: 3FT Hon
Entry Requirements: *GCE:* 260. *IB:* 24.

N5C8 BSc Marketing with Psychology
Duration: 3FT Hon
Entry Requirements: *GCE:* 260. *IB:* 24.

C8B9 BSc Psychology with Health Studies
Duration: 3FT Hon
Entry Requirements: *GCE:* 260. *IB:* 24.

C1C8 BSc/BA Biosciences with Psychology
Duration: 3FT Hon
Entry Requirements: *GCE:* 260. *IB:* 24.

G4CV BSc/BA Computing with Psychology
Duration: 3FT Hon
Entry Requirements: *GCE:* 260. *IB:* 24.

X3C8 BSc/BA Early Childhood Studies with Psychology
Duration: 3FT Hon   CRB Check: Required
Entry Requirements: *GCE:* 260. *IB:* 24.

FC48 BSc/BA Forensic Investigation and Psychology
Duration: 3FT Hon
Entry Requirements: *GCE:* 260. *IB:* 24.

F4C8 BSc/BA Forensic Investigation with Psychology
Duration: 3FT Hon
Entry Requirements: *GCE:* 260. *IB:* 24.

CV81 BSc/BA History and Psychology
Duration: 3FT Hon
Entry Requirements: *GCE:* 260. *IB:* 24.

V1C8 BSc/BA History with Psychology
Duration: 3FT Hon
Entry Requirements: *GCE:* 260. *IB:* 24.

C20 CARDIFF METROPOLITAN UNIVERSITY (UWIC)
ADMISSIONS UNIT
LLANDAFF CAMPUS
WESTERN AVENUE
CARDIFF CF5 2YB
t: 029 2041 6070 f: 029 2041 6286
e: admissions@cardiffmet.ac.uk
// www.cardiffmet.ac.uk

XC38 BA Educational Studies and Psychology
Duration: 3FT Hon   CRB Check: Required
Entry Requirements: *GCE:* 260. *IB:* 24.

C30 UNIVERSITY OF CENTRAL LANCASHIRE
PRESTON
LANCS PR1 2HE
t: 01772 201201 f: 01772 894954
e: uadmissions@uclan.ac.uk
// www.uclan.ac.uk

X3C8 BA/BSc Education and Psychology
Duration: 3FT Hon
Entry Requirements: *Foundation:* Distinction. *GCE:* 260-300. *IB:* 25. *BTEC Dip:* D*D*. *BTEC ExtDip:* DMM. *OCR NED:* M2

C8B1 BSc Forensic Psychology
Duration: 3FT Hon
Entry Requirements: *Foundation:* Distinction. *GCE:* 260-300. *SQAH:* BBBBC-BBCCC. *IB:* 30. *OCR NED:* M2

CN81 BSc Psychology and Business
Duration: 3FT Hon
Entry Requirements: *GCE:* 260-300. *SQAH:* ABBCC-BBBB. *SQAAH:* BBB-CCC. *IB:* 30.

C8B9 BSc Psychology and Counselling & Psychotherapy
Duration: 3FT Hon
Entry Requirements: *Foundation:* Distinction. *GCE:* 260-300. *IB:* 25. *BTEC Dip:* D*D*. *BTEC ExtDip:* DMM. *OCR NED:* M2

CMV9 BSc Psychology and Criminology
Duration: 3FT Hon
Entry Requirements: *Foundation:* Distinction. *GCE:* 260-300. *SQAH:* BBBBC-BBCCC. *IB:* 30. *OCR NED:* M2

CX83 BSc Psychology and Education Studies
Duration: 3FT Hon
Entry Requirements: *GCE:* 260-300. *IB:* 28. *OCR ND:* D *OCR NED:* M2

C55 UNIVERSITY OF CHESTER
PARKGATE ROAD
CHESTER CH1 4BJ
t: 01244 511000 f: 01244 511300
e: enquiries@chester.ac.uk
// www.chester.ac.uk

LC58 BA Counselling Skills and Psychology
Duration: 3FT Hon
Entry Requirements: *Foundation:* Pass. *GCE:* 260-300. *SQAH:* BBBB. *IB:* 28.

WC48 BA Drama & Theatre Studies and Psychology
Duration: 3FT Hon
Entry Requirements: *Foundation:* Pass. *GCE:* 260-300. *SQAH:* BBBB. *IB:* 28.

VC18 BA History and Psychology
Duration: 3FT Hon
Entry Requirements: *GCE:* 260-300. *SQAH:* BBBB. *IB:* 28.

MC18 BA Law and Psychology
Duration: 3FT Hon
Entry Requirements: *Foundation:* Pass. *GCE:* 260-300. *SQAH:* BBBB. *IB:* 28.

DC38 BSc Animal Behaviour and Psychology
Duration: 3FT Hon
Entry Requirements: *GCE:* 260-300. *SQAH:* BBBB. *IB:* 28.

CC18 BSc Biology and Psychology
Duration: 3FT Hon
Entry Requirements: *GCE:* 260-300. *SQAH:* BBBB. *IB:* 28.

MC98 BSc Criminology and Psychology
Duration: 3FT Hon
Entry Requirements: *Foundation:* Pass. *GCE:* 260-300. *SQAH:* BBBB. *IB:* 28.

FC48 BSc Forensic Biology and Psychology
Duration: 3FT Hon
Entry Requirements: *GCE:* 260-300. *SQAH:* BBBB. *IB:* 28.

FC88 BSc Geography and Psychology
Duration: 3FT Hon
Entry Requirements: *GCE:* 260-300. *SQAH:* BBBB. *IB:* 28.

GC18 BSc Mathematics and Psychology
Duration: 3FT Hon
Entry Requirements: *GCE:* 260-300. *SQAH:* BBBB. *IB:* 28.

FC78 BSc Natural Hazard Management and Psychology
Duration: 3FT Hon
Entry Requirements: *GCE:* 260-300. *SQAH:* BBBB. *IB:* 28.

LC38 BSc Psychology and Sociology
Duration: 3FT Hon
Entry Requirements: *Foundation:* Pass. *GCE:* 260-300. *SQAH:* BBBB. *IB:* 28.

C60 CITY UNIVERSITY
NORTHAMPTON SQUARE
LONDON EC1V 0HB
t: 020 7040 5060 f: 020 7040 8995
e: ugadmissions@city.ac.uk
// www.city.ac.uk

CP85 BA Journalism and Psychology (3 years or 4 year SW)
Duration: 3FT Hon
Entry Requirements: *GCE:* AAA. *IB:* 35.

LCH8 BSc Sociology/Psychology
Duration: 3FT Hon
Entry Requirements: *GCE:* AAB. *SQAH:* BBBBC. *IB:* 32.

CL82 Cert International Foundation (Social Sciences)
Duration: 1FT FYr
Entry Requirements: Contact the institution for details.

C78 CORNWALL COLLEGE
POOL
REDRUTH
CORNWALL TR15 3RD
t: 01209 616161 f: 01209 611612
e: he.admissions@cornwall.ac.uk
// www.cornwall.ac.uk

DC38 FdSc Animal Behaviour and Psychology
Duration: 2FT Fdg
Entry Requirements: *GCE:* 120. Interview required.

C85 COVENTRY UNIVERSITY
THE STUDENT CENTRE
COVENTRY UNIVERSITY
1 GULSON RD
COVENTRY CV1 2JH
t: 024 7615 2222 f: 024 7615 2223
e: studentenquiries@coventry.ac.uk
// www.coventry.ac.uk

CM89 BA Criminology and Psychology
Duration: 3FT/4SW Hon
Entry Requirements: *GCE:* BCC. *SQAH:* BCCCC. *IB:* 28. *BTEC ExtDip:* DMM. *OCR NED:* M2

LC38 BA Sociology and Psychology
Duration: 3FT/4SW Hon
Entry Requirements: *GCE:* BCC. *SQAH:* BCCCC. *IB:* 28. *BTEC ExtDip:* DMM. *OCR NED:* M2

CM82 BSc Psychology and Criminology
Duration: 3FT/4SW Hon
Entry Requirements: *GCE:* BBB. *SQAH:* BBBBC. *IB:* 28. *BTEC ExtDip:* DDM. *OCR NED:* M1

D26 DE MONTFORT UNIVERSITY
THE GATEWAY
LEICESTER LE1 9BH
t: 0116 255 1551 f: 0116 250 6204
e: enquiries@dmu.ac.uk
// www.dmu.ac.uk

L3C8 BA Criminology and Criminal Justice with Psychology
Duration: 3FT Hon
Entry Requirements: *GCE:* 260. *IB:* 28. *BTEC Dip:* D*D. *BTEC ExtDip:* DMM. *OCR NED:* M2

X3C8 BA Education Studies with Psychology
Duration: 3FT Hon
Entry Requirements: *GCE:* 280. *IB:* 28. *BTEC Dip:* D*D*. *BTEC ExtDip:* DMM. *OCR NED:* M2 Interview required.

CN86 BA Human Resource Management and Psychology
Duration: 3FT/4SW Hon
Entry Requirements: *GCE:* 280. *IB:* 28. *BTEC Dip:* D*D*. *BTEC ExtDip:* DMM. *OCR NED:* M2 Interview required.

CM81 BA Law and Psychology
Duration: 3FT Hon
Entry Requirements: *GCE:* 280. *IB:* 28. *BTEC Dip:* D*D*. *BTEC ExtDip:* DMM. *OCR NED:* M2 Interview required.

CN85 BA Marketing and Psychology
Duration: 3FT/4SW Hon
Entry Requirements: *GCE:* 280. *IB:* 28. *BTEC Dip:* D*D*. *BTEC ExtDip:* DMM. *OCR NED:* M2 Interview required.

C8X3 BA Psychology with Education Studies
Duration: 3FT Hon
Entry Requirements: *GCE:* 300. *IB:* 30. *BTEC ExtDip:* DDM. *OCR NED:* M1

CX83 BA/BSc Education Studies and Psychology
Duration: 3FT Hon
Entry Requirements: *GCE:* 280. *IB:* 28. *BTEC Dip:* D*D*. *BTEC ExtDip:* DMM. *OCR NED:* M2 Interview required.

C8L3 BSc Psychology with Criminology
Duration: 3FT Hon
Entry Requirements: *GCE:* 300. *IB:* 30. *BTEC ExtDip:* DDM. *OCR NED:* M1

C8B9 BSc Psychology with Health Studies
Duration: 3FT Hon
Entry Requirements: *GCE:* 300. *IB:* 30. *BTEC ExtDip:* DDM. *OCR NED:* M1

D39 UNIVERSITY OF DERBY
KEDLESTON ROAD
DERBY DE22 1GB
t: 01332 591167 f: 01332 597724
e: askadmissions@derby.ac.uk
// www.derby.ac.uk

MC28 BA Applied Criminology and Psychology
Duration: 3FT Hon
Entry Requirements: *Foundation:* Distinction. *GCE:* 260-300. *IB:* 28. *BTEC Dip:* D*D*. *BTEC ExtDip:* DMM. *OCR NED:* M2

CW89 BA Creative Writing and Psychology
Duration: 3FT Hon
Entry Requirements: *Foundation:* Distinction. *GCE:* 260-300. *IB:* 28. *BTEC Dip:* D*D*. *BTEC ExtDip:* DMM. *OCR NED:* M2

CM81 BA Law and Psychology
Duration: 3FT Hon
Entry Requirements: *Foundation:* Distinction. *GCE:* 260-300. *IB:* 28. *BTEC Dip:* D*D*. *BTEC ExtDip:* DMM. *OCR NED:* M2

CL8H BA Psychology and Sociology
Duration: 3FT Hon
Entry Requirements: *Foundation:* Distinction. *GCE:* 260-300. *IB:* 28. *BTEC Dip:* D*D*. *BTEC ExtDip:* DMM. *OCR NED:* M2

NC48 BA/BSc Accounting and Psychology
Duration: 3FT Hon
Entry Requirements: *Foundation:* Distinction. *GCE:* 260-300. *IB:* 28. *BTEC Dip:* D*D*. *BTEC ExtDip:* DMM. *OCR NED:* M2

KC1V BA/BSc Architectural Design and Psychology
Duration: 3FT Hon
Entry Requirements: *Foundation:* Distinction. *GCE:* 260-300. *IB:* 28. *BTEC Dip:* D*D*. *BTEC ExtDip:* DMM. *OCR NED:* M2

WC58 BA/BSc Dance & Movement Studies and Psychology
Duration: 3FT Hon
Entry Requirements: *Foundation:* Distinction. *GCE:* 260-300. *IB:* 28. *BTEC Dip:* D*D*. *BTEC ExtDip:* DMM. *OCR NED:* M2

LC58 BA/BSc Early Childhood Studies and Psychology
Duration: 3FT Hon
Entry Requirements: *Foundation:* Distinction. *GCE:* 260-300. *IB:* 28. *BTEC Dip:* D*D*. *BTEC ExtDip:* DMM. *OCR NED:* M2

PC3V BA/BSc Media Studies and Psychology
Duration: 3FT Hon
Entry Requirements: *Foundation:* Distinction. *GCE:* 260-300. *IB:* 28. *BTEC Dip:* D*D*. *BTEC ExtDip:* DMM. *OCR NED:* M2

WC88 BA/BSc Professional Writing and Psychology
Duration: 3FT Hon
Entry Requirements: *Foundation:* Distinction. *GCE:* 260-300. *IB:* 28. *BTEC Dip:* D*D*. *BTEC ExtDip:* DMM. *OCR NED:* M2

CW8K BA/BSc Psychology and Theatre Studies
Duration: 3FT Hon
Entry Requirements: *Foundation:* Distinction. *GCE:* 260-300. *IB:* 28. *BTEC Dip:* D*D*. *BTEC ExtDip:* DMM. *OCR NED:* M2

CC18 BSc Biology and Psychology
Duration: 3FT Hon
Entry Requirements: *Foundation:* Distinction. *GCE:* 260-300. *IB:* 28. *BTEC Dip:* D*D*. *BTEC ExtDip:* DMM. *OCR NED:* M2

CN8F BSc Business Management and Psychology
Duration: 3FT Hon
Entry Requirements: *Foundation:* Distinction. *GCE:* 260-300. *IB:* 28. *BTEC Dip:* D*D*. *BTEC ExtDip:* DMM. *OCR NED:* M2

FC68 BSc Geology and Psychology
Duration: 3FT Hon
Entry Requirements: *Foundation:* Distinction. *GCE:* 260-300. *IB:* 28. *BTEC Dip:* D*D*. *BTEC ExtDip:* DMM. *OCR NED:* M2

CN8P BSc Human Resource Management and Psychology
Duration: 3FT Hon
Entry Requirements: *Foundation:* Distinction. *GCE:* 260-300. *IB:* 28. *BTEC Dip:* D*D*. *BTEC ExtDip:* DMM. *OCR NED:* M2

CW83 BSc Psychology and Popular Music (Production)
Duration: 3FT Hon
Entry Requirements: *Foundation:* Distinction. *GCE:* 260-300. *IB:* 28. *BTEC Dip:* D*D*. *BTEC ExtDip:* DMM. *OCR NED:* M2

LC98 BSc Third World Development and Psychology
Duration: 3FT Hon
Entry Requirements: *Foundation:* Distinction. *GCE:* 260-300. *IB:* 28. *BTEC Dip:* D*D*. *BTEC ExtDip:* DMM. *OCR NED:* M2

CC38 BSc Zoology and Psychology
Duration: 3FT Hon
Entry Requirements: *Foundation:* Distinction. *GCE:* 260-300. *IB:* 28. *BTEC Dip:* D*D*. *BTEC ExtDip:* DMM. *OCR NED:* M2

D65 UNIVERSITY OF DUNDEE
NETHERGATE
DUNDEE DD1 4HN
t: 01382 383838 f: 01382 388150
e: contactus@dundee.ac.uk
// www.dundee.ac.uk/admissions/undergraduate/

CG81 BSc Mathematics and Psychology
Duration: 4FT Hon
Entry Requirements: *GCE:* BCC. *SQAH:* ABBB. *IB:* 30.

CG84 BSc Psychology and Applied Computing
Duration: 4FT Hon
Entry Requirements: *GCE:* BCC. *SQAH:* ABBB. *IB:* 30.

LNC0 MA Business Economics with Marketing and Psychology
Duration: 4FT Hon
Entry Requirements: *GCE:* BCC. *SQAH:* ABBB. *IB:* 30.

CL87 MA Geography and Psychology
Duration: 4FT Hon
Entry Requirements: *GCE:* BCC. *SQAH:* ABBB. *IB:* 30.

CV81 MA History and Psychology
Duration: 4FT Hon
Entry Requirements: *GCE:* BCC. *SQAH:* ABBB. *IB:* 30.

CV85 MA Philosophy and Psychology
Duration: 4FT Hon
Entry Requirements: *GCE:* BCC. *SQAH:* ABBB. *IB:* 30.

CL82 MA Politics and Psychology
Duration: 4FT Hon
Entry Requirements: *GCE:* BCC. *SQAH:* ABBB. *IB:* 30.

D86 DURHAM UNIVERSITY
DURHAM UNIVERSITY
UNIVERSITY OFFICE
DURHAM DH1 3HP
t: 0191 334 2000 f: 0191 334 6055
e: admissions@durham.ac.uk
// www.durham.ac.uk

X1C8 BA Education Studies (Psychology)
Duration: 3FT Hon
Entry Requirements: *GCE:* AAB. *SQAH:* AAABB. *SQAAH:* AAB. *IB:* 36.

CV85 BA Philosophy and Psychology
Duration: 3FT Hon
Entry Requirements: *GCE:* AAA. *SQAH:* AAAAB. *SQAAH:* AAA. *IB:* 37.

CFG0 BSc Natural Sciences option - Psychology
Duration: 3FT Hon
Entry Requirements: *GCE:* AAA. *SQAAH:* AAA. *IB:* 38.

E28 UNIVERSITY OF EAST LONDON
DOCKLANDS CAMPUS
UNIVERSITY WAY
LONDON E16 2RD
t: 020 8223 3333 f: 020 8223 2978
e: study@uel.ac.uk
// www.uel.ac.uk

L6C8 BA Anthropology with Psychology
Duration: 3FT Hon
Entry Requirements: *GCE:* 240. *IB:* 24.

CP89 BA Communication Studies/Psychosocial Studies
Duration: 3FT Hon
Entry Requirements: *GCE:* 240. *IB:* 24.

W8C8 BA Creative and Professional Writing with Psychology
Duration: 3FT Hon
Entry Requirements: *GCE:* 240. *IB:* 24.

M9C8 BA Criminology with Psychology
Duration: 3FT Hon
Entry Requirements: *GCE:* 240. *IB:* 24.

MC98 BA Criminology with Psychosocial Studies
Duration: 3FT Hon
Entry Requirements: *GCE:* 240. *IB:* 24.

M9CW BA Criminology/Psychosocial Studies
Duration: 3FT Hon
Entry Requirements: *GCE:* 240. *IB:* 24.

WFC8 BA Digital Fashion with Psychology
Duration: 3FT Hon
Entry Requirements: *GCE:* 240. *IB:* 24. Portfolio required.

X3C8 BA Early Childhood Studies with Psychology
Duration: 3FT Hon
Entry Requirements: *GCE:* 240. *IB:* 24.

CV81 BA History/Psychosocial Studies
Duration: 3FT Hon
Entry Requirements: *GCE:* 240. *IB:* 24.

N6C8 BA Human Resource Management with Psychology
Duration: 3FT Hon
Entry Requirements: *GCE:* 240. *IB:* 24.

CM81 BA Law/Psychosocial Studies
Duration: 3FT Hon
Entry Requirements: *GCE:* 240. *IB:* 28.

C8XH BA Psychosocial Studies with Early Childhood Studies
Duration: 3FT Hon
Entry Requirements: *GCE:* 240. *IB:* 24.

L3CV BA Sociology with Psychology
Duration: 3FT Hon
Entry Requirements: *GCE:* 240. *IB:* 24.

CL83 BA Sociology/Psychosocial Studies
Duration: 3FT Hon
Entry Requirements: *GCE:* 240. *IB:* 24.

X3CV BA Special Needs and Inclusive Education with Psychology
Duration: 3FT Hon
Entry Requirements: *GCE:* 240. *IB:* 24.

L5C8 BA Youth & Community Work with Psychology
Duration: 3FT Hon
Entry Requirements: *GCE:* 240. *IB:* 24.

LC68 BA/BSc Anthropology/Psychosocial Studies
Duration: 3FT Hon
Entry Requirements: *GCE:* 240. *IB:* 24.

B9CV BSc Clinical Science with Psychology
Duration: 3FT Hon
Entry Requirements: *GCE:* 240. *IB:* 24.

G4C8 BSc Computer Networks with Psychology
Duration: 3FT Hon
Entry Requirements: *GCE:* 240. *IB:* 24.

G4CW BSc Computing with Psychology
Duration: 3FT Hon
Entry Requirements: *GCE:* 240. *IB:* 24.

C1C8 BSc Human Biology with Psychology
Duration: 3FT Hon
Entry Requirements: *GCE:* 240. *IB:* 24.

C8N5 BSc Psychology with Advertising
Duration: 3FT Hon
Entry Requirements: *GCE:* 240. *IB:* 24.

C8I1 BSc Psychology with Computing
Duration: 3FT Hon
Entry Requirements: *GCE:* 240. *IB:* 24.

C8M9 BSc Psychology with Criminology
Duration: 3FT Hon
Entry Requirements: *GCE:* 240. *IB:* 24.

C8X3 BSc Psychology with Early Childhood Studies
Duration: 3FT Hon
Entry Requirements: *GCE:* 240. *IB:* 24.

C8W2 BSc Psychology with Graphic Design
Duration: 3FT Hon
Entry Requirements: *GCE:* 240. *IB:* 24.

C8C1 BSc Psychology with Human Biology
Duration: 3FT Hon
Entry Requirements: *GCE:* 240. *IB:* 24.

C8N6 BSc Psychology with Human Resource Management
Duration: 3FT Hon
Entry Requirements: *GCE:* 240. *IB:* 24.

C8L3 BSc Psychology with Sociology
Duration: 3FT Hon
Entry Requirements: *GCE:* 240. *IB:* 24.

C8X1 BSc Psychology with Special Needs and Inclusive Education
Duration: 3FT Hon
Entry Requirements: *GCE:* 240. *IB:* 24.

E56 THE UNIVERSITY OF EDINBURGH
STUDENT RECRUITMENT & ADMISSIONS
57 GEORGE SQUARE
EDINBURGH EH8 9JU
t: 0131 650 4360 f: 0131 651 1236
e: sra.enquiries@ed.ac.uk
// www.ed.ac.uk/studying/undergraduate/

VC58 MA Philosophy and Psychology
Duration: 4FT Hon
Entry Requirements: *GCE:* AAA-BBB. *SQAH:* AAAA-BBBB. *IB:* 34.

CN81 MA Psychology and Business Studies
Duration: 4FT Hon
Entry Requirements: *GCE:* AAA-BBB. *SQAH:* AAAA-BBBB. *IB:* 34.

LC38 MA Sociology and Psychology
Duration: 4FT Hon
Entry Requirements: *GCE:* AAA-BBB. *SQAH:* AABB-BBBB. *IB:* 34.

E59 EDINBURGH NAPIER UNIVERSITY
CRAIGLOCKHART CAMPUS
EDINBURGH EH14 1DJ
t: +44 (0)8452 60 60 40 f: 0131 455 6464
e: info@napier.ac.uk
// www.napier.ac.uk

CL83 BA Psychology and Sociology
Duration: 3FT/4FT Ord/Hon
Entry Requirements: *GCE:* 230.

LC38 BA Social Sciences
Duration: 3FT/4FT Ord/Hon
Entry Requirements: *GCE:* 230.

E70 THE UNIVERSITY OF ESSEX
WIVENHOE PARK
COLCHESTER
ESSEX CO4 3SQ
t: 01206 873666 f: 01206 874477
e: admit@essex.ac.uk
// www.essex.ac.uk

CLV3 BSc Social Psychology and Sociology (Including Year Abroad)
Duration: 4FT Hon
Entry Requirements: Contact the institution for details.

F66 FARNBOROUGH COLLEGE OF TECHNOLOGY
BOUNDARY ROAD
FARNBOROUGH
HAMPSHIRE GU14 6SB
t: 01252 407028 f: 01252 407041
e: admissions@farn-ct.ac.uk
// www.farn-ct.ac.uk

CN85 BA Psychology and Marketing
Duration: 2FT Hon
Entry Requirements: *GCE:* 240. *OCR ND:* M2 *OCR NED:* M3
Admissions Test required.

CL83 BSc Psychology and Criminology
Duration: 2FT Hon
Entry Requirements: *GCE:* 240.

G14 UNIVERSITY OF GLAMORGAN, CARDIFF AND PONTYPRIDD
ENQUIRIES AND ADMISSIONS UNIT
PONTYPRIDD CF37 1DL
t: 08456 434030 f: 01443 654050
e: enquiries@glam.ac.uk
// www.glam.ac.uk

M9C8 BSc Criminology with Psychology
Duration: 3FT Hon
Entry Requirements: *GCE:* BBC. *IB:* 25. *BTEC SubDip:* M. *BTEC Dip:* D*D*. *BTEC ExtDip:* DMM.

CX83 BSc Early Years Development and Education
Duration: 3FT Hon
Entry Requirements: *GCE:* BBC. *IB:* 25. *BTEC SubDip:* M. *BTEC Dip:* D*D*. *BTEC ExtDip:* DMM.

C8M9 BSc Psychology with Criminology
Duration: 3FT Hon
Entry Requirements: *GCE:* BBC. *IB:* 25. *BTEC SubDip:* M. *BTEC Dip:* D*D*. *BTEC ExtDip:* DMM.

C8X3 BSc Psychology with Education
Duration: 3FT Hon
Entry Requirements: *GCE:* BBC. *IB:* 25. *BTEC SubDip:* M. *BTEC Dip:* D*D*. *BTEC ExtDip:* DMM.

C8L3 BSc Psychology with Sociology
Duration: 3FT Hon
Entry Requirements: *GCE:* BBC. *IB:* 25. *BTEC SubDip:* M. *BTEC Dip:* D*D*. *BTEC ExtDip:* DMM.

L3C8 BSc Sociology with Psychology
Duration: 3FT Hon
Entry Requirements: *GCE:* BBC. *IB:* 25. *BTEC SubDip:* M. *BTEC Dip:* D*D*. *BTEC ExtDip:* DMM.

G28 UNIVERSITY OF GLASGOW
71 SOUTHPARK AVENUE
UNIVERSITY OF GLASGOW
GLASGOW G12 8QQ
t: 0141 330 6062 f: 0141 330 2961
e: student.recruitment@glasgow.ac.uk
// www.glasgow.ac.uk

GC18 BSc Applied Mathematics and Psychology
Duration: 4FT Hon
Entry Requirements: *GCE:* ABB. *SQAH:* AAAA-AABB. *IB:* 36.

CG84 BSc Computing Science/Psychology
Duration: 4FT Hon
Entry Requirements: *GCE:* ABB. *SQAH:* AAAA-AABB. *IB:* 36.

CG81 BSc Mathematics and Psychology
Duration: 4FT Hon
Entry Requirements: *GCE:* ABB. *SQAH:* AAAA-AABB. *IB:* 36.

BC18 BSc Physiology/Psychology
Duration: 4FT Hon
Entry Requirements: *GCE:* ABB. *SQAH:* AAAA-AABB. *IB:* 32.

CG83 BSc Psychology/Statistics
Duration: 4FT Hon
Entry Requirements: *GCE:* ABB. *SQAH:* AAAA-AABB. *IB:* 36.

CV84 MA Archaeology/Psychology
Duration: 4FT Hon
Entry Requirements: *GCE:* ABB. *SQAH:* AAAB-ABBB. *IB:* 36.

VC48 MA Archaeology/Psychology
Duration: 4FT Hon
Entry Requirements: *GCE:* ABB. *SQAH:* AAAA-AABB. *IB:* 36.

CN82 MA Business & Management/Psychology
Duration: 4FT Hon
Entry Requirements: *GCE:* ABB. *SQAH:* AAAA-AABB. *IB:* 36.

LC18 MA Business Economics/Psychology
Duration: 4FT Hon
Entry Requirements: *GCE:* ABB. *SQAH:* AAAA-AABB. *IB:* 36.

CGV4 MA Computing Science/Psychology
Duration: 4FT Hon
Entry Requirements: *GCE:* ABB. *SQAH:* AAAA-AABB. *IB:* 36.

GC48 MA Computing/Psychology
Duration: 4FT Hon
Entry Requirements: *GCE:* ABB. *SQAH:* AAAB-ABBB. *IB:* 36.

GC5V MA Digital Media & Information Studies/Psychology
Duration: 4FT Hon
Entry Requirements: *GCE:* ABB. *SQAH:* AAAB-ABBB. *IB:* 36.

CV83 MA Economic & Social History/Psychology
Duration: 4FT Hon
Entry Requirements: *GCE:* ABB. *SQAH:* AAAA-AABB. *IB:* 36.

CL81 MA Economics/Psychology
Duration: 4FT Hon
Entry Requirements: *GCE:* ABB. *SQAH:* AAAA-AABB. *IB:* 36.

CVV3 MA History of Art/Psychology
Duration: 4FT Hon
Entry Requirements: *GCE:* ABB. *SQAH:* AAAB-ABBB. *IB:* 36.

CV81 MA History/Psychology
Duration: 4FT Hon
Entry Requirements: *GCE:* ABB. *SQAH:* AAAB-ABBB. *IB:* 36.

VC18 MA History/Psychology
Duration: 4FT Hon
Entry Requirements: *GCE:* ABB. *SQAH:* AAAA-AABB. *IB:* 36.

CW83 MA Music/Psychology
Duration: 4FT Hon
Entry Requirements: *GCE:* ABB. *SQAH:* AAAB-ABBB. *IB:* 36.

CV85 MA Philosophy/Psychology
Duration: 4FT Hon
Entry Requirements: *GCE:* ABB. *SQAH:* AAAA-AABB. *IB:* 36.

CVV5 MA Philosophy/Psychology
Duration: 4FT Hon
Entry Requirements: *GCE:* ABB. *SQAH:* AAAB-ABBB. *IB:* 36.

CL82 MA Politics/Psychology
Duration: 4FT Hon
Entry Requirements: *GCE:* ABB. *SQAH:* AAAA-AABB. *IB:* 36.

LC48 MA Psychology/Public Policy
Duration: 4FT Hon
Entry Requirements: *GCE:* ABB. *SQAH:* AAAA-AABB. *IB:* 36.

CVV2 MA Psychology/Scottish History
Duration: 4FT Hon
Entry Requirements: *GCE:* ABB. *SQAH:* AAAA-AABB. *IB:* 36.

CVW2 MA Psychology/Scottish History
Duration: 4FT Hon
Entry Requirements: *GCE:* ABB. *SQAH:* AAAB-ABBB. *IB:* 36.

LC38 MA Psychology/Sociology
Duration: 4FT Hon
Entry Requirements: *GCE:* ABB. *SQAH:* AAAA-AABB. *IB:* 36.

CW84 MA Psychology/Theatre Studies
Duration: 4FT Hon
Entry Requirements: *GCE:* ABB. *SQAH:* AAAB-ABBB. *IB:* 36.

CV86 MA Psychology/Theology & Religious Studies
Duration: 4FT Hon
Entry Requirements: *GCE:* ABB. *SQAH:* AAAB-ABBB. *IB:* 36.

LC68 MA Sociology/Psychology
Duration: 4FT Hon
Entry Requirements: *GCE:* ABB. *SQAH:* AAAB-ABBB. *IB:* 36.

G42 GLASGOW CALEDONIAN UNIVERSITY
STUDENT RECRUITMENT & ADMISSIONS SERVICE
CITY CAMPUS
COWCADDENS ROAD
GLASGOW G4 0BA
t: 0141 331 3000 f: 0141 331 8676
e: undergraduate@gcu.ac.uk
// www.gcu.ac.uk

CL03 BSc Human Biology, Sociology and Psychology
Duration: 4FT Hon
Entry Requirements: *GCE:* BCC. *SQAH:* AAA-BBBC. *IB:* 24.

C8G4 BSc Psychology with Interactive Entertainment
Duration: 4FT Hon
Entry Requirements: *GCE:* CCC. *SQAH:* BBBCC-BBCC. *IB:* 28.
OCR NED: M3

G50 THE UNIVERSITY OF GLOUCESTERSHIRE
PARK CAMPUS
THE PARK
CHELTENHAM GL50 2RH
t: 01242 714501 f: 01242 714869
e: admissions@glos.ac.uk
// www.glos.ac.uk

LC38 BA/BSc Psychology and Sociology
Duration: 3FT Hon
Entry Requirements: *GCE:* 280-300.

MC98 BSc Criminology and Psychology
Duration: 3FT Hon
Entry Requirements: *GCE:* 280-300.

G70 UNIVERSITY OF GREENWICH
GREENWICH CAMPUS
OLD ROYAL NAVAL COLLEGE
PARK ROW
LONDON SE10 9LS
t: 020 8331 9000 f: 020 8331 8145
e: courseinfo@gre.ac.uk
// www.gre.ac.uk

XC38 BA Education and Psychology
Duration: 3FT Hon
Entry Requirements: *GCE:* 320. *IB:* 24.

X3C8 BA Education with Psychology
Duration: 3FT Hon
Entry Requirements: *GCE:* 320. *IB:* 24.

C8B9 BSc Psychology with Counselling
Duration: 3FT Hon
Entry Requirements: *GCE:* 320. *IB:* 24.

LC38 BSc Sociology and Psychology
Duration: 3FT Hon
Entry Requirements: *GCE:* 240. *IB:* 24.

H14 HAVERING COLLEGE OF FURTHER AND HIGHER EDUCATION
ARDLEIGH GREEN ROAD
HORNCHURCH
ESSEX RM11 2LL
t: 01708 462793 f: 01708 462736
e: HE@havering-college.ac.uk
// www.havering-college.ac.uk

BCX8 BA Integrative Counselling and Psychotherapy
Duration: 3FT Hon
Entry Requirements: Contact the institution for details.

H24 HERIOT-WATT UNIVERSITY, EDINBURGH
EDINBURGH CAMPUS
EDINBURGH EH14 4AS
t: 0131 449 5111 f: 0131 451 3630
e: ugadmissions@hw.ac.uk
// www.hw.ac.uk

G1C8 BSc Mathematics with Psychology
Duration: 3FT/4FT Hon
Entry Requirements: *GCE:* BBB. *SQAH:* ABBBC. *SQAAH:* BBB. *IB:* 26.

CF84 BSc Psychology (Forensic Science)
Duration: 4FT Hon
Entry Requirements: *GCE:* BBB. *SQAH:* BBBBC. *SQAAH:* BB. *IB:* 27.

C8B9 BSc Psychology with Human Health
Duration: 4FT Hon
Entry Requirements: *GCE:* BBB. *SQAH:* BBBBC. *SQAAH:* BB. *IB:* 27.

C8N2 BSc Psychology with Management
Duration: 4FT Hon
Entry Requirements: *GCE:* BBB. *SQAH:* BBBBC. *SQAAH:* BB. *IB:* 27.

H36 UNIVERSITY OF HERTFORDSHIRE
UNIVERSITY ADMISSIONS SERVICE
COLLEGE LANE
HATFIELD
HERTS AL10 9AB
t: 01707 284800
// www.herts.ac.uk

N1C8 BSc Business/Psychology
Duration: 3FT/4SW Hon
Entry Requirements: *GCE:* 320.

B9C8 BSc Health Studies/Psychology
Duration: 3FT/4SW Hon
Entry Requirements: *GCE:* 320.

B1C8 BSc Human Biology/Psychology
Duration: 3FT/4SW Hon
Entry Requirements: *GCE:* 320.

L7C8 BSc Human Geography/Psychology
Duration: 3FT/4SW Hon
Entry Requirements: *GCE:* 320.

M1C8 BSc Law/Psychology
Duration: 3FT/4SW Hon
Entry Requirements: *GCE:* 320.

G1C8 BSc Mathematics/Psychology
Duration: 3FT/4SW Hon
Entry Requirements: *GCE:* 320.

V5C8 BSc Philosophy/Psychology
Duration: 3FT/4SW Hon
Entry Requirements: *GCE:* 320.

C8N1 BSc Psychology/Business
Duration: 3FT/4SW Hon
Entry Requirements: *GCE:* 320.

C8B9 BSc Psychology/Health Studies
Duration: 3FT/4SW Hon
Entry Requirements: *GCE:* 320.

C8B1 BSc Psychology/Human Biology
Duration: 3FT/4SW Hon
Entry Requirements: *GCE:* 320.

C8L7 BSc Psychology/Human Geography
Duration: 3FT/4SW Hon
Entry Requirements: *GCE:* 320.

C8M1 BSc Psychology/Law
Duration: 3FT/4SW Hon
Entry Requirements: *GCE:* 320.

C8G1 BSc Psychology/Mathematics
Duration: 3FT/4SW Hon
Entry Requirements: *GCE:* 320.

C8V5 BSc Psychology/Philosophy
Duration: 3FT/4SW Hon
Entry Requirements: *GCE:* 320.

H60 THE UNIVERSITY OF HUDDERSFIELD
QUEENSGATE
HUDDERSFIELD HD1 3DH
t: 01484 473969 f: 01484 472765
e: admissionsandrecords@hud.ac.uk
// www.hud.ac.uk

NC18 BA Business and Psychology
Duration: 3FT/4SW Hon
Entry Requirements: *GCE:* 300. *SQAH:* BBBB. *IB:* 26.

C8B9 BSc Psychology with Counselling
Duration: 3FT Hon
Entry Requirements: *GCE:* 300. *SQAH:* BBBB.

C8M2 BSc Psychology with Criminology
Duration: 3FT Hon
Entry Requirements: *GCE:* 300.

CL83 BSc Sociology and Psychology
Duration: 3FT Hon
Entry Requirements: *GCE:* 280.

H72 THE UNIVERSITY OF HULL
THE UNIVERSITY OF HULL
COTTINGHAM ROAD
HULL HU6 7RX
t: 01482 466100 f: 01482 442290
e: admissions@hull.ac.uk
// www.hull.ac.uk

M9C8 BA Criminology with Psychology
Duration: 3FT Hon
Entry Requirements: *GCE:* 280-320. *IB:* 28. *BTEC ExtDip:* DMM.

V5C8 BSc Philosophy with Psychology
Duration: 3FT Hon
Entry Requirements: *GCE:* 280-320. *IB:* 28. *BTEC ExtDip:* DMM.

C8M9 BSc Psychology with Criminology
Duration: 3FT Hon
Entry Requirements: *GCE:* 280. *IB:* 32. *BTEC ExtDip:* DMM.

C8V5 BSc Psychology with Philosophy
Duration: 3FT Hon
Entry Requirements: *GCE:* 280. *IB:* 32. *BTEC ExtDip:* DMM.

C8L3 BSc Psychology with Sociology
Duration: 3FT Hon
Entry Requirements: *GCE:* 280. *IB:* 32. *BTEC ExtDip:* DMM.

K12 KEELE UNIVERSITY
KEELE UNIVERSITY
STAFFORDSHIRE ST5 5BG
t: 01782 734005 f: 01782 632343
e: undergraduate@keele.ac.uk
// www.keele.ac.uk

NC4V BSc Accounting and Psychology
Duration: 3FT Hon
Entry Requirements: *GCE:* ABB.

FC98 BSc Applied Environmental Science and Psychology
Duration: 3FT Hon
Entry Requirements: *GCE:* BBC.

CC87 BSc Biochemistry and Psychology
Duration: 3FT Hon
Entry Requirements: *GCE:* BBC.

CC81 BSc Biology and Psychology
Duration: 3FT Hon
Entry Requirements: *GCE:* BBC.

CN89 BSc Business Management and Psychology
Duration: 3FT Hon
Entry Requirements: *GCE:* ABB.

CF81 BSc Chemistry and Psychology
Duration: 3FT Hon
Entry Requirements: *GCE:* BBC.

CG84 BSc Computer Science and Psychology
Duration: 3FT Hon
Entry Requirements: *GCE:* BBC.

GC4V BSc Creative Computing and Psychology
Duration: 3FT Hon
Entry Requirements: *GCE:* BBC.

CM81 BSc Criminology and Psychology
Duration: 3FT Hon
Entry Requirements: *GCE:* BBC.

CL81 BSc Economics and Psychology
Duration: 3FT Hon
Entry Requirements: *GCE:* ABB.

CX83 BSc Educational Studies and Psychology
Duration: 3FT Hon
Entry Requirements: *GCE:* BBC.

FC48 BSc Forensic Science and Psychology
Duration: 3FT Hon
Entry Requirements: *GCE:* BBC.

CF86 BSc Geology and Psychology
Duration: 3FT Hon
Entry Requirements: *GCE:* BBC.

CV81 BSc History and Psychology
Duration: 3FT Hon
Entry Requirements: *GCE:* BBB.

CC1V BSc Human Biology and Psychology
Duration: 3FT Hon
Entry Requirements: *GCE:* BBC.

CN86 BSc Human Resource Management and Psychology
Duration: 3FT Hon
Entry Requirements: *GCE:* ABB.

NC18 BSc International Business and Psychology
Duration: 3FT Hon
Entry Requirements: *GCE:* ABB.

CN85 BSc Marketing and Psychology
Duration: 3FT Hon
Entry Requirements: *GCE:* ABB.

CG81 BSc Mathematics and Psychology
Duration: 3FT Hon
Entry Requirements: *GCE:* BBC.

PC38 BSc Media, Communications & Culture and Psychology
Duration: 3FT Hon
Entry Requirements: *GCE:* BBC.

CFV1 BSc Medicinal Chemistry and Psychology
Duration: 3FT Hon
Entry Requirements: *GCE:* BBC.

CWV3 BSc Music Technology and Psychology
Duration: 3FT Hon
Entry Requirements: *GCE:* BBC.

CW83 BSc Music and Psychology
Duration: 3FT Hon
Entry Requirements: *GCE:* BBC.

BC18 BSc Neuroscience and Psychology
Duration: 3FT Hon
Entry Requirements: *GCE:* BBC.

CV85 BSc Philosophy and Psychology
Duration: 3FT Hon
Entry Requirements: *GCE:* BBB.

CL82 BSc Politics and Psychology
Duration: 3FT Hon
Entry Requirements: *GCE:* BBB.

CG8L BSc Psychology and Information Systems
Duration: 3FT Hon
Entry Requirements: *GCE:* BBC.

CL83 BSc Psychology and Sociology
Duration: 3FT Hon
Entry Requirements: *GCE:* BBC.

GC78 BSc Smart Systems and Psychology
Duration: 3FT Hon
Entry Requirements: *GCE:* BBC.

K24 THE UNIVERSITY OF KENT
RECRUITMENT & ADMISSIONS OFFICE
REGISTRY
UNIVERSITY OF KENT
CANTERBURY, KENT CT2 7NZ
t: 01227 827272 f: 01227 827077
e: information@kent.ac.uk
// www.kent.ac.uk

CM81 BSc Psychology and Law (4 years)
Duration: 4FT Hon
Entry Requirements: *GCE:* AAB. *SQAH:* AAAAB. *SQAAH:* AAB. *IB:* 33. *OCR ND:* D *OCR NED:* D1

CL86 BSc Psychology and Social Anthropology
Duration: 3FT Hon
Entry Requirements: *GCE:* AAB. *SQAH:* AAAAB. *SQAAH:* AAB. *IB:* 33. *OCR ND:* D *OCR NED:* D1

CL83 BSc Psychology and Sociology
Duration: 3FT Hon
Entry Requirements: *GCE:* AAB. *SQAH:* AAAAB. *SQAAH:* AAB. *IB:* 33. *OCR ND:* D *OCR NED:* D1

K84 KINGSTON UNIVERSITY
STUDENT INFORMATION & ADVICE CENTRE
COOPER HOUSE
40-46 SURBITON ROAD
KINGSTON UPON THAMES KT1 2HX
t: 0844 8552177 f: 020 8547 7080
e: aps@kingston.ac.uk
// www.kingston.ac.uk

WC88 BA Creative Writing and Psychology
Duration: 3FT Hon
Entry Requirements: *GCE:* 220-360.

W8C8 BA Creative Writing with Psychology
Duration: 3FT Hon
Entry Requirements: *GCE:* 220-360.

LC38 BA Criminology and Psychology
Duration: 3FT Hon
Entry Requirements: *GCE:* 240-320. *SQAH:* BBCCC. *SQAAH:* BBC.

M9C8 BA Criminology with Psychology
Duration: 3FT Hon
Entry Requirements: *GCE:* 240-320. *SQAH:* BBCCC. *SQAAH:* BBC.

WC48 BA Drama and Psychology
Duration: 3FT Hon
Entry Requirements: *GCE:* 300-360. *SQAH:* BBCCC. *SQAAH:* BBC.

W4C8 BA Drama with Psychology
Duration: 3FT Hon
Entry Requirements: *GCE:* 300-360. *SQAH:* BBCCC. *SQAAH:* BBC.

VC18 BA History and Psychology
Duration: 3FT Hon
Entry Requirements: *GCE:* 240-360.

V1C8 BA History with Psychology
Duration: 3FT Hon
Entry Requirements: *GCE:* 240-360.

LC28 BA Human Rights and Psychology
Duration: 3FT Hon
Entry Requirements: *GCE:* 240-360.

L2CV BA Human Rights with Psychology
Duration: 3FT Hon
Entry Requirements: *GCE:* 240-360.

LCF8 BA International Relations and Psychology
Duration: 3FT Hon
Entry Requirements: *GCE:* 240-360.

PC58 BA Journalism and Psychology
Duration: 3FT Hon
Entry Requirements: *GCE:* 340. *SQAH:* BBCCC. *SQAAH:* BBC. *IB:* 25.

P5C8 BA Journalism with Psychology
Duration: 3FT Hon
Entry Requirements: *GCE:* 340. *SQAH:* BBCCC. *SQAAH:* BBC. *IB:* 25.

PC38 BA Media & Cultural Studies and Psychology
Duration: 3FT Hon
Entry Requirements: *GCE:* 260-360.

P3C8 BA Media & Cultural Studies with Psychology
Duration: 3FT Hon
Entry Requirements: *GCE:* 260-360.

LCG8 BA Politics and Psychology
Duration: 3FT Hon
Entry Requirements: *GCE:* 240-360.

L2C8 BA Politics with Psychology
Duration: 3FT Hon
Entry Requirements: *GCE:* 240-360.

CP83 BA Psychology and Television & New Broadcasting Media
Duration: 3FT Hon
Entry Requirements: *GCE:* 240-360.

C8N1 BA Psychology with Business
Duration: 3FT Hon
Entry Requirements: *GCE:* 280.

CN81 BA Psychology with Business Studies
Duration: 3FT Hon
Entry Requirements: *GCE:* 280.

C8W8 BA Psychology with Creative Writing
Duration: 3FT Hon
Entry Requirements: *GCE:* 240-360.

C8M9 BA Psychology with Criminology
Duration: 3FT Hon
Entry Requirements: *GCE:* 240-320.

C8LF BA Psychology with Human Rights
Duration: 3FT Hon
Entry Requirements: *GCE:* 240-360.

C8LG BA Psychology with International Relations
Duration: 3FT Hon
Entry Requirements: *GCE:* 240-360.

C8P5 BA Psychology with Journalism
Duration: 3FT Hon
Entry Requirements: *GCE:* 340.

C8P3 BA Psychology with Media & Cultural Studies
Duration: 3FT Hon
Entry Requirements: *GCE:* 260-360.

C8PH BA Psychology with Television & New Broadcasting Media
Duration: 3FT Hon
Entry Requirements: *GCE:* 240-360.

P3CV BA Television & New Broadcasting Media with Psychology
Duration: 3FT Hon
Entry Requirements: *GCE:* 240-360.

NC18 BSc Business and Psychology
Duration: 3FT Hon
Entry Requirements: *GCE:* 280.

L2CW BSc International Relations with Psychology
Duration: 3FT Hon
Entry Requirements: *GCE:* 240-360.

CL83 BSc Psychology and Sociology
Duration: 3FT Hon
Entry Requirements: *GCE:* 240-360.

C8W4 BSc Psychology with Drama
Duration: 3FT Hon
Entry Requirements: *GCE:* 300-360.

C8V1 BSc Psychology with History
Duration: 3FT Hon
Entry Requirements: *GCE:* 240-360.

C8L2 BSc Psychology with Politics
Duration: 3FT Hon
Entry Requirements: *GCE:* 240-360.

C8L3 BSc Psychology with Sociology
Duration: 3FT Hon
Entry Requirements: *GCE:* 240-360.

L3C8 BSc Sociology with Psychology
Duration: 3FT Hon
Entry Requirements: *GCE:* 240-360.

L14 LANCASTER UNIVERSITY
THE UNIVERSITY
LANCASTER
LANCASHIRE LA1 4YW
t: 01524 592029 f: 01524 846243
e: ugadmissions@lancaster.ac.uk
// www.lancs.ac.uk

CN82 BA Organisation Studies and Psychology
Duration: 3FT Hon
Entry Requirements: *GCE:* AAB. *SQAH:* ABBBB. *SQAAH:* AAB. *IB:* 35.

C1C8 BSc Biology with Psychology
Duration: 3FT Hon
Entry Requirements: *GCE:* AAB. *SQAH:* ABBBB. *SQAAH:* AAB. *IB:* 35.

N5C8 BSc Marketing with Psychology
Duration: 3FT Hon
Entry Requirements: *GCE:* AAB. *SQAH:* ABBBB. *SQAAH:* AAB. *IB:* 35.

CG83 BSc Psychology and Statistics
Duration: 3FT Hon
Entry Requirements: *GCE:* AAB. *SQAH:* ABBBB. *SQAAH:* ABB. *IB:* 35.

L27 LEEDS METROPOLITAN UNIVERSITY
COURSE ENQUIRIES OFFICE
CITY CAMPUS
LEEDS LS1 3HE
t: 0113 81 23113 f: 0113 81 23129
// www.leedsmet.ac.uk

MC98 BA Criminology & Psychology
Duration: 3FT Hon
Entry Requirements: *GCE:* 200. *IB:* 24.

C8M9 BSc Psychology with Criminology
Duration: 3FT Hon
Entry Requirements: *GCE:* 260. *IB:* 24.

L34 UNIVERSITY OF LEICESTER
UNIVERSITY ROAD
LEICESTER LE1 7RH
t: 0116 252 5281 f: 0116 252 2447
e: admissions@le.ac.uk
// www.le.ac.uk

C8C9 BSc Psychology with Biological Sciences
Duration: 3FT Hon
Entry Requirements: Contact the institution for details.

C8BC BSc Psychology with Cognitive Neuroscience
Duration: 3FT Hon
Entry Requirements: *GCE:* AAB. *SQAH:* AAAAB-AAABB. *SQAAH:* AAB. *IB:* 34.

C8L3 BSc Psychology with Sociology
Duration: 3FT Hon
Entry Requirements: *GCE:* ABB. *SQAH:* AABBB. *SQAAH:* ABB. *IB:* 32.

L39 UNIVERSITY OF LINCOLN
ADMISSIONS
BRAYFORD POOL
LINCOLN LN6 7TS
t: 01522 886097 f: 01522 886146
e: admissions@lincoln.ac.uk
// www.lincoln.ac.uk

CN85 BA/BSc Marketing and Psychology
Duration: 3FT Hon
Entry Requirements: *GCE:* 300.

CM89 BA/BSc Psychology and Criminology
Duration: 3FT Hon
Entry Requirements: *GCE:* 300.

CL84 BA/BSc Psychology and Social Policy
Duration: 3FT Hon
Entry Requirements: *GCE:* 300.

L41 THE UNIVERSITY OF LIVERPOOL
THE FOUNDATION BUILDING
BROWNLOW HILL
LIVERPOOL L69 7ZX
t: 0151 794 2000 f: 0151 708 6502
e: ugrecruitment@liv.ac.uk
// www.liv.ac.uk

BCG0 BSc Combined Honours option - Psychology
Duration: 3FT Hon
Entry Requirements: *GCE:* AAB-BBC. *SQAAH:* AAB-BBC.

L46 LIVERPOOL HOPE UNIVERSITY
HOPE PARK
LIVERPOOL L16 9JD
t: 0151 291 3331 f: 0151 291 3434
e: administration@hope.ac.uk
// www.hope.ac.uk

N4C8 BA Accounting and Psychology
Duration: 3FT Hon
Entry Requirements: *GCE:* 300-320. *IB:* 25.

VC38 BA Art & Design History and Psychology
Duration: 3FT Hon
Entry Requirements: *GCE:* 300-320. *IB:* 25. Interview required.

VC68 BA Christian Theology and Psychology
Duration: 3FT Hon
Entry Requirements: *GCE:* 300-320. *IB:* 25.

LC38 BA Criminology and Psychology
Duration: 3FT Hon
Entry Requirements: *GCE:* 300-320. *IB:* 25.

W5C8 BA Dance and Psychology
Duration: 3FT Hon
Entry Requirements: *GCE:* 300-320. *IB:* 25.

W1C8 BA Fine Art & Psychology
Duration: 3FT Hon
Entry Requirements: *GCE:* 300-320. *IB:* 25.

VC1V BA History and Psychology
Duration: 3FT Hon
Entry Requirements: *GCE:* 300-320. *IB:* 25.

LC2V BA International Relations and Psychology
Duration: 3FT Hon
Entry Requirements: *GCE:* 300-320. *IB:* 25.

MC18 BA Law and Psychology
Duration: 3FT Hon
Entry Requirements: *GCE:* 300-320. *IB:* 25.

WC38 BA Music and Psychology
Duration: 3FT Hon
Entry Requirements: *GCE:* 300-320. *IB:* 25. Interview required.

CC18 BSc Biology and Psychology
Duration: 3FT Hon
Entry Requirements: *GCE:* 300-320. *IB:* 25.

GC4V BSc Computing and Psychology
Duration: 3FT Hon
Entry Requirements: *GCE:* 300-320.

FLC8 BSc Geography and Psychology
Duration: 3FT Hon
Entry Requirements: *GCE:* 300-320. *IB:* 25.

BCX8 BSc Health and Psychology
Duration: 3FT Hon
Entry Requirements: *GCE:* 300-320. *IB:* 25.

BC18 BSc Human Biology and Psychology
Duration: 3FT Hon
Entry Requirements: *GCE:* 300-320. *IB:* 25.

GC58 BSc Information Technology and Psychology
Duration: 3FT Hon
Entry Requirements: *GCE:* 300-320. *IB:* 25.

GC18 BSc Mathematics and Psychology
Duration: 3FT Hon
Entry Requirements: *GCE:* 300-320. *IB:* 25.

CB84 BSc Nutrition and Psychology
Duration: 3FT Hon
Entry Requirements: *GCE:* 300-320. *IB:* 25.

L51 LIVERPOOL JOHN MOORES UNIVERSITY
KINGSWAY HOUSE
HATTON GARDEN
LIVERPOOL L3 2AJ
t: 0151 231 5090 f: 0151 904 6368
e: courses@ljmu.ac.uk
// www.ljmu.ac.uk

MC2W BSc Criminology and Psychology
Duration: 3FT Hon
Entry Requirements: *GCE:* 280. *IB:* 29. *OCR ND:* D *OCR NED:* M3

L62 THE LONDON COLLEGE, UCK
VICTORIA GARDENS
NOTTING HILL GATE
LONDON W11 3PE
t: 020 7243 4000 f: 020 7243 1484
e: admissions@lcuck.ac.uk
// www.lcuck.ac.uk

38LC Dip Psychology and Social Sciences
Duration: 1FT Oth
Entry Requirements: Contact the institution for details.

L68 LONDON METROPOLITAN UNIVERSITY
166-220 HOLLOWAY ROAD
LONDON N7 8DB
t: 020 7133 4200
e: admissions@londonmet.ac.uk
// www.londonmet.ac.uk

CM8X BSc Criminology and Psychology
Duration: 3FT Hon
Entry Requirements: *GCE:* 300. *IB:* 28.

CL83 BSc Psychology and Sociology
Duration: 3FT Hon
Entry Requirements: *GCE:* 300. *IB:* 28.

L75 LONDON SOUTH BANK UNIVERSITY
ADMISSIONS AND RECRUITMENT CENTRE
90 LONDON ROAD
LONDON SE1 6LN
t: 0800 923 8888 f: 020 7815 8273
e: course.enquiry@lsbu.ac.uk
// www.lsbu.ac.uk

M9C8 BSc Criminology with Psychology
Duration: 3FT Hon
Entry Requirements: *GCE:* 240. *IB:* 24.

C8X3 BSc Psychology (Child Development)
Duration: 3FT Hon
Entry Requirements: *GCE:* 260. *IB:* 24.

C8M9 BSc (Hons) Psychology with Criminology
Duration: 3FT Hon
Entry Requirements: *GCE:* 260. *IB:* 24.

M1C8 LLB Law with Psychology
Duration: 3FT Hon
Entry Requirements: *GCE:* 260. *IB:* 24.

M20 THE UNIVERSITY OF MANCHESTER
RUTHERFORD BUILDING
OXFORD ROAD
MANCHESTER M13 9PL
t: 0161 275 2077 f: 0161 275 2106
e: ug-admissions@manchester.ac.uk
// www.manchester.ac.uk

BC18 BSc Cognitive Neuroscience and Psychology
Duration: 3FT Hon
Entry Requirements: *GCE:* AAA-ABB. *SQAH:* AAAAA-AAAAB. *SQAAH:* AAA-ABB. Interview required.

BCC8 BSc Cognitive Neuroscience and Psychology with Industrial/Professional Experience
Duration: 4SW Hon
Entry Requirements: *GCE:* AAA-ABB. *SQAH:* AAAAA-AAABB. *SQAAH:* AAA-ABB. Interview required.

M40 THE MANCHESTER METROPOLITAN UNIVERSITY
ADMISSIONS OFFICE
ALL SAINTS (GMS)
ALL SAINTS
MANCHESTER M15 6BH
t: 0161 247 2000
// www.mmu.ac.uk

LC58 BA/BSc Abuse Studies/Psychology
Duration: 3FT Hon
Entry Requirements: *GCE:* 280. *IB:* 28. *BTEC Dip:* D*D*. *BTEC ExtDip:* DMM.

NC18 BA/BSc Business/Psychology
Duration: 3FT Hon
Entry Requirements: *GCE:* 280. *IB:* 28. *BTEC Dip:* D*D*. *BTEC ExtDip:* DMM.

NC1V BA/BSc Business/Psychology
Duration: 3FT Hon
Entry Requirements: *GCE:* 300. *IB:* 30.

CL85 BA/BSc Childhood & Youth Studies/Psychology
Duration: 3FT Hon
Entry Requirements: *GCE:* 280. *IB:* 28. *BTEC Dip:* D*D*. *BTEC ExtDip:* DMM.

WC88 BA/BSc Creative Writing/Psychology
Duration: 3FT Hon
Entry Requirements: *GCE:* 280. *IB:* 28. *BTEC Dip:* D*D*. *BTEC ExtDip:* DMM. Portfolio required.

LC38 BA/BSc Crime Studies/Psychology
Duration: 3FT Hon
Entry Requirements: *GCE:* 280. *IB:* 28. *BTEC Dip:* D*D*. *BTEC ExtDip:* DMM.

MC98 BA/BSc Criminology/Psychology
Duration: 3FT Hon
Entry Requirements: *GCE:* 300. *IB:* 30.

WC48 BA/BSc Drama/Psychology
Duration: 3FT Hon
Entry Requirements: *GCE:* 280. *IB:* 28. *BTEC Dip:* D*D*. *BTEC ExtDip:* DMM. Interview required.

X3C8 BA/BSc Early Years/Psychology
Duration: 3FT Hon   CRB Check: Required
Entry Requirements: *GCE:* 280. *IB:* 28. *BTEC Dip:* D*D*. *BTEC ExtDip:* DMM.

XC38 BA/BSc Education Studies/Psychology
Duration: 3FT Hon
Entry Requirements: *GCE:* 280. *IB:* 28. *BTEC Dip:* D*D*. *BTEC ExtDip:* DMM.

XCH8 BA/BSc Education Studies/Psychology
Duration: 3FT Hon   CRB Check: Required
Entry Requirements: *GCE:* 300. *IB:* 30.

CN86 BA/BSc Human Resource Management/Psychology
Duration: 3FT Hon
Entry Requirements: *GCE:* 280. *IB:* 28. *BTEC Dip:* D*D*. *BTEC ExtDip:* DMM.

CN85 BA/BSc Marketing/Psychology
Duration: 3FT Hon
Entry Requirements: *GCE:* 280. *IB:* 28. *BTEC Dip:* D*D*. *BTEC ExtDip:* DMM.

WC38 BA/BSc Music/Psychology
Duration: 3FT Hon
Entry Requirements: *GCE:* 280. *IB:* 28. *BTEC Dip:* D*D*. *BTEC ExtDip:* DMM. Interview required.

VC58 BA/BSc Philosophy/Psychology
Duration: 3FT Hon
Entry Requirements: *GCE:* 280. *IB:* 28. *BTEC Dip:* D*D*. *BTEC ExtDip:* DMM.

VCM8 BA/BSc Philosophy/Psychology
Duration: 3FT Hon
Entry Requirements: *GCE:* 300. *IB:* 30.

CL83 BA/BSc Psychology/Sociology
Duration: 3FT Hon
Entry Requirements: *GCE:* 300. *IB:* 30.

CLV3 BA/BSc Psychology/Sociology
Duration: 3FT Hon
Entry Requirements: *GCE:* 280. *IB:* 28. *BTEC Dip:* D*D*. *BTEC ExtDip:* DMM.

CC18 BSc Biology/Psychology
Duration: 3FT Hon
Entry Requirements: *GCE:* 300. *IB:* 30.

FC48 BSc Forensic Science/Psychology
Duration: 3FT Hon
Entry Requirements: *GCE:* 300. *IB:* 30.

BC68 BSc Psychology and Speech Pathology
Duration: 4FT Hon   CRB Check: Required
Entry Requirements: *GCE:* BBB. *SQAH:* AAAAA-BBBBB. *SQAAH:* AAA-BBB. *IB:* 30. *BTEC Dip:* D*D*. *BTEC ExtDip:* DDM. *OCR ND:* D *OCR NED:* D2 Interview required. Portfolio required.

M80 MIDDLESEX UNIVERSITY
MIDDLESEX UNIVERSITY
THE BURROUGHS
LONDON NW4 4BT
t: 020 8411 5555 f: 020 8411 5649
e: enquiries@mdx.ac.uk
// www.mdx.ac.uk

L3CW BA Criminology with Psychology
Duration: 3FT/4SW Hon
Entry Requirements: *GCE:* 200-300. *IB:* 28.

L3CV BA Sociology with Psychology
Duration: 3FT Hon
Entry Requirements: *GCE:* 200-300. *IB:* 28.

C8B9 BSc Psychology with Counselling Skills
Duration: 3FT Hon
Entry Requirements: *GCE:* 200-300. *IB:* 28.

CM89 BSc Psychology with Criminology
Duration: 3FT/4SW Hon
Entry Requirements: *GCE:* 200-300. *IB:* 28.

C8X3 BSc Psychology with Education
Duration: 3FT/4SW Hon/Ord
Entry Requirements: Contact the institution for details.

C8N6 BSc Psychology with Human Resource Management
Duration: 3FT Hon
Entry Requirements: *GCE:* 200-300. *IB:* 28.

C8N5 BSc Psychology with Marketing
Duration: 3FT Hon
Entry Requirements: *GCE:* 200-300. *IB:* 28.

N21 NEWCASTLE UNIVERSITY
KING'S GATE
NEWCASTLE UPON TYNE NE1 7RU
t: 01912083333
// www.ncl.ac.uk

CC18 BSc Biology and Psychology
Duration: 3FT Hon
Entry Requirements: *GCE:* AAB. *SQAH:* AAABB. *IB:* 35.

CG81 BSc Mathematics and Psychology
Duration: 3FT Hon
Entry Requirements: *GCE:* AAB. *SQAH:* AAABB. *IB:* 35.

BC48 BSc Nutrition and Psychology
Duration: 3FT/4SW Hon
Entry Requirements: *GCE:* AAB. *SQAH:* AAAAB. *IB:* 35. *BTEC ExtDip:* DDD.

N31 NEWHAM COLLEGE OF FURTHER EDUCATION
EAST HAM CAMPUS
HIGH STREET SOUTH
LONDON E6 6ER
t: 020 8257 4000 f: 020 8257 4325
e: admissions@newham.ac.uk
// www.newham.ac.uk

XC38 BA Education Studies and Psychology
Duration: 3FT Hon
Entry Requirements: Contact the institution for details.

LC28 BA Politics and Psychology
Duration: 3FT Hon
Entry Requirements: Contact the institution for details.

CL83 BA Psychology and Sociology
Duration: 3FT Hon
Entry Requirements: Contact the institution for details.

CN82 BA (Hons) Psychology and Business Management
Duration: 3FT Hon
Entry Requirements: Contact the institution for details.

BC9W BA/BSc Counselling Studies and Psychology
Duration: 3FT Hon
Entry Requirements: Contact the institution for details.

N36 NEWMAN UNIVERSITY COLLEGE, BIRMINGHAM
GENNERS LANE
BARTLEY GREEN
BIRMINGHAM B32 3NT
t: 0121 476 1181 f: 0121 476 1196
e: Admissions@newman.ac.uk
// www.newman.ac.uk

C8VC BA Psychology with Ancient History
Duration: 3FT Hon
Entry Requirements: *Foundation:* Distinction. *GCE:* 280. *IB:* 25.
BTEC ExtDip: DMM. *OCR ND:* M2 *OCR NED:* M2

C8W1 BA Psychology with Art & Design
Duration: 3FT Hon
Entry Requirements: *Foundation:* Distinction. *GCE:* 280. *IB:* 25.
BTEC ExtDip: DMM. *OCR ND:* M2 *OCR NED:* M2

C8B9 BA Psychology with Counselling Studies
Duration: 3FT Hon
Entry Requirements: *Foundation:* Distinction. *GCE:* 280. *IB:* 25.
BTEC ExtDip: DMM. *OCR ND:* M2 *OCR NED:* M2

C8W8 BA Psychology with Creative Writing
Duration: 3FT Hon
Entry Requirements: *Foundation:* Distinction. *GCE:* 280. *IB:* 25.
BTEC ExtDip: DMM. *OCR ND:* M2 *OCR NED:* M2

C8W4 BA Psychology with Drama
Duration: 3FT Hon
Entry Requirements: *Foundation:* Distinction. *GCE:* 280. *IB:* 25.
BTEC ExtDip: DMM. *OCR ND:* M2 *OCR NED:* M2

C8V3 BA Psychology with Local History & Heritage
Duration: 3FT Hon
Entry Requirements: *Foundation:* Distinction. *GCE:* 280. *IB:* 25.
BTEC ExtDip: DMM. *OCR ND:* M2 *OCR NED:* M2

C8N2 BA Psychology with Management & Business
Duration: 3FT Hon
Entry Requirements: *Foundation:* Distinction. *GCE:* 280. *IB:* 25.
BTEC ExtDip: DMM. *OCR ND:* M2 *OCR NED:* M2

C8P3 BA Psychology with Media & Communication
Duration: 3FT Hon
Entry Requirements: *Foundation:* Distinction. *GCE:* 280. *IB:* 25.
BTEC ExtDip: DMM. *OCR ND:* M2 *OCR NED:* M2

C8V5 BA Psychology with Philosophy & Theology
Duration: 3FT Hon
Entry Requirements: *Foundation:* Distinction. *GCE:* 280. *IB:* 25.
BTEC ExtDip: DMM. *OCR ND:* M2 *OCR NED:* M2

C8VM BA Psychology with Philosophy, Religion & Ethics
Duration: 3FT Hon
Entry Requirements: *Foundation:* Distinction. *GCE:* 280. *IB:* 25.
BTEC ExtDip: DMM. *OCR ND:* M2 *OCR NED:* M2

N37 UNIVERSITY OF WALES, NEWPORT
ADMISSIONS
LODGE ROAD
CAERLEON
NEWPORT NP18 3QT
t: 01633 432030 f: 01633 432850
e: admissions@newport.ac.uk
// www.newport.ac.uk

CL83 BA/BSc Psychology and Criminology & Criminal Justice
Duration: 3FT Hon
Entry Requirements: *GCE:* 240. *IB:* 24. Interview required.

C8B9 BA/BSc Psychology with Counselling Studies
Duration: 3FT Hon
Entry Requirements: *GCE:* 240. *IB:* 24. Interview required.

CL8H BSc Psychology and Social Studies
Duration: 3FT Hon
Entry Requirements: *GCE:* 240. *IB:* 24. Interview required.

N38 UNIVERSITY OF NORTHAMPTON
PARK CAMPUS
BOUGHTON GREEN ROAD
NORTHAMPTON NN2 7AL
t: 0800 358 2232 f: 01604 722083
e: admissions@northampton.ac.uk
// www.northampton.ac.uk

N4C8 BA Accounting/Psychology
Duration: 3FT Hon
Entry Requirements: *GCE:* 260-280. *SQAH:* AAA-BBBB. *IB:* 24.
BTEC Dip: DD. *BTEC ExtDip:* DMM. *OCR ND:* D *OCR NED:* M2

N5CV BA Advertising/Psychology
Duration: 3FT Hon
Entry Requirements: *GCE:* 260-280. *SQAH:* AAA-BBBB. *IB:* 24.
BTEC Dip: DD. *BTEC ExtDip:* DMM. *OCR ND:* D *OCR NED:* M2

N1CV BA Business Entrepreneurship/Psychology
Duration: 3FT Hon
Entry Requirements: *GCE:* 260-280. *SQAH:* AAA-BBBB. *IB:* 24.
BTEC Dip: DD. *BTEC ExtDip:* DMM. *OCR ND:* D *OCR NED:* M2

N1C8 BA Business/Psychology
Duration: 3FT Hon
Entry Requirements: *GCE:* 260-280. *SQAH:* AAA-BBBB. *IB:* 24.
BTEC Dip: DD. *BTEC ExtDip:* DMM. *OCR ND:* D *OCR NED:* M2

M9C8 BA Criminology/Psychology
Duration: 3FT Hon
Entry Requirements: *GCE:* 260-280. *SQAH:* AAA-BBBB. *IB:* 24.
BTEC Dip: DD. *BTEC ExtDip:* DMM. *OCR ND:* D *OCR NED:* M2

W5C8 BA Dance/Psychology
Duration: 3FT Hon
Entry Requirements: *GCE:* 260-280. *SQAH:* AAA-BBBB. *IB:* 24.
BTEC Dip: DD. *BTEC ExtDip:* DMM. *OCR ND:* D *OCR NED:* M2
Interview required.

W4C8 BA Drama/Psychology
Duration: 3FT Hon
Entry Requirements: *GCE:* 260-280. *SQAH:* AAA-BBBB. *IB:* 24.
BTEC Dip: DD. *BTEC ExtDip:* DMM. *OCR ND:* D *OCR NED:* M2
Interview required.

X3C8 BA Education Studies/Psychology
Duration: 3FT Hon
Entry Requirements: *GCE:* 260-280. *SQAH:* AAA-BBBB. *IB:* 24.
BTEC Dip: DD. *BTEC ExtDip:* DMM. *OCR ND:* D *OCR NED:* M2

N8CV BA Events Management/Psychology
Duration: 3FT Hon
Entry Requirements: *GCE:* 260-280. *SQAH:* AAA-BBBB. *IB:* 24.
BTEC Dip: DD. *BTEC ExtDip:* DMM. *OCR ND:* D *OCR NED:* M2

W6C8 BA Film & Television Studies/Psychology
Duration: 3FT Hon
Entry Requirements: *GCE:* 260-280. *SQAH:* AAA-BBBB. *IB:* 24.
BTEC Dip: DD. *BTEC ExtDip:* DMM. *OCR ND:* D *OCR NED:* M2

W1C8 BA Fine Art Painting & Drawing/Psychology
Duration: 3FT Hon
Entry Requirements: *GCE:* 260-280. *SQAH:* AAA-BBBB. *IB:* 24.
BTEC Dip: DD. *BTEC ExtDip:* DMM. *OCR ND:* D *OCR NED:* M2

L4C8 BA Health Studies/Psychology
Duration: 3FT Hon
Entry Requirements: *GCE:* 260-280. *SQAH:* AAA-BBBB. *IB:* 24.
BTEC Dip: DD. *BTEC ExtDip:* DMM. *OCR ND:* D *OCR NED:* M2

V1C8 BA History/Psychology
Duration: 3FT Hon
Entry Requirements: *GCE:* 260-280. *SQAH:* AAA-BBBB. *IB:* 24.
BTEC Dip: DD. *BTEC ExtDip:* DMM. *OCR ND:* D *OCR NED:* M2

L7C8 BA Human Geography/Psychology
Duration: 3FT Hon
Entry Requirements: *GCE:* 260-280. *SQAH:* AAA-BBBB. *IB:* 24.
BTEC Dip: DD. *BTEC ExtDip:* DMM. *OCR ND:* D *OCR NED:* M2

N6C8 BA Human Resource Management/Psychology
Duration: 3FT Hon
Entry Requirements: *GCE:* 260-280. *SQAH:* AAA-BBBB. *IB:* 24.
BTEC Dip: DD. *BTEC ExtDip:* DMM. *OCR ND:* D *OCR NED:* M2

L9CV BA International Development/Psychology
Duration: 3FT Hon
Entry Requirements: *GCE:* 260-280. *SQAH:* AAA-BBBB. *IB:* 24.
BTEC Dip: DD. *BTEC ExtDip:* DMM. *OCR ND:* D *OCR NED:* M2

P5C8 BA Journalism/Psychology
Duration: 3FT Hon
Entry Requirements: *GCE:* 260-280. *SQAH:* AAA-BBBB. *IB:* 24.
BTEC Dip: DD. *BTEC ExtDip:* DMM. *OCR ND:* D *OCR NED:* M2

M1C8 BA Law/Psychology
Duration: 3FT Hon
Entry Requirements: *GCE:* 260-280. *SQAH:* AAA-BBBB. *IB:* 24.
BTEC Dip: DD. *BTEC ExtDip:* DMM. *OCR ND:* D *OCR NED:* M2

N2C8 BA Management/Psychology
Duration: 3FT Hon
Entry Requirements: *GCE:* 260-280. *SQAH:* AAA-BBBB. *IB:* 24.
BTEC Dip: DD. *BTEC ExtDip:* DMM. *OCR ND:* D *OCR NED:* M2

N5C8 BA Marketing/Psychology
Duration: 3FT Hon
Entry Requirements: *GCE:* 260-280. *SQAH:* AAA-BBBB. *IB:* 24.
BTEC Dip: DD. *BTEC ExtDip:* DMM. *OCR ND:* D *OCR NED:* M2

P3CV BA Media Production/Psychology
Duration: 3FT Hon
Entry Requirements: *GCE:* 260-280. *SQAH:* AAA-BBBB. *IB:* 24.
BTEC Dip: DD. *BTEC ExtDip:* DMM. *OCR ND:* D *OCR NED:* M2

C8N4 BA Psychology/Accounting
Duration: 3FT Hon
Entry Requirements: *GCE:* 260-280. *SQAH:* AAA-BBBB. *IB:* 24.
BTEC Dip: DD. *BTEC ExtDip:* DMM. *OCR ND:* D *OCR NED:* M2

C8NM BA Psychology/Advertising
Duration: 3FT Hon
Entry Requirements: *GCE:* 260-280. *SQAH:* AAA-BBBB. *IB:* 24.
BTEC Dip: DD. *BTEC ExtDip:* DMM. *OCR ND:* D *OCR NED:* M2

C8N1 BA Psychology/Business
Duration: 3FT Hon
Entry Requirements: *GCE:* 260-280. *SQAH:* AAA-BBBB. *IB:* 24.
BTEC Dip: DD. *BTEC ExtDip:* DMM. *OCR ND:* D *OCR NED:* M2

C8NF BA Psychology/Business Entrepreneurship
Duration: 3FT Hon
Entry Requirements: *GCE:* 260-280. *SQAH:* AAA-BBBB. *IB:* 24.
BTEC Dip: DD. *BTEC ExtDip:* DMM. *OCR ND:* D *OCR NED:* M2

C8M9 BA Psychology/Criminology
Duration: 3FT Hon
Entry Requirements: *GCE:* 260-280. *SQAH:* AAA-BBBB. *IB:* 24.
BTEC Dip: DD. *BTEC ExtDip:* DMM. *OCR ND:* D *OCR NED:* M2

C8W5 BA Psychology/Dance
Duration: 3FT Hon
Entry Requirements: *GCE:* 260-280. *SQAH:* AAA-BBBB. *IB:* 24.
BTEC Dip: DD. *BTEC ExtDip:* DMM. *OCR ND:* D *OCR NED:* M2
Interview required.

C8W4 BA Psychology/Drama
Duration: 3FT Hon
Entry Requirements: *GCE:* 260-280. *SQAH:* AAA-BBBB. *IB:* 24.
BTEC Dip: DD. *BTEC ExtDip:* DMM. *OCR ND:* D *OCR NED:* M2
Interview required.

C8X3 BA Psychology/Education Studies
Duration: 3FT Hon
Entry Requirements: *GCE:* 260-280. *SQAH:* AAA-BBBB. *IB:* 24.
BTEC Dip: DD. *BTEC ExtDip:* DMM. *OCR ND:* D *OCR NED:* M2

C8NV BA Psychology/Events Management
Duration: 3FT Hon
Entry Requirements: *GCE:* 260-280. *SQAH:* AAA-BBBB. *IB:* 24.
BTEC Dip: DD. *BTEC ExtDip:* DMM. *OCR ND:* D *OCR NED:* M2

C8W6 BA Psychology/Film & Television Studies
Duration: 3FT Hon
Entry Requirements: *GCE:* 260-280. *SQAH:* AAA-BBBB. *IB:* 24.
BTEC Dip: DD. *BTEC ExtDip:* DMM. *OCR ND:* D *OCR NED:* M2

C8W1 BA Psychology/Fine Art Painting & Drawing
Duration: 3FT Hon
Entry Requirements: *GCE:* 260-280. *SQAH:* AAA-BBBB. *IB:* 24.
BTEC Dip: DD. *BTEC ExtDip:* DMM. *OCR ND:* D *OCR NED:* M2

C8L4 BA Psychology/Health Studies
Duration: 3FT Hon
Entry Requirements: *GCE:* 260-280. *SQAH:* AAA-BBBB. *IB:* 24.
BTEC Dip: DD. *BTEC ExtDip:* DMM. *OCR ND:* D *OCR NED:* M2

C8V1 BA Psychology/History
Duration: 3FT Hon
Entry Requirements: *GCE:* 260-280. *SQAH:* AAA-BBBB. *IB:* 24.
BTEC Dip: DD. *BTEC ExtDip:* DMM. *OCR ND:* D *OCR NED:* M2

C8L7 BA Psychology/Human Geography
Duration: 3FT Hon
Entry Requirements: *GCE:* 260-280. *SQAH:* AAA-BBBB. *IB:* 24.
BTEC Dip: DD. *BTEC ExtDip:* DMM. *OCR ND:* D *OCR NED:* M2

C8N6 BA Psychology/Human Resource Management
Duration: 3FT Hon
Entry Requirements: *GCE:* 260-280. *SQAH:* AAA-BBBB. *IB:* 24.
BTEC Dip: DD. *BTEC ExtDip:* DMM. *OCR ND:* D *OCR NED:* M2

C8LX BA Psychology/International Development
Duration: 3FT Hon
Entry Requirements: *GCE:* 260-280. *SQAH:* AAA-BBBB. *IB:* 24.
BTEC Dip: DD. *BTEC ExtDip:* DMM. *OCR ND:* D *OCR NED:* M2

C8P5 BA Psychology/Journalism
Duration: 3FT Hon
Entry Requirements: *GCE:* 260-280. *SQAH:* AAA-BBBB. *IB:* 24.
BTEC Dip: DD. *BTEC ExtDip:* DMM. *OCR ND:* D *OCR NED:* M2

C8M1 BA Psychology/Law
Duration: 3FT Hon
Entry Requirements: *GCE:* 260-280. *SQAH:* AAA-BBBB. *IB:* 24.
BTEC Dip: DD. *BTEC ExtDip:* DMM. *OCR ND:* D *OCR NED:* M2

C8N2 BA Psychology/Management
Duration: 3FT Hon
Entry Requirements: *GCE:* 260-280. *SQAH:* AAA-BBBB. *IB:* 24.
BTEC Dip: DD. *BTEC ExtDip:* DMM. *OCR ND:* D *OCR NED:* M2

C8N5 BA Psychology/Marketing
Duration: 3FT Hon
Entry Requirements: *GCE:* 260-280. *SQAH:* AAA-BBBB. *IB:* 24.
BTEC Dip: DD. *BTEC ExtDip:* DMM. *OCR ND:* D *OCR NED:* M2

C8PH BA Psychology/Media Production
Duration: 3FT Hon
Entry Requirements: *GCE:* 260-280. *SQAH:* AAA-BBBB. *IB:* 24.
BTEC Dip: DD. *BTEC ExtDip:* DMM. *OCR ND:* D *OCR NED:* M2

C8L5 BA Psychology/Social Care
Duration: 3FT Hon
Entry Requirements: *GCE:* 260-280. *SQAH:* AAA-BBBB. *IB:* 24.
BTEC Dip: DD. *BTEC ExtDip:* DMM. *OCR ND:* D *OCR NED:* M2

C8L3 BA Psychology/Sociology
Duration: 3FT Hon
Entry Requirements: *GCE:* 260-280. *SQAH:* AAA-BBBB. *IB:* 24.
BTEC Dip: DD. *BTEC ExtDip:* DMM. *OCR ND:* D *OCR NED:* M2

C8N8 BA Psychology/Tourism
Duration: 3FT Hon
Entry Requirements: *GCE:* 260-280. *SQAH:* AAA-BBBB. *IB:* 24.
BTEC Dip: DD. *BTEC ExtDip:* DMM. *OCR ND:* D *OCR NED:* M2

L5C8 BA Social Care/Psychology
Duration: 3FT Hon
Entry Requirements: *GCE:* 260-280. *SQAH:* AAA-BBBB. *IB:* 24.
BTEC Dip: DD. *BTEC ExtDip:* DMM. *OCR ND:* D *OCR NED:* M2

L3C8 BA Sociology/Psychology
Duration: 3FT Hon
Entry Requirements: *GCE:* 260-280. *SQAH:* AAA-BBBB. *IB:* 24.
BTEC Dip: DD. *BTEC ExtDip:* DMM. *OCR ND:* D *OCR NED:* M2

XC38 BA Special Educational Needs & Inclusion/Psychology
Duration: 3FT Hon
Entry Requirements: *GCE:* 260-280. *SQAH:* AAA-BBBB. *IB:* 24.
BTEC Dip: DD. *BTEC ExtDip:* DMM. *OCR ND:* D *OCR NED:* M2

N8C8 BA Tourism/Psychology
Duration: 3FT Hon
Entry Requirements: *GCE:* 260-280. *SQAH:* AAA-BBBB. *IB:* 24.
BTEC Dip: DD. *BTEC ExtDip:* DMM. *OCR ND:* D *OCR NED:* M2

C1C8 BSc Biological Conservation/Psychology
Duration: 3FT Hon
Entry Requirements: *GCE:* 260-280. *SQAH:* AAA-BBBB. *IB:* 24.
BTEC Dip: DD. *BTEC ExtDip:* DMM. *OCR ND:* D *OCR NED:* M2

G4C8 BSc Computing/Psychology
Duration: 3FT Hon
Entry Requirements: *GCE:* 260-280. *SQAH:* AAA-BBBB. *IB:* 24.
BTEC Dip: DD. *BTEC ExtDip:* DMM. *OCR ND:* D *OCR NED:* M2

B1C8 BSc Human Bioscience/Psychology
Duration: 3FT Hon
Entry Requirements: *GCE:* 260-280. *SQAH:* AAA-BBBB. *IB:* 24.
BTEC Dip: DD. *BTEC ExtDip:* DMM. *OCR ND:* D *OCR NED:* M2

BC98 BSc Psychology and Counselling
Duration: 3FT Hon
Entry Requirements: *GCE:* 280-320. *SQAH:* AABB. *IB:* 26. *BTEC Dip:* DD. *BTEC ExtDip:* DMM. *OCR ND:* D *OCR NED:* M2 Interview required.

C8NA BSc Psychology with Applied Management
Duration: 3FT Hon
Entry Requirements: *GCE:* 260-280. *SQAH:* AAA-BBBB. *IB:* 24.
BTEC Dip: DD. *BTEC ExtDip:* DMM. *OCR ND:* D *OCR NED:* M2

C8C1 BSc Psychology/Biological Conservation
Duration: 3FT Hon
Entry Requirements: *GCE:* 260-280. *SQAH:* AAA-BBBB. *IB:* 24.
BTEC Dip: DD. *BTEC ExtDip:* DMM. *OCR ND:* D *OCR NED:* M2

C8G4 BSc Psychology/Computing
Duration: 3FT Hon
Entry Requirements: *GCE:* 260-280. *SQAH:* AAA-BBBB. *IB:* 24.
BTEC Dip: DD. *BTEC ExtDip:* DMM. *OCR ND:* D *OCR NED:* M2

C8B1 BSc Psychology/Human Bioscience
Duration: 3FT Hon
Entry Requirements: *GCE:* 260-280. *SQAH:* AAA-BBBB. *IB:* 24.
BTEC Dip: DD. *BTEC ExtDip:* DMM. *OCR ND:* D *OCR NED:* M2

N77 NORTHUMBRIA UNIVERSITY
TRINITY BUILDING
NORTHUMBERLAND ROAD
NEWCASTLE UPON TYNE NE1 8ST
t: 0191 243 7420 f: 0191 227 4561
e: er.admissions@northumbria.ac.uk
// www.northumbria.ac.uk

C8M9 BSc Psychology with Criminology
Duration: 3FT Hon
Entry Requirements: *GCE:* 320. *SQAH:* BBBBC. *SQAAH:* BBC. *IB:* 26. *OCR ND:* D *OCR NED:* M2

N84 THE UNIVERSITY OF NOTTINGHAM
THE ADMISSIONS OFFICE
THE UNIVERSITY OF NOTTINGHAM
UNIVERSITY PARK
NOTTINGHAM NG7 2RD
t: 0115 951 5151 f: 0115 951 4668
// www.nottingham.ac.uk

C850 BSc Psychology and Cognitive Neuroscience
Duration: 3FT Hon
Entry Requirements: *GCE:* ABB. *SQAAH:* ABB. *IB:* 32.

CV85 BSc Psychology and Philosophy
Duration: 3FT Hon
Entry Requirements: *GCE:* AAB. *SQAAH:* AAB. *IB:* 34.

N91 NOTTINGHAM TRENT UNIVERSITY
DRYDEN BUILDING
BURTON STREET
NOTTINGHAM NG1 4BU
t: +44 (0) 115 848 4200 f: +44 (0) 115 848 8869
e: applications@ntu.ac.uk
// www.ntu.ac.uk

CX83 BA Psychology and Educational Development
Duration: 3FT Hon   CRB Check: Required
Entry Requirements: *GCE:* 280. *BTEC Dip:* D*D*. *BTEC ExtDip:* DMM. *OCR NED:* M2

XC38 BA Psychology and Special & Inclusive Education
Duration: 3FT Hon   CRB Check: Required
Entry Requirements: *GCE:* 280. *BTEC Dip:* D*D*. *BTEC ExtDip:* DMM. *OCR NED:* M2

CX8H BA Psychology, Business and Education
Duration: 3FT Hon   CRB Check: Required
Entry Requirements: *GCE:* 280. *BTEC Dip:* D*D*. *BTEC ExtDip:* DMM. *OCR NED:* M2

C8M2 BSc Psychology with Criminology
Duration: 3FT Hon
Entry Requirements: *GCE:* 300. *OCR NED:* D2

C8LH BSc Psychology with Sociology
Duration: 3FT Hon
Entry Requirements: *GCE:* 280. *OCR NED:* M2

M1C8 LLB Law with Psychology
Duration: 3FT Hon
Entry Requirements: *GCE:* 280. *OCR NED:* M2

O33 OXFORD UNIVERSITY
UNDERGRADUATE ADMISSIONS OFFICE
UNIVERSITY OF OXFORD
WELLINGTON SQUARE
OXFORD OX1 2JD
t: 01865 288000 f: 01865 270212
e: undergraduate.admissions@admin.ox.ac.uk
// www.admissions.ox.ac.uk

BC98 BA Biomedical Sciences
Duration: 3FT Hon
Entry Requirements: *GCE:* AAA. *SQAH:* AAAAA. *SQAAH:* AAB.
Interview required. Admissions Test required.

CV85 BA Psychology and Philosophy
Duration: 3FT Hon
Entry Requirements: *GCE:* AAA. *SQAH:* AAAAA-AAAAB. *SQAAH:* AAB. Interview required. Admissions Test required.

O66 OXFORD BROOKES UNIVERSITY
ADMISSIONS OFFICE
HEADINGTON CAMPUS
GIPSY LANE
OXFORD OX3 0BP
t: 01865 483040 f: 01865 483983
e: admissions@brookes.ac.uk
// www.brookes.ac.uk

CL86 BA/BSc Anthropology/Psychology
Duration: 3FT Hon
Entry Requirements: *GCE:* ABB.

NC28 BA/BSc Business Management/Psychology
Duration: 3FT Hon
Entry Requirements: *GCE:* BBC.

XC38 BA/BSc Education Studies/Psychology
Duration: 3FT Hon
Entry Requirements: Contact the institution for details.

CW83 BA/BSc Music/Psychology
Duration: 3FT Hon
Entry Requirements: *GCE:* BBB.

CV85 BA/BSc Philosophy/Psychology
Duration: 3FT Hon
Entry Requirements: *GCE:* ABB.

CL83 BA/BSc Psychology/Sociology
Duration: 3FT Hon
Entry Requirements: *GCE:* ABB.

BCD8 BSc Human Biosciences/Psychology
Duration: 3FT Hon
Entry Requirements: Contact the institution for details.

P51 PETROC
OLD STICKLEPATH HILL
BARNSTAPLE
NORTH DEVON EX31 2BQ
t: 01271 852365 f: 01271 338121
e: he@petroc.ac.uk
// www.petroc.ac.uk

C8L3 FdSc Psychology with Sociology
Duration: 2FT Fdg
Entry Requirements: Contact the institution for details.

P60 PLYMOUTH UNIVERSITY
DRAKE CIRCUS
PLYMOUTH PL4 8AA
t: 01752 585858 f: 01752 588055
e: admissions@plymouth.ac.uk
// www.plymouth.ac.uk

M9CV BSc Criminology & Criminal Justice Studies with Psychology
Duration: 3FT Hon
Entry Requirements: *GCE:* 260. *IB:* 24.

L2CV BSc International Relations with Psychology
Duration: 3FT Hon
Entry Requirements: *GCE:* 240. *IB:* 24.

C8MX BSc Psychology with Criminology and Criminal Justice Studies
Duration: 3FT Hon
Entry Requirements: *GCE:* 320. *IB:* 28.

C8C1 BSc Psychology with Human Biology
Duration: 3FT Hon
Entry Requirements: *GCE:* 320. *IB:* 28.

C8M2 BSc Psychology with Law
Duration: 3FT Hon
Entry Requirements: *GCE:* 320. *IB:* 28.

C8L3 BSc Psychology with Sociology
Duration: 3FT Hon
Entry Requirements: *GCE:* 320. *IB:* 28.

P80 UNIVERSITY OF PORTSMOUTH
ACADEMIC REGISTRY
UNIVERSITY HOUSE
WINSTON CHURCHILL AVENUE
PORTSMOUTH PO1 2UP
t: 023 9284 8484 f: 023 9284 3082
e: admissions@port.ac.uk
// www.port.ac.uk

L5C8 BA Childhood and Youth Studies with Psychology
Duration: 3FT Hon
Entry Requirements: *GCE:* 240-300. *BTEC Dip:* DD. *BTEC ExtDip:* MMM.

X3C8 BA Early Childhood Studies with Psychology
Duration: 3FT Hon
Entry Requirements: *GCE:* 240-300. *BTEC Dip:* DD. *BTEC ExtDip:* MMM.

N6C8 BA Human Resource Management with Psychology
Duration: 3FT/4SW Hon
Entry Requirements: *GCE:* 280. *IB:* 28. *BTEC Dip:* D*D*. *BTEC ExtDip:* DMM.

N5C8 BA Marketing with Psychology
Duration: 3FT/4SW Hon
Entry Requirements: *GCE:* 280. *IB:* 28. *BTEC Dip:* D*D*. *BTEC ExtDip:* DMM.

M9C8 BSc Criminology with Psychology
Duration: 3FT Hon
Entry Requirements: *GCE:* 240-300. *BTEC Dip:* DD. *BTEC ExtDip:* DMM.

L3C8 BSc Sociology with Psychology
Duration: 3FT Hon
Entry Requirements: *GCE:* 240-300. *BTEC Dip:* DD. *BTEC ExtDip:* DMM.

Q25 QUEEN MARGARET UNIVERSITY, EDINBURGH
QUEEN MARGARET UNIVERSITY DRIVE
EDINBURGH EH21 6UU
t: 0131474 0000 f: 0131 474 0001
e: admissions@qmu.ac.uk
// www.qmu.ac.uk

CL83 BSc Psychology and Sociology
Duration: 4FT Hon
Entry Requirements: *GCE:* 220. *IB:* 26.

Q50 QUEEN MARY, UNIVERSITY OF LONDON
QUEEN MARY, UNIVERSITY OF LONDON
MILE END ROAD
LONDON E1 4NS
t: 020 7882 5555 f: 020 7882 5500
e: admissions@qmul.ac.uk
// www.qmul.ac.uk

C1C8 BSc Biology with Psychology
Duration: 3FT Hon
Entry Requirements: *GCE:* 300. *IB:* 32.

G1C8 BSc Mathematics with Psychology
Duration: 3FT Hon
Entry Requirements: *GCE:* 340. *IB:* 36.

R12 THE UNIVERSITY OF READING
THE UNIVERSITY OF READING
PO BOX 217
READING RG6 6AH
t: 0118 378 8619 f: 0118 378 8924
e: student.recruitment@reading.ac.uk
// www.reading.ac.uk

CW81 BA Art and Psychology
Duration: 4FT Hon
Entry Requirements: *GCE:* AAB. *SQAH:* AAABB. *SQAAH:* AAB. *BTEC Dip:* DD. *BTEC ExtDip:* DDD. Interview required. Portfolio required.

CV85 BA Psychology and Philosophy
Duration: 3FT Hon
Entry Requirements: *GCE:* AAB. *SQAH:* AAABB. *SQAAH:* AAB. *BTEC Dip:* DD. *BTEC ExtDip:* DDD. Interview required.

GC18 BSc Mathematics and Psychology
Duration: 3FT Hon
Entry Requirements: *GCE:* AAB. *SQAH:* AABBB. *SQAAH:* AAB. *BTEC Dip:* DD. *BTEC ExtDip:* DDD. *OCR ND:* D *OCR NED:* M3

CC18 BSc Psychology and Biology
Duration: 3FT Hon
Entry Requirements: *GCE:* AAB. *SQAH:* AAABB. *SQAAH:* AAB. Interview required.

R48 ROEHAMPTON UNIVERSITY
ROEHAMPTON LANE
LONDON SW15 5PU
t: 020 8392 3232 f: 020 8392 3470
e: enquiries@roehampton.ac.uk
// www.roehampton.ac.uk

MC98 BA Criminology and Psychology
Duration: 3FT Hon
Entry Requirements: *GCE:* 300. *IB:* 26. *BTEC ExtDip:* DDM. *OCR NED:* D2 Interview required.

CL86 BSc Biological Anthropology and Psychology
Duration: 3FT Hon
Entry Requirements: *Foundation:* Distinction. *GCE:* 300. *IB:* 25. *BTEC Dip:* D*D*. *BTEC ExtDip:* DMM. *OCR NED:* M2 Interview required.

R72 ROYAL HOLLOWAY, UNIVERSITY OF LONDON
ROYAL HOLLOWAY, UNIVERSITY OF LONDON
EGHAM
SURREY TW20 0EX
t: 01784 414944 f: 01784 473662
e: Admissions@rhul.ac.uk
// www.rhul.ac.uk

GC18 BSc Mathematics and Psychology
Duration: 3FT Hon
Entry Requirements: *IB:* 35.

S03 THE UNIVERSITY OF SALFORD
SALFORD M5 4WT
t: 0161 295 4545 f: 0161 295 4646
e: ug-admissions@salford.ac.uk
// www.salford.ac.uk

CL85 BSc Psychology Studies and Counselling Studies
Duration: 3FT Hon
Entry Requirements: *GCE:* 300. *IB:* 27. *OCR NED:* M1

CM89 BSc Psychology and Criminology
Duration: 3FT Hon
Entry Requirements: *GCE:* 300. *IB:* 27. *OCR NED:* M1

S21 SHEFFIELD HALLAM UNIVERSITY
CITY CAMPUS
HOWARD STREET
SHEFFIELD S1 1WB
t: 0114 225 5555 f: 0114 225 2167
e: admissions@shu.ac.uk
// www.shu.ac.uk

CX83 BA Education Studies with Psychology & Counselling
Duration: 3FT Hon
Entry Requirements: *GCE:* 260.

MC98 BSc Criminology and Psychology
Duration: 3FT Hon
Entry Requirements: *GCE:* 280.

CL83 BSc Psychology and Sociology
Duration: 3FT Hon
Entry Requirements: *GCE:* 280.

S27 UNIVERSITY OF SOUTHAMPTON
HIGHFIELD
SOUTHAMPTON SO17 1BJ
t: 023 8059 4732 f: 023 8059 3037
e: admissions@soton.ac.uk
// www.southampton.ac.uk

LC3V BSc Applied Social Sciences (Criminology and Psychological Studies)
Duration: 3FT Hon
Entry Requirements: *GCE:* AAB. *SQAH:* AABBB. *SQAAH:* BB. *IB:* 32.

CX83 BSc Education Studies and Psychology
Duration: 3FT Hon
Entry Requirements: Contact the institution for details.

S30 SOUTHAMPTON SOLENT UNIVERSITY
EAST PARK TERRACE
SOUTHAMPTON
HAMPSHIRE SO14 0RT
t: +44 (0) 23 8031 9039 f: + 44 (0)23 8022 2259
e: admissions@solent.ac.uk
// www.solent.ac.uk/

L4C8 BA Criminal Investigation with Psychology
Duration: 3FT Hon
Entry Requirements: *Foundation:* Distinction. *GCE:* 240. *SQAAH:* AA-CCD. *IB:* 24. *BTEC ExtDip:* MMM. *OCR ND:* D *OCR NED:* M3

MC98 BA Criminology and Psychology
Duration: 3FT Hon
Entry Requirements: *Foundation:* Distinction. *GCE:* 240. *SQAAH:* AA-CCD. *IB:* 24. *BTEC ExtDip:* MMM. *OCR ND:* D *OCR NED:* M3

C8B9 BSc Psychology (Counselling)
Duration: 3FT Hon
Entry Requirements: *Foundation:* Distinction. *GCE:* 240. *SQAAH:* AA-CCD. *IB:* 24. *BTEC ExtDip:* MMM. *OCR ND:* D *OCR NED:* M3

C8M9 BSc Psychology (Criminal Behaviour)
Duration: 3FT Hon
Entry Requirements: *Foundation:* Distinction. *GCE:* 240. *SQAAH:* AA-CCD. *IB:* 24. *BTEC ExtDip:* MMM. *OCR ND:* D *OCR NED:* M3

S32 SOUTH DEVON COLLEGE
LONG ROAD
PAIGNTON
DEVON TQ4 7EJ
t: 08000 213181 f: 01803 540541
e: university@southdevon.ac.uk
// www.southdevon.ac.uk/
welcome-to-university-level

CL83 FdSc Psychology with Sociology
Duration: 2FT Fdg
Entry Requirements: Contact the institution for details.

S36 UNIVERSITY OF ST ANDREWS
ST KATHARINE'S WEST
16 THE SCORES
ST ANDREWS
FIFE KY16 9AX
t: 01334 462150 f: 01334 463330
e: admissions@st-andrews.ac.uk
// www.st-andrews.ac.uk

CC18 BSc Biology and Psychology
Duration: 4FT Hon
Entry Requirements: *GCE:* AAA. *SQAH:* AAAB. *IB:* 36.

CG84 BSc Computer Science and Psychology
Duration: 4FT Hon
Entry Requirements: *GCE:* AAA. *SQAH:* AAAB. *IB:* 36.

LC18 BSc Economics and Psychology
Duration: 4FT Hon
Entry Requirements: *GCE:* AAA. *SQAH:* AAAB. *IB:* 38.

GC18 BSc Mathematics and Psychology
Duration: 4FT Hon
Entry Requirements: *GCE:* AAA. *SQAH:* AAAB. *IB:* 36.

C8C1 BSc Psychology with Biology
Duration: 4FT Hon
Entry Requirements: *GCE:* AAA. *SQAH:* AAAB. *IB:* 36.

CV83 MA Art History and Psychology
Duration: 4FT Hon
Entry Requirements: *GCE:* AAA. *SQAH:* AAAB. *IB:* 36.

CL81 MA Economics and Psychology
Duration: 4FT Hon
Entry Requirements: *GCE:* AAA. *SQAH:* AAAB. *IB:* 38.

CP83 MA Film Studies and Psychology
Duration: 4FT Hon
Entry Requirements: *GCE:* AAA. *SQAH:* AAAB. *IB:* 36.

CL87 MA Geography and Psychology
Duration: 4FT Hon
Entry Requirements: *GCE:* AAA. *SQAH:* AAAB. *IB:* 36.

CL82 MA International Relations and Psychology
Duration: 4FT Hon
Entry Requirements: *GCE:* AAA. *SQAH:* AAAA. *IB:* 38.

CN82 MA Management and Psychology
Duration: 4FT Hon
Entry Requirements: *GCE:* AAA. *SQAH:* AAAA. *IB:* 38.

CG81 MA Mathematics and Psychology
Duration: 4FT Hon
Entry Requirements: *GCE:* AAA. *SQAH:* AAAB. *IB:* 36.

CV81 MA Mediaeval History and Psychology
Duration: 4FT Hon
Entry Requirements: *GCE:* AAA. *SQAH:* AAAB. *IB:* 36.

CV8C MA Modern History and Psychology
Duration: 4FT Hon
Entry Requirements: *GCE:* AAA. *SQAH:* AAAB. *IB:* 36.

CV85 MA Philosophy and Psychology
Duration: 4FT Hon
Entry Requirements: *GCE:* AAA. *SQAH:* AAAB. *IB:* 36.

CL86 MA Psychology and Social Anthropology
Duration: 4FT Hon
Entry Requirements: *GCE:* AAA. *SQAH:* AAAB. *IB:* 36.

CV86 MA Psychology and Theological Studies
Duration: 4FT Hon
Entry Requirements: *GCE:* AAA. *SQAH:* AAAB. *IB:* 36.

C8P3 MA Psychology with Film Studies
Duration: 4FT Hon
Entry Requirements: *GCE:* AAA. *SQAH:* AAAB. *IB:* 36.

C8L7 MA Psychology with Geography
Duration: 4FT Hon
Entry Requirements: *GCE:* AAA. *SQAH:* AAAB. *IB:* 36.

S64 ST MARY'S UNIVERSITY COLLEGE, TWICKENHAM
WALDEGRAVE ROAD
STRAWBERRY HILL
MIDDLESEX TW1 4SX
t: 020 8240 4029 f: 020 8240 2361
e: admit@smuc.ac.uk
// www.smuc.ac.uk

XC38 BA/BSc Education & Social Science and Psychology
Duration: 3FT Hon
Entry Requirements: *GCE:* 240. *SQAH:* BBBC. *IB:* 28. *OCR ND:* D *OCR NED:* M3 Interview required.

NC28 BA/BSc Management Studies and Psychology
Duration: 3FT Hon
Entry Requirements: *GCE:* 240. *SQAH:* BBBC. *IB:* 28. *OCR ND:* D *OCR NED:* M3 Interview required.

CV85 BA/BSc Philosophy and Psychology
Duration: 3FT Hon
Entry Requirements: *GCE:* 240. *SQAH:* BBBC. *IB:* 28. *OCR ND:* D *OCR NED:* M3 Interview required.

BC4V BSc Nutrition and Psychology
Duration: 3FT Hon
Entry Requirements: *GCE:* 240. *SQAH:* BBBC. *IB:* 28. *OCR ND:* D *OCR NED:* M3 Interview required.

CL83 BSc Psychology and Sociology
Duration: 3FT Hon
Entry Requirements: *GCE:* 240. *SQAH:* BBBC. *IB:* 28. *OCR ND:* D *OCR NED:* M3 Interview required.

CB89 FdSc Psychology and Counselling
Duration: 2FT Fdg
Entry Requirements: **SQAH:** BBBC. Interview required.

S72 STAFFORDSHIRE UNIVERSITY
COLLEGE ROAD
STOKE ON TRENT ST4 2DE
t: 01782 292753 f: 01782 292740
e: admissions@staffs.ac.uk
// www.staffs.ac.uk

C891 BSc Psychology and Child Development
Duration: 3FT Hon
Entry Requirements: **GCE:** 200-280. **IB:** 24.

CB89 BSc Psychology and Counselling
Duration: 3FT Hon
Entry Requirements: **GCE:** 200-280. **IB:** 24.

CMV1 BSc Psychology and Criminology
Duration: 3FT Hon
Entry Requirements: **GCE:** 200-280. **IB:** 24.

S75 THE UNIVERSITY OF STIRLING
STUDENT RECRUITMENT & ADMISSIONS SERVICE
UNIVERSITY OF STIRLING
STIRLING
SCOTLAND FK9 4LA
t: 01786 467044 f: 01786 466800
e: admissions@stir.ac.uk
// www.stir.ac.uk

CP83 BA Film & Media and Psychology
Duration: 4FT Hon
Entry Requirements: **GCE:** BBC. **SQAH:** BBBB. **SQAAH:** AAA-CCC.
IB: 32. **BTEC ExtDip:** DMM.

NC68 BA Human Resource Management and Psychology
Duration: 4FT Hon
Entry Requirements: **GCE:** BBC. **SQAH:** BBBB. **SQAAH:** AAA-CCC.
IB: 32. **BTEC ExtDip:** DMM.

CN85 BA Marketing and Psychology
Duration: 4FT Hon
Entry Requirements: **GCE:** BBC. **SQAH:** BBBB. **SQAAH:** AAA-CCC.
IB: 32. **BTEC ExtDip:** DMM.

CV85 BA Philosophy and Psychology
Duration: 4FT Hon
Entry Requirements: **GCE:** BBC. **SQAH:** BBBB. **SQAAH:** AAA-CCC.
IB: 32. **BTEC ExtDip:** DMM.

LC28 BA Politics and Psychology
Duration: 4FT Hon
Entry Requirements: **GCE:** BBC. **SQAH:** BBBB. **SQAAH:** AAA-CCC.
IB: 32. **BTEC ExtDip:** DMM.

CL83 BA Psychology and Sociology
Duration: 4FT Hon
Entry Requirements: **GCE:** BBC. **SQAH:** BBBB. **SQAAH:** AAA-CCC.
IB: 32. **BTEC ExtDip:** DMM.

CC18 BSc Biology and Psychology
Duration: 4FT Hon
Entry Requirements: **GCE:** BBC. **SQAH:** BBBB. **SQAAH:** AAA-CCC.
IB: 32. **BTEC ExtDip:** DMM.

CN81 BSc Business Studies and Psychology
Duration: 4FT Hon
Entry Requirements: **GCE:** BBC. **SQAH:** BBBB. **SQAAH:** AAA-CCC.
IB: 32. **BTEC ExtDip:** DMM.

CG81 BSc Mathematics and Psychology
Duration: 4FT Hon
Entry Requirements: **GCE:** BBC. **SQAH:** BBBB. **SQAAH:** AAA-CCC.
IB: 32. **BTEC ExtDip:** DMM.

S78 THE UNIVERSITY OF STRATHCLYDE
GLASGOW G1 1XQ
t: 0141 552 4400 f: 0141 552 0775
// www.strath.ac.uk

LC18 BA Economics and Psychology
Duration: 4FT Hon
Entry Requirements: **GCE:** AAB. **SQAH:** AAAABB-AAAB. **IB:** 36.

VC18 BA History and Psychology
Duration: 4FT Hon
Entry Requirements: **GCE:** ABB. **SQAH:** AAABB-AAAB. **IB:** 34.

NC68 BA Human Resource Management and Psychology
Duration: 4FT Hon
Entry Requirements: **GCE:** AAB. **SQAH:** AAAABB-AAAB. **IB:** 36.

MC18 BA Law and Psychology
Duration: 4FT Hon
Entry Requirements: **GCE:** ABB. **SQAH:** AAABB-AAAB. **IB:** 34.

NC58 BA Marketing and Psychology
Duration: 4FT Hon
Entry Requirements: **GCE:** AAB. **SQAH:** AAAABB-AAAB. **IB:** 36.

LC28 BA Politics and Psychology
Duration: 4FT Hon
Entry Requirements: **GCE:** ABB. **SQAH:** AAABB-AAAB. **IB:** 34.

CL81 BA Psychology and Economics
Duration: 4FT Hon
Entry Requirements: **GCE:** ABB. **SQAH:** AAABB-AAAB. **IB:** 34.

CX83 BA Psychology and Education
Duration: 4FT Hon
Entry Requirements: Contact the institution for details.

CN86 BA Psychology and Human Resource Management
Duration: 4FT Hon
Entry Requirements: **GCE:** ABB. **SQAH:** AAABB-AAAB. **IB:** 34.

CG81 BA Psychology and Mathematics
Duration: 4FT Hon
Entry Requirements: *GCE:* ABB. *SQAH:* AAABB-AAAB. *IB:* 34.

S82 UNIVERSITY CAMPUS SUFFOLK (UCS)
WATERFRONT BUILDING
NEPTUNE QUAY
IPSWICH
SUFFOLK IP4 1QJ
t: 01473 338833 f: 01473 339900
e: info@ucs.ac.uk
// www.ucs.ac.uk

NC18 BA Business Management and Psychology
Duration: 3FT Hon
Entry Requirements: *GCE:* 280. *IB:* 28. *BTEC ExtDip:* DMM.
Interview required.

XC38 BA Early Childhood Studies and Psychology
Duration: 3FT Hon
Entry Requirements: *GCE:* 280. *IB:* 28. *BTEC ExtDip:* DMM.
Interview required.

CX8H BSc Psychology and Early Childhood Studies
Duration: 3FT Hon
Entry Requirements: *GCE:* 240-280. *IB:* 28. *BTEC ExtDip:* DMM.

LC38 BSc Psychology and Sociology
Duration: 3FT Hon
Entry Requirements: *GCE:* 240-280. *IB:* 28. *BTEC ExtDip:* DMM.

CL85 BSc Psychology and Youth Studies
Duration: 3FT Hon
Entry Requirements: *GCE:* 240-280. *IB:* 28. *BTEC ExtDip:* DMM.

S84 UNIVERSITY OF SUNDERLAND
STUDENT HELPLINE
THE STUDENT GATEWAY
CHESTER ROAD
SUNDERLAND SR1 3SD
t: 0191 515 3000 f: 0191 515 3805
e: student.helpline@sunderland.ac.uk
// www.sunderland.ac.uk

N1C8 BA Business Management with Psychology
Duration: 3FT Hon
Entry Requirements: *GCE:* 260-360. *IB:* 31. *OCR ND:* D *OCR NED:* M3

X3C8 BA Childhood Studies with Psychology
Duration: 3FT Hon
Entry Requirements: *GCE:* 260-360.

CM89 BA Criminology and Psychology
Duration: 3FT Hon
Entry Requirements: *GCE:* 260-360. *OCR ND:* D *OCR NED:* M3

M9C8 BA Criminology with Psychology
Duration: 3FT Hon
Entry Requirements: *GCE:* 260-360. *OCR ND:* D *OCR NED:* M3

W5C8 BA Dance with Psychology
Duration: 3FT Hon
Entry Requirements: *GCE:* 260-360. *IB:* 31. *OCR ND:* D *OCR NED:* M3

W4C8 BA Drama with Psychology
Duration: 3FT Hon
Entry Requirements: *GCE:* 260-360. *OCR ND:* D *OCR NED:* M3

V1C8 BA History with Psychology
Duration: 3FT Hon
Entry Requirements: *GCE:* 260-360. *IB:* 31. *OCR ND:* D *OCR NED:* M3

CP85 BA Journalism and Psychology
Duration: 3FT Hon
Entry Requirements: *GCE:* 260-360. *IB:* 32. *OCR ND:* D *OCR NED:* M3

P5C8 BA Journalism with Psychology
Duration: 3FT Hon
Entry Requirements: *GCE:* 260-360. *IB:* 32. *OCR ND:* D *OCR NED:* M3

P3C8 BA Media Studies with Psychology
Duration: 3FT Hon
Entry Requirements: *GCE:* 260-360. *IB:* 32. *OCR ND:* D *OCR NED:* M3

WC68 BA Photography and Psychology
Duration: 3FT Hon
Entry Requirements: *GCE:* 260-360. *OCR ND:* D *OCR NED:* M3

L2C8 BA Politics with Psychology
Duration: 3FT Hon
Entry Requirements: *GCE:* 260-360. *IB:* 31. *OCR ND:* D *OCR NED:* M3

CX81 BA Psychology and TESOL
Duration: 3FT Hon
Entry Requirements: *GCE:* 260-360. *OCR ND:* D *OCR NED:* M3

C8X1 BA Psychology with TESOL
Duration: 3FT Hon
Entry Requirements: *GCE:* 260-360. *OCR ND:* D *OCR NED:* M3

PC28 BA Public Relations and Psychology
Duration: 3FT Hon
Entry Requirements: *GCE:* 260-360. *IB:* 31. *OCR ND:* D *OCR NED:* M3

L3C8 BA Sociology with Psychology
Duration: 3FT Hon
Entry Requirements: *GCE:* 260-360. *IB:* 31. *OCR ND:* D *OCR NED:* M3

X1C8 BA TESOL with Psychology/Psychological Studies
Duration: 3FT Hon
Entry Requirements: *GCE:* 260-360. *OCR ND:* D *OCR NED:* M3

NC88 BA Tourism and Psychology
Duration: 3FT Hon
Entry Requirements: *GCE:* 260-360. *IB:* 31. *OCR ND:* D *OCR NED:* M3

NC18 BA/BSc Business Management and Psychology
Duration: 3FT Hon
Entry Requirements: *GCE:* 260-360. *IB:* 31. *OCR ND:* D *OCR NED:* M3

XCH8 BA/BSc Childhood Studies and Psychology
Duration: 3FT Hon
Entry Requirements: *GCE:* 260-360.

CW85 BA/BSc Dance and Psychology
Duration: 3FT Hon
Entry Requirements: *GCE:* 260-360. *IB:* 31. *OCR ND:* D *OCR NED:* M3

LC58 BA/BSc Health & Social Care and Psychology
Duration: 3FT Hon
Entry Requirements: *GCE:* 260-360.

L5C8 BA/BSc Health & Social Care with Psychology
Duration: 3FT Hon
Entry Requirements: *GCE:* 260-360.

VC18 BA/BSc History and Psychology
Duration: 3FT Hon
Entry Requirements: *GCE:* 260-360. *IB:* 32. *OCR ND:* D *OCR NED:* M3

CM81 BA/BSc Law and Psychology
Duration: 3FT Hon
Entry Requirements: *GCE:* 260-360. *OCR ND:* D *OCR NED:* M3

PC38 BA/BSc Media Studies and Psychology
Duration: 3FT Hon
Entry Requirements: *GCE:* 260-360. *IB:* 32. *OCR ND:* D *OCR NED:* M3

LC28 BA/BSc Politics and Psychology
Duration: 3FT Hon
Entry Requirements: *GCE:* 260-360. *IB:* 31. *OCR ND:* D *OCR NED:* M3

CW84 BA/BSc Psychology and Drama
Duration: 3FT Hon
Entry Requirements: *GCE:* 260-360. *OCR ND:* D *OCR NED:* M3

CX83 BA/BSc Psychology and Education
Duration: 3FT Hon
Entry Requirements: *GCE:* 260-360. *OCR ND:* D *OCR NED:* M3

CL83 BA/BSc Psychology and Sociology
Duration: 3FT Hon
Entry Requirements: *GCE:* 260-360. *IB:* 32. *OCR ND:* D *OCR NED:* M3

C8L5 BA/BSc Psychology with Health & Social Care
Duration: 3FT Hon
Entry Requirements: *GCE:* 260-360.

P2C8 BA/BSc Public Relations with Psychology
Duration: 3FT Hon
Entry Requirements: *GCE:* 260-360. *OCR ND:* D *OCR NED:* M3

C8N1 BSc Psychology with Business Management
Duration: 3FT Hon
Entry Requirements: *GCE:* 260-360. *IB:* 32. *OCR ND:* D *OCR NED:* M3

C8XH BSc Psychology with Childhood Studies
Duration: 3FT Hon
Entry Requirements: *GCE:* 260-360.

C8BX BSc Psychology with Counselling
Duration: 3FT Hon
Entry Requirements: *GCE:* 260-360. *IB:* 24. *OCR ND:* D

C8M9 BSc Psychology with Criminology
Duration: 3FT Hon
Entry Requirements: *GCE:* 260-360. *IB:* 32. *OCR ND:* D *OCR NED:* M3

C8W5 BSc Psychology with Dance
Duration: 3FT Hon
Entry Requirements: *GCE:* 260-360. *IB:* 31. *OCR ND:* D *OCR NED:* M3

C8W4 BSc Psychology with Drama
Duration: 3FT Hon
Entry Requirements: *GCE:* 260-360. *OCR ND:* D *OCR NED:* M3

C8X3 BSc Psychology with Education
Duration: 3FT Hon
Entry Requirements: *GCE:* 260-360. *IB:* 32. *OCR ND:* D *OCR NED:* M3

C8V1 BSc Psychology with History
Duration: 3FT Hon
Entry Requirements: *GCE:* 260-360. *IB:* 32. *OCR ND:* D *OCR NED:* M3

C8P5 BSc Psychology with Journalism
Duration: 3FT Hon
Entry Requirements: *GCE:* 260-360. *OCR ND:* D *OCR NED:* M3

C8P3 BSc Psychology with Media Studies
Duration: 3FT Hon
Entry Requirements: *GCE:* 260-360. *IB:* 32. *OCR ND:* D *OCR NED:* M3

C8W6 BSc Psychology with Photography
Duration: 3FT Hon
Entry Requirements: *GCE:* 260-360. *IB:* 32. *OCR ND:* D *OCR NED:* M3

C8L2 BSc Psychology with Politics
Duration: 3FT Hon
Entry Requirements: *GCE:* 260-360. *IB:* 32. *OCR ND:* D *OCR NED:* M3

C8L3 BSc Psychology with Sociology
Duration: 3FT Hon
Entry Requirements: *GCE:* 260-360. *IB:* 32. *OCR ND:* D *OCR NED:* M3

S90 UNIVERSITY OF SUSSEX
UNDERGRADUATE ADMISSIONS
SUSSEX HOUSE
UNIVERSITY OF SUSSEX
BRIGHTON BN1 9RH
t: 01273 678416 f: 01273 678545
e: ug.applicants@sussex.ac.uk
// www.sussex.ac.uk

CG87 BSc Psychology with Cognitive Science
Duration: 3FT Hon
Entry Requirements: *GCE:* AAB. *SQAH:* AAABB. *IB:* 35. *BTEC SubDip:* D. *BTEC Dip:* DD. *BTEC ExtDip:* DDD. *OCR ND:* D *OCR NED:* D1

CB81 BSc Psychology with Neuroscience
Duration: 3FT Hon
Entry Requirements: *GCE:* AAB. *SQAH:* AAABB. *IB:* 35. *BTEC SubDip:* D. *BTEC Dip:* DD. *BTEC ExtDip:* DDD. *OCR ND:* D *OCR NED:* D1

C8L3 BSc Psychology with Sociology
Duration: 3FT Hon
Entry Requirements: *GCE:* AAB. *SQAH:* AAABB. *IB:* 35. *BTEC SubDip:* D. *BTEC Dip:* DD. *BTEC ExtDip:* DDD. *OCR ND:* D *OCR NED:* D1

S96 SWANSEA METROPOLITAN UNIVERSITY
MOUNT PLEASANT CAMPUS
SWANSEA SA1 6ED
t: 01792 481000 f: 01792 481061
e: gemma.green@smu.ac.uk
// www.smu.ac.uk

BC98 BA Counselling and Psychology
Duration: 3FT Hon
Entry Requirements: *GCE:* 180-360. *IB:* 24. Interview required.

WC84 BA Drama and Psychology
Duration: 3FT Hon
Entry Requirements: *GCE:* 180-360. *IB:* 24. Interview required.

XC38 BA Educational Studies and Psychology
Duration: 3FT Hon   CRB Check: Required
Entry Requirements: *GCE:* 180-360. *IB:* 24. Interview required.

T20 TEESSIDE UNIVERSITY
MIDDLESBROUGH TS1 3BA
t: 01642 218121 f: 01642 384201
e: registry@tees.ac.uk
// www.tees.ac.uk

M9C8 BSc Criminology with Psychology
Duration: 3FT Hon
Entry Requirements: *GCE:* 240.

L550 BSc Psychology and Counselling
Duration: 3FT Hon
Entry Requirements: *GCE:* 260.

CM89 BSc Psychology and Criminology
Duration: 3FT Hon
Entry Requirements: *GCE:* 260.

U20 UNIVERSITY OF ULSTER
COLERAINE
CO. LONDONDERRY
NORTHERN IRELAND BT52 1SA
t: 028 7012 4221 f: 028 7012 4908
e: online@ulster.ac.uk
// www.ulster.ac.uk

W4C8 BA Drama with Psychology
Duration: 3FT Hon
Entry Requirements: *GCE:* BBC. *IB:* 24. Interview required.

V1C8 BA History with Psychology
Duration: 3FT Hon
Entry Requirements: *GCE:* 280. *IB:* 24.

P5C8 BA Journalism with Psychology
Duration: 3FT Hon
Entry Requirements: *GCE:* 280-300.

P3C8 BA Media Studies with Psychology
Duration: 3FT Hon
Entry Requirements: *GCE:* 280. *IB:* 24.

W3C8 BA Music with Psychology
Duration: 3FT Hon
Entry Requirements: *GCE:* CCC. *IB:* 24. Interview required.

N5C8 BSc Advertising with Psychology
Duration: 4FT Hon
Entry Requirements: *GCE:* 240. *IB:* 24.

N1C8 BSc Business Studies with Psychology
Duration: 3FT Hon
Entry Requirements: *GCE:* 240. *IB:* 24.

N1CV BSc Business with Psychology
Duration: 3FT Hon
Entry Requirements: *GCE:* 240-280. *IB:* 24.

G4CV BSc Computing with Psychology
Duration: 4SW Hon
Entry Requirements: *GCE:* 280. *IB:* 24. Interview required.
Admissions Test required.

F8C8 BSc Environmental Science with Psychology
Duration: 3FT Hon
Entry Requirements: *GCE:* 220. *IB:* 24.

F8CV BSc Geography with Psychology
Duration: 3FT Hon
Entry Requirements: *GCE:* 220. *IB:* 24.

L3C8 BSc Sociology with Psychology
Duration: 3FT Hon
Entry Requirements: *GCE:* 240. *IB:* 24.

U40 UNIVERSITY OF THE WEST OF SCOTLAND
PAISLEY
RENFREWSHIRE
SCOTLAND PA1 2BE
t: 0141 848 3727 f: 0141 848 3623
e: admissions@uws.ac.uk
// www.uws.ac.uk

CC98 BSc Applied Bioscience and Psychology
Duration: 3FT/4FT Ord/Hon
Entry Requirements: *GCE:* CD. *SQAH:* BBC-BCCC.

U80 UNIVERSITY COLLEGE LONDON (UNIVERSITY OF LONDON)
GOWER STREET
LONDON WC1E 6BT
t: 020 7679 3000 f: 020 7679 3001
// www.ucl.ac.uk

CB86 BSc Psychology and Language Sciences
Duration: 3FT Hon
Entry Requirements: *GCE:* A*AAe-AAAe. *SQAAH:* AAA. Interview required.

W05 THE UNIVERSITY OF WEST LONDON
ST MARY'S ROAD
EALING
LONDON W5 5RF
t: 0800 036 8888 f: 020 8566 1353
e: learning.advice@uwl.ac.uk
// www.uwl.ac.uk

M2C8 BA Criminology with Psychology
Duration: 3FT Hon
Entry Requirements: *GCE:* 260. *IB:* 28. Interview required.

C8B9 BSc Psychology with Counselling Theory
Duration: 3FT Hon
Entry Requirements: *GCE:* 200. *IB:* 28. Interview required.

C8L3 BSc Psychology with Criminology
Duration: 3FT Hon
Entry Requirements: *GCE:* 200. *IB:* 28. Interview required.

W20 THE UNIVERSITY OF WARWICK
COVENTRY CV4 8UW
t: 024 7652 3723 f: 024 7652 4649
e: ugadmissions@warwick.ac.uk
// www.warwick.ac.uk

V5C8 BA Philosophy with Psychology
Duration: 3FT Hon
Entry Requirements: *GCE:* AAA. *SQAAH:* AA. *IB:* 38.

W76 UNIVERSITY OF WINCHESTER
WINCHESTER
HANTS SO22 4NR
t: 01962 827234 f: 01962 827288
e: course.enquiries@winchester.ac.uk
// www.winchester.ac.uk

VC48 BA Archaeology and Psychology
Duration: 3FT Hon
Entry Requirements: *Foundation:* Distinction. *GCE:* 260-300. *IB:* 25. *OCR ND:* D *OCR NED:* M2

CN81 BA Business Management and Psychology
Duration: 3FT Hon
Entry Requirements: *Foundation:* Distinction. *GCE:* 260-300. *IB:* 25. *OCR ND:* D *OCR NED:* M2

LC58 BA Childhood,Youth & Community Studies and Psychology
Duration: 3FT Hon
Entry Requirements: *Foundation:* Distinction. *GCE:* 260-300. *IB:* 25. *OCR ND:* D *OCR NED:* M2

CW85 BA Choreography & Dance and Psychology
Duration: 3FT Hon
Entry Requirements: *Foundation:* Distinction. *GCE:* 260-300. *IB:* 25. *OCR ND:* D *OCR NED:* M2

LC3V BA Criminology and Psychology
Duration: 3FT Hon
Entry Requirements: *Foundation:* Distinction. *GCE:* 260-300. *IB:* 25. *OCR ND:* D *OCR NED:* M2

CW84 BA Drama and Psychology
Duration: 3FT Hon
Entry Requirements: *Foundation:* Distinction. *GCE:* 260-300. *IB:* 25. *OCR ND:* D *OCR NED:* M2

XCJ8 BA Education Studies (Early Childhood) and Psychology
Duration: 3FT Hon
Entry Requirements: *Foundation:* Distinction. *GCE:* 260-300. *IB:* 25. *OCR ND:* D *OCR NED:* M2

CX83 BA Education Studies and Psychology
Duration: 3FT Hon
Entry Requirements: *Foundation:* Distinction. *GCE:* 260-300. *IB:* 25. *OCR ND:* D *OCR NED:* M2

WC68 BA Film & Cinema Technologies and Psychology
Duration: 3FT Hon
Entry Requirements: *Foundation:* Distinction. *GCE:* 260-300. *IB:* 25. *OCR ND:* D *OCR NED:* M2

CPX3 BA Film Studies and Psychology
Duration: 3FT Hon
Entry Requirements: *Foundation:* Distinction. *GCE:* 260-300. *IB:* 25. *OCR ND:* D *OCR NED:* M2

CV81 BA History and Psychology
Duration: 3FT Hon
Entry Requirements: *Foundation:* Distinction. *GCE:* 260-300. *IB:* 25. *OCR ND:* D *OCR NED:* M2

PC58 BA Journalism Studies and Psychology
Duration: 3FT Hon
Entry Requirements: *Foundation:* Distinction. *GCE:* 260-300. *IB:* 25. *OCR ND:* D *OCR NED:* M2

MC18 BA Law and Psychology
Duration: 3FT Hon
Entry Requirements: *Foundation:* Distinction. *GCE:* 260-300. *IB:* 25. *OCR ND:* D *OCR NED:* M2

PC38 BA Media Production and Psychology
Duration: 3FT Hon
Entry Requirements: *Foundation:* Distinction. *GCE:* 260-300. *IB:* 25. *OCR ND:* D *OCR NED:* M2

CP83 BA Media Studies and Psychology
Duration: 3FT Hon
Entry Requirements: *Foundation:* Distinction. *GCE:* 260-300. *IB:* 25. *OCR ND:* D *OCR NED:* M2

WC98 BA Modern Liberal Arts and Psychology
Duration: 3FT Hon
Entry Requirements: *Foundation:* Distinction. *GCE:* 260-300. *IB:* 25. *OCR ND:* D *OCR NED:* M2

WCLV BA Performing Arts (Contemporary Performance) and Psychology
Duration: 3FT Hon
Entry Requirements: *Foundation:* Distinction. *GCE:* 260-300. *IB:* 25. *OCR ND:* D *OCR NED:* M2

LC2V BA Politics & Global Studies and Psychology
Duration: 3FT Hon
Entry Requirements: *Foundation:* Distinction. *GCE:* 260-300. *IB:* 25. *OCR ND:* D *OCR NED:* M2

CLV3 BA Psychology and Sociology
Duration: 3FT Hon
Entry Requirements: *Foundation:* Distinction. *GCE:* 260-300. *IB:* 25. *OCR ND:* D *OCR NED:* M2

CV8P BA Psychology and Theology & Religious Studies
Duration: 3FT Hon
Entry Requirements: *Foundation:* Distinction. *GCE:* 260-300. *IB:* 25. *OCR ND:* D *OCR NED:* M2

C891 BSc Psychology & Child Development
Duration: 3FT Hon
Entry Requirements: *Foundation:* Distinction. *GCE:* 260-300. *IB:* 25. *OCR ND:* D *OCR NED:* M2

C890 BSc Psychology & Cognition
Duration: 3FT Hon
Entry Requirements: *Foundation:* Distinction. *GCE:* 260-300. *IB:* 25. *OCR ND:* D *OCR NED:* M2

W80 UNIVERSITY OF WORCESTER
HENWICK GROVE
WORCESTER WR2 6AJ
t: 01905 855111 f: 01905 855377
e: admissions@worc.ac.uk
// www.worcester.ac.uk

WC98 BA/BSc Art & Design and Psychology
Duration: 3FT Hon
Entry Requirements: *GCE:* 280-300. *IB:* 25. *OCR ND:* D *OCR NED:* M3

NC28 BA/BSc Business Management and Psychology
Duration: 3FT Hon
Entry Requirements: *GCE:* 280. *IB:* 25. *OCR ND:* D *OCR NED:* M3

WC48 BA/BSc Drama & Performance and Psychology
Duration: 3FT Hon
Entry Requirements: *GCE:* 280-300. *IB:* 25. *OCR ND:* D *OCR NED:* M3

XC38 BA/BSc Education Studies and Psychology
Duration: 3FT Hon
Entry Requirements: *GCE:* 280. *IB:* 25. *OCR ND:* D *OCR NED:* M3

CL85 BA/BSc Psychology and Social Welfare
Duration: 3FT Hon
Entry Requirements: *GCE:* 280. *IB:* 25. *OCR ND:* D *OCR NED:* M3

CL83 BA/BSc Psychology and Sociology
Duration: 3FT Hon
Entry Requirements: *GCE:* 280-300. *IB:* 25. *OCR ND:* D *OCR NED:* M3

CC18 BSc Biology and Psychology
Duration: 3FT Hon
Entry Requirements: *Foundation:* Merit. *GCE:* 280. *IB:* 25. *OCR ND:* D *OCR NED:* M3

CCC8 BSc Human Biology and Psychology
Duration: 3FT Hon
Entry Requirements: *GCE:* 280. *IB:* 25. *OCR ND:* D *OCR NED:* M3

BCK8 BSc Human Nutrition and Psychology
Duration: 3FT Hon
Entry Requirements: Contact the institution for details.

OTHER PSYCHOLOGY

A30 UNIVERSITY OF ABERTAY DUNDEE
BELL STREET
DUNDEE DD1 1HG
t: 01382 308080 f: 01382 308081
e: sro@abertay.ac.uk
// www.abertay.ac.uk

B130 BSc Forensic Psychobiology
Duration: 4FT Hon
Entry Requirements: *GCE:* CC. *SQAH:* BBB. *IB:* 26.

A80 ASTON UNIVERSITY, BIRMINGHAM
ASTON TRIANGLE
BIRMINGHAM B4 7ET
t: 0121 204 4444 f: 0121 204 3696
e: admissions@aston.ac.uk   (automatic response)
// www.aston.ac.uk/prospective-students/ug

CL83 BSc Psychology and Sociology
Duration: 4SW Hon
Entry Requirements: *GCE:* AAB-ABB. *SQAH:* AABBB. *SQAAH:* AAB-ABB. *IB:* 33. *BTEC ExtDip:* DDD. *OCR ND:* D *OCR NED:* D1

B80 UNIVERSITY OF THE WEST OF ENGLAND, BRISTOL
FRENCHAY CAMPUS
COLDHARBOUR LANE
BRISTOL BS16 1QY
t: +44 (0)117 32 83333 f: +44 (0)117 32 82810
e: admissions@uwe.ac.uk
// www.uwe.ac.uk

C8X9 FdA Therapeutic Work with Children and Young People
Duration: 2FT Fdg
Entry Requirements: Contact the institution for details.

B94 BUCKINGHAMSHIRE NEW UNIVERSITY
QUEEN ALEXANDRA ROAD
HIGH WYCOMBE
BUCKINGHAMSHIRE HP11 2JZ
t: 0800 0565 660 f: 01494 605 023
e: admissions@bucks.ac.uk
// bucks.ac.uk

C890 BSc Criminological Psychology
Duration: 3FT Hon
Entry Requirements: *GCE:* 240-280. *IB:* 25. *OCR ND:* D *OCR NED:* M2

C30 UNIVERSITY OF CENTRAL LANCASHIRE
PRESTON
LANCS PR1 2HE
t: 01772 201201 f: 01772 894954
e: uadmissions@uclan.ac.uk
// www.uclan.ac.uk

C860 BSc Neuropsychology
Duration: 3FT Hon
Entry Requirements: *Foundation:* Distinction. *GCE:* 260-300. *SQAH:* BBBBC-BBCCC. *IB:* 30. *OCR NED:* M2

E28 UNIVERSITY OF EAST LONDON
DOCKLANDS CAMPUS
UNIVERSITY WAY
LONDON E16 2RD
t: 020 8223 3333 f: 020 8223 2978
e: study@uel.ac.uk
// www.uel.ac.uk

C823 BSc Developmental Psychology
Duration: 3FT Hon
Entry Requirements: *GCE:* 240. *IB:* 24.

G14 UNIVERSITY OF GLAMORGAN, CARDIFF AND PONTYPRIDD
ENQUIRIES AND ADMISSIONS UNIT
PONTYPRIDD CF37 1DL
t: 08456 434030 f: 01443 654050
e: enquiries@glam.ac.uk
// www.glam.ac.uk

C820 BSc Developmental Psychology
Duration: 3FT Hon
Entry Requirements: *GCE:* BBC. *IB:* 25. *BTEC SubDip:* M. *BTEC Dip:* D*D*. *BTEC ExtDip:* DMM.

G53 GLYNDWR UNIVERSITY
PLAS COCH
MOLD ROAD
WREXHAM LL11 2AW
t: 01978 293439 f: 01978 290008
e: sid@glyndwr.ac.uk
// www.glyndwr.ac.uk

C866 BSc Equestrian Psychology
Duration: 1FT Hon
Entry Requirements: Contact the institution for details.

C865 FdSc Equestrian Psychology
Duration: 2FT Fdg
Entry Requirements: *GCE:* 120.

N31 NEWHAM COLLEGE OF FURTHER EDUCATION
EAST HAM CAMPUS
HIGH STREET SOUTH
LONDON E6 6ER
t: 020 8257 4000 f: 020 8257 4325
e: admissions@newham.ac.uk
// www.newham.ac.uk

C821 BSc Child and Adolescent Psychology
Duration: 3FT Hon
Entry Requirements: Contact the institution for details.

R12 THE UNIVERSITY OF READING
THE UNIVERSITY OF READING
PO BOX 217
READING RG6 6AH
t: 0118 378 8619 f: 0118 378 8924
e: student.recruitment@reading.ac.uk
// www.reading.ac.uk

CN85 BSc Consumer Behaviour and Marketing
Duration: 3FT Hon
Entry Requirements: *GCE:* 320.

S72 STAFFORDSHIRE UNIVERSITY
COLLEGE ROAD
STOKE ON TRENT ST4 2DE
t: 01782 292753 f: 01782 292740
e: admissions@staffs.ac.uk
// www.staffs.ac.uk

C890 BSc Forensic Psychology
Duration: 3FT Hon
Entry Requirements: *GCE:* 200-280. *IB:* 24.

S90 UNIVERSITY OF SUSSEX
UNDERGRADUATE ADMISSIONS
SUSSEX HOUSE
UNIVERSITY OF SUSSEX
BRIGHTON BN1 9RH
t: 01273 678416 f: 01273 678545
e: ug.applicants@sussex.ac.uk
// www.sussex.ac.uk

B141 BSc Neuroscience with Cognitive Science
Duration: 3FT Hon
Entry Requirements: *GCE:* AAB. *SQAH:* AAABB. *SQAAH:* AAB. *IB:* 35. *BTEC SubDip:* D. *BTEC Dip:* DD. *BTEC ExtDip:* DDD. *OCR ND:* D *OCR NED:* D1

T20 TEESSIDE UNIVERSITY
MIDDLESBROUGH TS1 3BA
t: 01642 218121 f: 01642 384201
e: registry@tees.ac.uk
// www.tees.ac.uk

C890 BSc Forensic Psychology
Duration: 3FT Hon
Entry Requirements: *GCE:* 260.

U20 UNIVERSITY OF ULSTER
COLERAINE
CO. LONDONDERRY
NORTHERN IRELAND BT52 1SA
t: 028 7012 4221 f: 028 7012 4908
e: online@ulster.ac.uk
// www.ulster.ac.uk

C820 BSc Psychology with DPP/DIAS
Duration: 4SW Hon
Entry Requirements: *GCE:* 280-300.

W80 UNIVERSITY OF WORCESTER
HENWICK GROVE
WORCESTER WR2 6AJ
t: 01905 855111 f: 01905 855377
e: admissions@worc.ac.uk
// www.worcester.ac.uk

C820 BSc Developmental Psychology
Duration: 3FT Hon
Entry Requirements: *GCE:* 280. *IB:* 25. *OCR ND:* D *OCR NED:* M3

PS